# Trent's Trust

## And Other Stories

Bret Harte

## Alpha Editions

This edition published in 2024

ISBN : 9789362092809

Design and Setting By
**Alpha Editions**
www.alphaedis.com
Email - info@alphaedis.com

As per information held with us this book is in Public Domain.
This book is a reproduction of an important historical work. Alpha Editions uses the best technology to reproduce historical work in the same manner it was first published to preserve its original nature. Any marks or number seen are left intentionally to preserve its true form.

# Contents

TRENT'S TRUST ................................................................... - 1 -
I ............................................................................................ - 1 -
MR. MACGLOWRIE'S WIDOW .............................................. - 65 -
A WARD OF COLONEL STARBOTTLE'S ............................ - 81 -
PROSPER'S "OLD MOTHER" ................................................ - 103 -
THE CONVALESCENCE OF JACK HAMLIN ..................... - 119 -
A PUPIL OF CHESTNUT RIDGE ......................................... - 138 -
DICK BOYLE'S BUSINESS CARD ........................................ - 150 -

# TRENT'S TRUST

## I

Randolph Trent stepped from the Stockton boat on the San Francisco wharf, penniless, friendless, and unknown. Hunger might have been added to his trials, for, having paid his last coin in passage money, he had been a day and a half without food. Yet he knew it only by an occasional lapse into weakness as much mental as physical. Nevertheless, he was first on the gangplank to land, and hurried feverishly ashore, in that vague desire for action and change of scene common to such irritation; yet after mixing for a few moments with the departing passengers, each selfishly hurrying to some rendezvous of rest or business, he insensibly drew apart from them, with the instinct of a vagabond and outcast. Although he was conscious that he was neither, but merely an unsuccessful miner suddenly reduced to the point of soliciting work or alms of any kind, he took advantage of the first crossing to plunge into a side street, with a vague sense of hiding his shame.

A rising wind, which had rocked the boat for the last few hours, had now developed into a strong sou'wester, with torrents of rain which swept the roadway. His well-worn working clothes, fitted to the warmer Southern mines, gave him more concern from their visible, absurd contrast to the climate than from any actual sense of discomfort, and his feverishness defied the chill of his soaking garments, as he hurriedly faced the blast through the dimly lighted street. At the next corner he paused; he had reached another, and, from its dilapidated appearance, apparently an older wharf than that where he had landed, but, like the first, it was still a straggling avenue leading toward the higher and more animated part of the city. He again mechanically—for a part of his trouble was a vague, undefined purpose—turned toward it.

In his feverish exaltation his powers of perception seemed to be quickened: he was vividly alive to the incongruous, half-marine, half-backwoods character of the warehouses and commercial buildings; to the hull of a stranded ship already built into a block of rude tenements; to the dark stockaded wall of a house framed of corrugated iron, and its weird contiguity to a Swiss chalet, whose galleries were used only to bear the signs of the shops, and whose frame had been carried across seas in sections to be set up at random here.

Moving past these, as in a nightmare dream, of which even the turbulency of the weather seemed to be a part, he stumbled, blinded, panting, and unexpectedly, with no consciousness of his rapid pace beyond his breathlessness, upon the dazzling main thoroughfare of the city. In spite of the weather, the slippery pavements were thronged by hurrying crowds of well-dressed people, again all intent on their own purposes,—purposes that seemed so trifling and unimportant beside his own. The shops were brilliantly lighted, exposing their brightest wares through plate-glass windows; a jeweler's glittered with precious stones; a fashionable apothecary's next to it almost outrivaled it with its gorgeous globes, the gold and green precision of its shelves, and the marble and silver soda fountain like a shrine before it. All this specious show of opulence came upon him with the shock of contrast, and with it a bitter revulsion of feeling more hopeless than his feverish anxiety,—the bitterness of disappointment.

For during his journey he had been buoyed up with the prospect of finding work and sympathy in this youthful city,—a prospect founded solely on his inexperienced hopes. For this he had exchanged the poverty of the mining district,—a poverty that had nothing ignoble about it, that was a part of the economy of nature, and shared with his fellow men and the birds and beasts in their rude encampments. He had given up the brotherhood of the miner, and that practical help and sympathy which brought no degradation with it, for this rude shock of self-interested, self-satisfied civilization. He, who would not have shrunk from asking rest, food, or a night's lodging at the cabin of a brother miner or woodsman, now recoiled suddenly from these well-dressed citizens. What madness had sent him here, an intruder, or, even, as it seemed to him in his dripping clothes, an impostor? And yet these were the people to whom he had confidently expected to tell his story, and who would cheerfully assist him with work! He could almost anticipate the hard laugh or brutal hurried negative in their faces. In his foolish heart he thanked God he had not tried it. Then the apathetic recoil which is apt to follow any keen emotion overtook him. He was dazedly conscious of being rudely shoved once or twice, and even heard the epithet "drunken lout" from one who had run against him.

He found himself presently staring vacantly in the apothecary's window. How long he stood there he could not tell, for he was aroused only by the door opening in front of him, and a young girl emerging with some purchase in her hand. He could see that she was handsomely dressed and quite pretty, and as she passed out she lifted to his withdrawing figure a pair of calm, inquiring eyes, which, however, changed to a look of half-wondering, half-amused pity as she gazed. Yet that look of pity stung his pride more deeply than all. With a deliberate effort he recovered his energy. No, he would not beg, he would not ask assistance from these people; he would go back—anywhere! To the steamboat first; they might let him sleep there, give him a meal, and allow him to work his passage back to Stockton. He might be refused. Well, what then? Well, beyond, there was the bay! He laughed bitterly—his mind was sane enough for that—but he kept on repeating it vaguely to himself, as he crossed the street again, and once more made his way to the wharf.

The wind and rain had increased, but he no longer heeded them in his feverish haste and his consciousness that motion could alone keep away that dreadful apathy which threatened to overcloud his judgment. And he wished while he was able to reason logically to make up his mind to end this unsupportable situation that night. He was scarcely twenty, yet it seemed to him that it had already been demonstrated that his life was a failure; he was an orphan, and when he left college to seek his own fortune in California, he believed he had staked his all upon that venture—and lost.

That bitterness which is the sudden recoil of boyish enthusiasm, and is none the less terrible for being without experience to justify it,—that melancholy we are too apt to look back upon with cynical jeers and laughter in middle age,—is more potent than we dare to think, and it was in no mere pose of youthful pessimism that Randolph Trent now contemplated suicide. Such scraps of philosophy as his education had given him pointed to that one conclusion. And it was the only refuge that pride—real or false—offered him from the one supreme terror of youth—shame.

The street was deserted, and the few lights he had previously noted in warehouses and shops were extinguished. It had grown darker with the storm; the incongruous buildings on either side had become misshapen shadows; the long perspective of the wharf was a strange gloom from which the spars of a ship stood out like the cross he remembered as a boy to have once seen in a picture of the tempest-smitten Calvary. It was his only fancy connected with the future—it might have been his last, for suddenly one of the planks of the rotten wharf gave way beneath his feet, and he felt himself violently precipitated toward the gurgling and oozing tide below. He threw out his arms desperately, caught at a strong girder, drew himself up with the energy of desperation, and staggered to his feet again, safe—and sane. For with this terrible automatic struggle to avoid that death he was courting came a flash of reason. If he had resolutely thrown himself from the pier head as he intended, would he have undergone a hopeless revulsion like this? Was he sure that this might not be, after all, the terrible penalty of self-destruction—this inevitable fierce protest of mind and body when TOO LATE? He was momentarily touched with a sense of gratitude at his escape, but his reason told him it was not from his ACCIDENT, but from his intention.

He was trying carefully to retrace his steps, but as he did so he saw the figure of a man dimly lurching toward him out of the darkness of the wharf and the crossed yards of the ship. A gleam of hope came over him, for the emotion of the last few minutes had rudely displaced his pride and self-love. He would appeal to this stranger, whoever he was; there was more chance that in this rude locality he would be a belated sailor or some humbler wayfarer, and the darkness and solitude made him feel less ashamed. By the last flickering street lamp he could see that he was a man about his own size, with something of the rolling gait of a sailor, which was increased by the weight of a traveling portmanteau he was swinging in his hand. As he approached he evidently detected Randolph's waiting figure, slackened his speed slightly, and changed his portmanteau from his right hand to his left as a precaution for defense.

Randolph felt the blood flush his cheek at this significant proof of his disreputable appearance, but determined to accost him. He scarcely recognized the sound of his own voice now first breaking the silence for hours, but he made his appeal. The man listened, made a slight gesture forward with his disengaged hand, and impelled Randolph slowly up to the street lamp until it shone on both their faces. Randolph saw a man a few years his senior, with a slightly trimmed beard on his dark, weather-beaten cheeks, well-cut features, a quick, observant eye, and a sailor's upward glance and bearing. The stranger saw a thin, youthful, anxious, yet refined and handsome face beneath straggling damp curls, and dark eyes preternaturally bright with suffering. Perhaps his experienced ear, too, detected some harmony with all this in Randolph's voice.

"And you want something to eat, a night's lodging, and a chance of work afterward," the stranger repeated with good-humored deliberation.

"Yes," said Randolph.

"You look it."

Randolph colored faintly.

"Do you ever drink?"

"Yes," said Randolph wonderingly.

"I thought I'd ask," said the stranger, "as it might play hell with you just now if you were not accustomed to it. Take that. Just a swallow, you know—that's as good as a jugful."

He handed him a heavy flask. Randolph felt the burning liquor scald his throat and fire his empty stomach. The stranger turned and looked down the vacant wharf to the darkness from which he came. Then he turned to Randolph again and said abruptly,—

"Strong enough to carry this bag?"

"Yes," said Randolph. The whiskey—possibly the relief—had given him new strength. Besides, he might earn his alms.

"Take it up to room 74, Niantic Hotel—top of next street to this, one block that way—and wait till I come."

"What name shall I say?" asked Randolph.

"Needn't say any. I ordered the room a week ago. Stop; there's the key. Go in; change your togs; you'll find something in that bag that'll fit you. Wait for me. Stop—no; you'd better get some grub there first." He fumbled in his pockets, but fruitlessly. "No matter. You'll find a buckskin purse, with some scads in it, in the bag. So long." And before Randolph could thank him, he lurched away again into the semi-darkness of the wharf.

Overflowing with gratitude at a hospitality so like that of his reckless brethren of the mines, Randolph picked up the portmanteau and started for the hotel. He walked warily now, with a new interest in life, and then, suddenly thinking of his own miraculous escape, he paused, wondering if he ought not to warn his benefactor of the perils of the rotten wharf; but he had already disappeared. The bag was not heavy, but he found that in his exhausted state this new exertion was telling, and he was glad when he reached the hotel. Equally glad was he in his dripping clothes to slip by the porter, and with the key in his pocket ascend unnoticed to 74.

Yet had his experience been larger he might have spared himself that sensitiveness. For the hotel was one of those great caravansaries popular with the returning miner. It received him and his gold dust in his worn-out and bedraggled working clothes, and returned him the next day as a well-dressed citizen on Montgomery Street. It was hard indeed to recognize the unshaven, unwashed, and unkempt "arrival" one met on the principal staircase at night in the scrupulously neat stranger one sat opposite to at breakfast the next morning. In this daily whirl of mutation all identity was swamped, as Randolph learned to know.

At present, finding himself in a comfortable bedroom, his first act was to change his wet clothes, which in the warmer temperature and the decline of his feverishness now began to chill him. He opened the portmanteau and found a complete suit of clothing, evidently a foreign make, well preserved, as if for "shore-going." His pride would have preferred a humbler suit as lessening his obligation, but there was no other. He discovered the purse, a chamois leather bag such as miners and travelers carried, which contained a dozen gold pieces and some paper notes. Taking from it a single coin to defray the expenses of a meal, he restrapped the bag, and leaving the key in the door lock for the benefit of his returning host, made his way to the dining room.

For a moment he was embarrassed when the waiter approached him inquisitively, but it was only to learn the number of his room to "charge" the meal. He ate it quickly, but not voraciously, for his appetite had not yet returned, and he was eager to get back to the room and see the stranger again and return to him the coin which was no longer necessary.

But the stranger had not yet arrived when he reached the room. Over an hour had elapsed since their strange meeting. A new fear came upon him: was it possible he had mistaken the hotel, and his benefactor was awaiting him elsewhere, perhaps even beginning to suspect not only his gratitude but his honesty! The thought made him hot again, but he was helpless. Not knowing the stranger's name, he could not inquire without exposing his situation to the landlord. But again, there was the key, and it was scarcely possible that it fitted another 74 in another hotel. He did not dare to leave the room, but sat by the window, peering through the streaming panes into the storm-swept street below. Gradually the fatigue his excitement had hitherto kept away began to overcome him; his eyes once or twice closed during his vigil, his head nodded against the pane. He rose and walked up and down the room to shake off his drowsiness. Another hour passed—nine o'clock, blown in fitful, far-off strokes from some wind-rocked steeple. Still no stranger. How inviting the bed looked to his weary eyes! The man had told him he wanted rest; he could lie down on the bed in his clothes until he came. He would waken quickly and be ready for his benefactor's directions. It was a great temptation. He yielded to it. His head had scarcely sunk upon the pillow before he slipped into a profound and dreamless sleep.

He awoke with a start, and for a few moments lay vaguely staring at the sunbeams that stretched across his bed before he could recall himself. The room was exactly as before, the portmanteau strapped and pushed under the table as he had left it. There came a tap at the door—the chambermaid to do up the room. She had been there once already, but seeing him asleep, she had forborne to wake him. Apparently the spectacle of a gentleman lying on the bed fully dressed, even to his boots, was not an unusual one at that hotel, for she made no comment. It was twelve o'clock, but she would come again later.

He was bewildered. He had slept the round of the clock—that was natural after his fatigue—but where was his benefactor? The lateness of the time forbade the conclusion that he had merely slept elsewhere; he would assuredly have returned by this time to claim his portmanteau. The portmanteau! He unstrapped it and examined the contents again. They were undisturbed as he had left them the night before. There was a further change of linen, the buckskin bag, which he could see now contained a couple of Bank of England notes, with some foreign gold mixed with American half-eagles, and a cheap, rough memorandum book clasped with elastic, containing a letter in a boyish hand addressed "Dear Daddy" and signed "Bobby," and a photograph of a boy taken by a foreign photographer at

Callao, as the printed back denoted, but nothing giving any clue whatever to the name of the owner.

A strange idea seized him: did the portmanteau really belong to the man who had given it to him? Had he been the innocent receiver of stolen goods from some one who wished to escape detection? He recalled now that he had heard stories of robbery of luggage by thieves "Sydney ducks"—on the deserted wharves, and remembered, too,—he could not tell why the thought had escaped him before,—that the man had spoken with an English accent. But the next moment he recalled his frank and open manner, and his mind cleared of all unworthy suspicion. It was more than likely that his benefactor had taken this delicate way of making a free, permanent gift for that temporary service. Yet he smiled faintly at the return of that youthful optimism which had caused him so much suffering.

Nevertheless, something must be done: he must try to find the man; still more important, he must seek work before this dubious loan was further encroached upon. He restrapped the portmanteau and replaced it under the table, locked the door, gave the key to the office clerk, saying that any one who called upon him was to await his return, and sallied forth. A fresh wind and a blue sky of scudding clouds were all that remained of last night's storm. As he made his way to the fateful wharf, still deserted except by an occasional "wharf-rat,"—as the longshore vagrant or petty thief was called,—he wondered at his own temerity of last night, and the trustfulness of his friend in yielding up his portmanteau to a stranger in such a place. A low drinking saloon, feebly disguised as a junk shop, stood at the corner, with slimy green steps leading to the water.

The wharf was slowly decaying, and here and there were occasional gaps in the planking, as dangerous as the one from which he had escaped the night before. He thought again of the warning he might have given to the stranger; but he reflected that as a seafaring man he must have been familiar with the locality where he had landed. But had he landed there? To Randolph's astonishment, there was no sign or trace of any late occupation of the wharf, and the ship whose crossyards he had seen dimly through the darkness the night before was no longer there. She might have "warped out" in the early morning, but there was no trace of her in the stream or offing beyond. A bark and brig quite dismantled at an adjacent wharf seemed to accent the loneliness. Beyond, the open channel between him and Verba Buena Island was racing with white-maned seas and sparkling in the shifting sunbeams. The scudding clouds above him drove down the steel-blue sky. The lateen sails of the Italian fishing boats were like shreds of cloud, too, blown over the blue and distant bay. His ears sang, his eyes blinked, his pulses throbbed, with the untiring, fierce activity of a San Francisco day.

With something of its restlessness he hurried back to the hotel. Still the stranger was not there, and no one had called for him. The room had been put in order; the portmanteau, that sole connecting link with his last night's experience, was under the table. He drew it out again, and again subjected it to a minute examination. A few toilet articles, not of the best quality, which he had overlooked at first, the linen, the buckskin purse, the memorandum book, and the suit of clothes he stood in, still comprised all he knew of his benefactor. He counted the money in the purse; it amounted, with the Bank of England notes, to about seventy dollars, as he could roughly guess. There was a scrap of paper, the torn-off margin of a newspaper, lying in the purse, with an address hastily scribbled in pencil. It gave, however, no name, only a number: "85 California Street." It might be a clue. He put it, with the purse, carefully in his pocket, and after hurriedly partaking of his forgotten breakfast, again started out.

He presently found himself in the main thoroughfare of last night, which he now knew to be Montgomery Street. It was more thronged than then, but he failed to be impressed, as then, with the selfish activity of the crowd. Yet he was half conscious that his own brighter fortune, more decent attire, and satisfied hunger had something to do with this change, and he glanced hurriedly at the druggist's broad plate-glass windows, with a faint hope that the young girl whose amused pity he had awakened might be there again. He found California Street quickly, and in a few moments he stood before No. 85. He was a little disturbed to find it a rather large building, and that it bore the inscription "Bank." Then came the usual shock to his mercurial temperament, and for the first time he began to consider the absurd hopelessness of his clue.

He, however, entered desperately, and approaching the window of the receiving teller, put the question he had formulated in his mind: Could they give him any information concerning a customer or correspondent who had just arrived in San Francisco and was putting up at the Niantic Hotel, room 74? He felt his face flushing, but, to his astonishment, the clerk manifested no surprise. "And you don't know his name?" said the clerk quietly. "Wait a moment." He moved away, and Randolph saw him speaking to one of the other clerks, who consulted a large register. In a few minutes he returned. "We don't have many customers," he began politely, "who leave only their hotel-room addresses," when he was interrupted by a mumbling protest from one of the other clerks. "That's very different," he replied to his fellow clerk, and then turned to Randolph. "I'm afraid we cannot help you; but I'll make other inquiries if you'll come back in ten minutes." Satisfied to be relieved from the present perils of his questioning, and doubtful of returning, Randolph turned away. But as he left the building he saw a written notice on the swinging door, "Wanted: a Night Porter;" and this one chance of employment determined his return.

When he again presented himself at the window the clerk motioned him to step inside through a lifted rail. Here he found himself confronted by the clerk and another man, distinguished by a certain air of authority, a keen gray eye, and singularly compressed lips set in a closely clipped beard. The clerk indicated him deferentially but briefly—everybody was astonishingly brief and businesslike there—as the president. The president absorbed and possessed Randolph with eyes that never seemed to leave him. Then leaning back against the counter, which he lightly grasped with both hands, he said: "We've sent to the Niantic Hotel to inquire about your man. He ordered his room by letter, giving no name. He arrived there on time last night, slept there, and has occupied the room No. 74 ever since. WE don't know him from Adam, but"—his eyes never left Randolph's—"from the description the landlord gave our clerk, you're the man himself."

For an instant Randolph flushed crimson. The natural mistake of the landlord flashed upon him, his own stupidity in seeking this information, the suspicious predicament in which he was now placed, and the necessity of telling the whole truth. But the president's eye was at once a threat and an invitation. He felt himself becoming suddenly cool, and, with a business brevity equal to their own, said:—

"I was looking for work last night on the wharf. He employed me to carry his bag to the hotel, saying I was to wait for him. I have waited since nine o'clock last night in his room, and he has not come."

"What are you in such a d——d hurry for? He's trusted you; can't you trust him? You've got his bag?" returned the president.

Randolph was silent for a moment. "I want to know what to do with it," he said.

"Hang on to it. What's in it?"

"Some clothes and a purse containing about seventy dollars."

"That ought to pay you for carrying it and storage afterward," said the president decisively. "What made you come here?"

"I found this address in the purse," said Randolph, producing it.

"Is that all?"

"Yes."

"And that's the only reason you came here, to find an owner for that bag?"

"Yes."

The president disengaged himself from the counter.

"I'm sorry to have given you so much trouble," said Randolph concludingly. "Thank you and good-morning."

"Good-morning."

As Randolph turned away he remembered the advertisement for the night watchman. He hesitated and turned back. He was a little surprised to find that the president had not gone away, but was looking after him.

"I beg your pardon, but I see you want a night watchman. Could I do?" said Randolph resolutely.

"No. You're a stranger here, and we want some one who knows the city,—Dewslake," he returned to the receiving teller, "who's taken Larkin's place?"

"No one yet," returned the teller, "but," he added parenthetically, "Judge Boompointer, you know, was speaking to you about his son."

"Yes, I know that." To Randolph: "Go round to my private room and wait for me. I won't be as long as your friend last night." Then he added to a negro porter, "Show him round there."

He moved away, stopping at one or two desks to give an order to the clerks, and once before the railing to speak to a depositor. Randolph followed the negro into the hall, through a "board room," and into a handsomely furnished office. He had not to wait long. In a few moments the president appeared with an older man whose gray side whiskers, cut with a certain precision, and whose black and white checked neckerchief, tied in a formal bow, proclaimed the English respectability of the period. At the president's dictation he took down Randolph's name, nativity, length of residence, and occupation in California. This concluded, the president, glancing at his companion, said briefly,—

"Well?"

"He had better come to-morrow morning at nine," was the answer.

"And ask for Mr. Dingwall, the deputy manager," added the president, with a gesture that was at once an introduction and a dismissal to both.

Randolph had heard before of this startling brevity of San Francisco business detail, yet he lingered until the door closed on Mr. Dingwall. His heart was honestly full.

"You have been very kind, sir," he stammered.

"I haven't run half the risks of that chap last night," said the president grimly, the least tremor of a smile on his set mouth.

"If you would only let me know what I can do to thank you," persisted Randolph.

"Trust the man that trusts you, and hang on to your trust," returned the president curtly, with a parting nod.

Elated and filled with high hopes as Randolph was, he felt some trepidation in returning to his hotel. He had to face his landlord with some explanation of the bank's inquiry. The landlord might consider him an impostor, and request him to leave, or, more dreadful still, insist upon keeping the bag. He thought of the parting words of the president, and resolved upon "hanging on to his trust," whatever happened. But he was agreeably surprised to find that he was received at the office with a certain respect not usually shown to the casual visitor. "Your caller turned up to-day"—Randolph started—"from the Eureka bank," continued the clerk. "Sorry we could not give your name, but you know you only left a deposit in your letter and sent a messenger for your key yesterday afternoon. When you came you went straight to your room. Perhaps you would like to register now." Randolph no longer hesitated, reflecting that he could explain it all later to his unknown benefactor, and wrote his name boldly. But he was still more astonished when the clerk continued: "I reckon it was a case of identifying you for a draft—it often happens here—and we'd have been glad to do it for you. But the bank clerk seemed satisfied with out description of you—you're easily described, you know" (this in a parenthesis, complimentarily intended)—"so it's all right. We can give you a better room lower down, if you're going to stay longer." Not knowing whether to laugh or to be embarrassed at this extraordinary conclusion of the blunder, Randolph answered that he had just come from the bank, adding, with a pardonable touch of youthful pride, that he was entering the bank's employment the next day.

Another equally agreeable surprise met him on his arrival there the next morning. Without any previous examination or trial he was installed at once as a corresponding clerk in the place of one just promoted to a sub-agency in the interior. His handwriting, his facility of composition, had all been taken for granted, or perhaps predicated upon something the president had discerned in that one quick, absorbing glance. He ventured to express the thought to his neighbor.

"The boss," said that gentleman, "can size a man in and out, and all through, in about the time it would take you and me to tell the color of his hair. HE don't make mistakes, you bet; but old Dingy—the dep—you settled with your clothes."

"My clothes!" echoed Randolph, with a faint flush.

"Yes, English cut—that fetched him."

And so his work began. His liberal salary, which seemed to him munificent in comparison with his previous earnings in the mines, enabled him to keep the contents of the buckskin purse intact, and presently to return the borrowed suit of clothes to the portmanteau. The mysterious owner should find everything as when he first placed it in his hands. With the quick mobility of youth and his own rather mercurial nature, he had begun to forget, or perhaps to be a little ashamed of his keen emotions and sufferings the night of his arrival, until that night was recalled to him in a singular way.

One Sunday a vague sense of duty to his still missing benefactor impelled him to spend part of his holiday upon the wharves. He had rambled away among the shipping at the newer pier slips, and had gazed curiously upon decks where a few seamen or officers in their Sunday apparel smoked, paced, or idled, trying vainly to recognize the face and figure which had once briefly flashed out under the flickering wharf lamp. Was the stranger a shipmaster who had suddenly transferred himself to another vessel on another voyage? A crowd which had gathered around some landing steps nearer shore presently attracted his attention. He lounged toward it and looked over the shoulders of the bystanders down upon the steps. A boat was lying there, which had just towed in the body of a man found floating on the water. Its features were already swollen and defaced like a hideous mask; its body distended beyond all proportion, even to the bursting of its sodden clothing. A tremulous fascination came over Randolph as he gazed. The bystanders made their brief comments, a few authoritatively and with the air of nautical experts.

"Been in the water about a week, I reckon."

"'Bout that time; just rucked up and floated with the tide."

"Not much chance o' spottin' him by his looks, eh?"

"Nor anything else, you bet. Reg'larly cleaned out. Look at his pockets."

"Wharf-rats or shanghai men?"

"Betwixt and between, I reckon. Man who found him says he's got an ugly cut just back of his head. Ye can't see it for his floating hair."

"Wonder if he got it before or after he got in the water."

"That's for the coroner to say."

"Much he knows or cares," said another cynically. "It'll just be a case of 'Found drowned' and the regular twenty-five dollars to HIM, and five to the man who found the body. That's enough for him to know."

Thrilled with a vague anxiety, Randolph edged forward for a nearer view of the wretched derelict still gently undulating on the towline. The closer he looked the more he was impressed by the idea of some frightful mask that hid a face that refused to be recognized. But his attention became fixed on a man who was giving some advice or orders and examining the body scrutinizingly. Without knowing why, Randolph felt a sudden aversion to him, which was deepened when the man, lifting his head, met Randolph's eyes with a pair of shifting yet aggressive ones. He bore, nevertheless, an odd, weird likeness to the missing man Randolph was seeking, which strangely troubled him. As the stranger's eyes followed him and lingered with a singular curiosity on Randolph's dress, he remembered with a sudden alarm that he was wearing the suit of the missing man. A quick impulse to conceal himself came upon him, but he as quickly conquered it, and returned the man's cold stare with an anger he could not account for, but which made the stranger avert his eyes. Then the man got into the boat beside the boatman, and the two again towed away the corpse. The head rose and fell with the swell, as if nodding a farewell. But it was still defiant, under its shapeless mask, that even wore a smile, as if triumphant in its hideous secret.

II

The opinion of the cynical bystander on the wharf proved to be a correct one. The coroner's jury brought in the usual verdict of "Found drowned," which was followed by the usual newspaper comment upon the insecurity of the wharves and the inadequate protection of the police.

Randolph Trent read it with conflicting emotions. The possibility he had conceived of the corpse being that of his benefactor was dismissed when he had seen its face, although he was sometimes tortured with doubt, and a wonder if he might not have learned more by attending the inquest. And there was still the suggestion that the mysterious disappearance might have been accomplished by violence like this. He was satisfied that if he had attempted publicly to identify the corpse as his missing friend he would have laid himself open to suspicion with a story he could hardly corroborate.

He had once thought of confiding his doubts to Mr. Revelstoke, the bank president, but he had a dread of that gentleman's curt conclusions and remembered his injunction to "hang on to his trust." Since his installation, Mr. Revelstoke had merely acknowledged his presence by a good-humored nod now and then, although Randolph had an instinctive feeling that he was perfectly informed as to his progress. It was wiser for Randolph to confine himself strictly to his duty and keep his own counsel.

Yet he was young, and it was not strange that in his idle moments his thoughts sometimes reverted to the pretty girl he had seen on the night of his arrival, nor that he should wish to parade his better fortune before her curious eyes. Neither was it strange that in this city, whose day-long sunshine brought every one into the public streets, he should presently have that opportunity. It chanced that one afternoon, being in the residential quarter, he noticed a well-dressed young girl walking before him in company with a delicate looking boy of seven or eight years. Something in the carriage of her graceful figure, something in a certain consciousness and ostentation of coquetry toward her youthful escort, attracted his attention. Yet it struck him that she was neither related to the child nor accustomed to children's ways, and that she somewhat unduly emphasized this to the passers-by, particularly those of his own sex, who seemed to be greatly attracted by her evident beauty. Presently she ascended the steps of a handsome dwelling, evidently their home, and as she turned he saw her face. It was the girl he remembered. As her eye caught his, he blushed with the consciousness of their former meeting; yet, in the very embarrassment of the moment, he lifted his hat in recognition. But the salutation was met only by a cold, critical stare. Randolph bit his lip and passed on. His reason told him she was right, his instinct told him she was unfair; the contradiction fascinated him.

Yet he was destined to see her again. A month later, while seated at his desk, which overlooked the teller's counter, he was startled to see her enter the bank and approach the counter. She was already withdrawing a glove from her little hand, ready to affix her signature to the receipted form to be proffered by the teller. As she received the gold in exchange, he could see, by the increased politeness of that official, his evident desire to prolong the transaction, and the sidelong glances of his fellow clerks, that she was apparently no stranger but a recognized object of admiration. Although her face was slightly flushed at the moment, Randolph observed that she wore a certain proud reserve, which he half hoped was intended as a check to these attentions. Her eyes were fixed upon the counter, and this gave him a brief opportunity to study her delicate beauty. For in a few moments she was gone; whether she had in her turn observed him he could not say. Presently he rose and sauntered, with what he believed was a careless air, toward the paying teller's counter and the receipt, which, being the last, was plainly exposed on the file of that day's "taking." He was startled by a titter of laughter from the clerks and by the teller ironically lifting the file and placing it before him.

"That's her name, sonny, but I didn't think that you'd tumble to it quite as quick as the others. Every new man manages to saunter round here to get a sight of that receipt, and I've seen hoary old depositors outside edge around inside, pretendin' they wanted to see the dep, jest to feast their eyes on that girl's name. Take a good look at it and paste a copy in your hat, for that's all you'll know of her, you bet. Perhaps you think she's put her address and her 'at home' days on the receipt. Look hard and maybe you'll see 'em."

The instinct of youthful retaliation to say he knew her address already stirred Randolph, but he shut his lips in time, and moved away. His desk neighbor informed him that the young lady came there once a month and drew a hundred dollars from some deposit to her credit, but that was all they knew. Her name was Caroline Avondale, yet there was no one of that name in the San Francisco Directory.

But Randolph's romantic curiosity would not allow the incident to rest there. A favorable impression he had produced on Mr. Dingwall enabled him to learn more, and precipitated what seemed to him a singular discovery. "You will find," said the deputy manager, "the statement of the first deposit to Miss Avondale's credit in letters in your own department. The account was opened two years ago through a South American banker. But I am afraid it will not satisfy your curiosity." Nevertheless, Randolph remained after office hours and spent some time in examining the correspondence of two years ago. He was rewarded at last by a banker's letter from Callao advising the remittance of one thousand dollars to the credit of Miss Avondale of San Francisco. The letter was written in Spanish, of which Randolph had a fair knowledge, but it was made plainer by a space having been left in the formal letter for the English name, which was written in another hand, together with a copy of Miss Avondale's signature for identification—the usual proceeding in those early days, when personal identification was difficult to travelers, emigrants, and visitors in a land of strangers.

But here he was struck by a singular resemblance which he at first put down to mere coincidence of names. The child's photograph which he had found in the portmanteau was taken at Callao. That was a mere coincidence, but it suggested to his mind a more singular one—that the handwriting of the address was, in some odd fashion, familiar to him. That night when he went home he opened the portmanteau and took from the purse the scrap of paper with the written address of the bank, and on comparing it with the banker's letter the next day he was startled to find that the handwriting of the bank's address and that in which the girl's name was introduced in the banker's letter were apparently the same. The letters in the words "Caroline" and "California" appeared as if formed by the same hand. How this might have struck a chirographical expert he did not know. He could not consult the paying teller, who was supposed to be familiar with signatures, without exposing his secret and himself to ridicule. And, after all, what did it prove? Nothing. Even if this girl were cognizant of the man who supplied her address to the Callao banker two years ago, and he was really the missing owner of the portmanteau, would she know where he was now? It might make an opening for conversation if he ever met her familiarly, but nothing more. Yet I am afraid another idea occasionally took possession of Randolph's romantic fancy. It was pleasant to think that the patron of his own fortunes might be in some mysterious way the custodian of hers. The money was placed to her credit—a liberal sum for a girl so young. The large house in which she lived was sufficient to prove to the optimistic Randolph that this income was something personal and distinct from her family. That his unknown benefactor was in the habit of mysteriously rewarding deserving merit after the fashion of a marine fairy godmother, I fear did not strike him as being ridiculous.

But an unfortunate query in that direction, addressed to a cynical fellow clerk, who had the exhaustive experience with the immature mustaches of twenty-three, elicited a reply which shocked him. To his indignant protest the young man continued:—

"Look here; a girl like that who draws money regularly from some man who doesn't show up by name, who comes for it herself, and hasn't any address, and calls herself 'Avondale'—only an innocent from Dutch Flat, like you, would swallow."

"Impossible," said Randolph indignantly. "Anybody could see she's a lady by her dress and bearing."

"Dress and bearing!" echoed the clerk, with the derision of blase youth. "If that's your test, you ought to see Florry ———."

But here one may safely leave the young gentleman as abruptly as Randolph did. Yet a drop of this corrosive criticism irritated his sensitiveness, and it was not until he recalled his last meeting with her and her innocent escort that he was himself again. Fortunately, he did not relate it to the critic, who would in all probability have added a precocious motherhood to the young lady's possible qualities.

He could now only look forward to her reappearance at the bank, and here he was destined to a more serious disappointment. For when she made her customary appearance at the counter, he noticed a certain businesslike gravity in the paying teller's reception of her, and that he was consulting a small register before him instead of handing her the usual receipt form. "Perhaps you are unaware, Miss Avondale, that your account is overdrawn," Randolph distinctly heard him say, although in a politely lowered voice.

The young girl stopped in taking off her glove; her delicate face expressed her wonder, and paled slightly; she cast a quick and apparently involuntary glance in the direction of Randolph, but said quietly,—

"I don't think I understand."

"I thought you did not—ladies so seldom do," continued the paying teller suavely. "But there are no funds to your credit. Has not your banker or correspondent advised you?"

The girl evidently did not comprehend. "I have no correspondent or banker," she said. "I mean—I have heard nothing."

"The original credit was opened from Callao," continued the official, "but since then it has been added to by drafts from Melbourne. There may be one nearly due now."

The young girl seemed scarcely to comprehend, yet her face remained pale and thoughtful. It was not until the paying teller resumed with suggestive politeness that she roused herself: "If you would like to see the president, he might oblige you until you hear from your friends. Of course, my duty is simply to"—

"I don't think I require you to exceed it," returned the young girl quietly, "or that I wish to see the president." Her delicate little face was quite set with resolution and a mature dignity, albeit it was still pale, as she drew away from the counter.

"If you would leave your address," continued the official with persistent politeness, "we could advise you of any later deposit to your credit."

"It is hardly necessary," returned the young lady. "I should learn it myself, and call again. Thank you. Good-morning." And settling her veil over her face, she quietly passed out.

The pain and indignation with which Randolph overheard this colloquy he could with the greatest difficulty conceal. For one wild moment he had thought of calling her back while he made a personal appeal to Revelstoke; but the conviction borne in upon him by her resolute bearing that she would refuse it, and he would only lay himself open to another rebuff, held him to his seat. Yet he could not entirely repress his youthful indignation.

"Where I come from," he said in an audible voice to his neighbor, "a young lady like that would have been spared this public disappointment. A dozen men would have made up that sum and let her go without knowing anything about her account being overdrawn." And he really believed it.

"Nice, comf'able way of doing banking business in Dutch Flat," returned the cynic. "And I suppose you'd have kept it up every month? Rather a tall price to pay for looking at a pretty girl once a month! But I suppose they're scarcer up there than here. All the same, it ain't too late now. Start up your subscription right here, sonny, and we'll all ante up."

But Randolph, who seldom followed his heroics to their ultimate prosaic conclusions, regretted he had spoken, although still unconvinced. Happily for his temper, he did not hear the comment of the two tellers.

"Won't see HER again, old boy," said one.

"I reckon not," returned the other, "now that she's been chucked by her fancy man—until she gets another. But cheer up; a girl like that won't want friends long."

It is not probable that either of these young gentlemen believed what they said, or would have been personally disrespectful or uncivil to any woman; they were fairly decent young fellows, but the rigors of business demanded this appearance of worldly wisdom between themselves. Meantime, for a week after, Randolph indulged in wild fancies of taking his benefactor's capital of seventy dollars, adding thirty to it from his own hard-earned savings, buying a draft with it from the bank for one hundred dollars, and in some mysterious way getting it to Miss Avondale as the delayed remittance.

The brief wet winter was nearly spent; the long dry season was due, although there was still the rare beauty of cloud scenery in the steel-blue sky, and the sudden return of quick but transient showers. It was on a Sunday of weather like this that the nature-loving Randolph extended his usual holiday excursion as far as Contra Costa by the steamer after his dutiful round of the wharves and shipping. It was with a gayety born equally of his youth and the weather that he overcame his constitutional shyness, and not only mingled without restraint among the pleasure-seekers that thronged the crowded boat, but, in the consciousness of his good looks and a new suit of clothes, even penetrated into the aristocratic seclusion of the "ladies' cabin"—sacred to the fair sex and their attendant swains or chaperones.

But he found every seat occupied, and was turning away, when he suddenly recognized Miss Avondale sitting beside her little escort. She appeared, however, in a somewhat constrained attitude, sustaining with one hand the boy, who had clambered on the seat. He was looking out of the cabin window, which she was also trying to do, with greater difficulty on account of her position. He could see her profile presented with such marked persistency that he was satisfied she had seen him and was avoiding him. He turned and left the cabin.

Yet, once on the deck again, he repented his haste. Perhaps she had not actually recognized him; perhaps she wished to avoid him only because she was in plainer clothes—a circumstance that, with his knowledge of her changed fortunes, struck him to the heart. It seemed to him that even as a humble employee of the bank he was in some way responsible for it, and wondered if she associated him with her humiliation. He longed to speak with her and assure her of his sympathy, and yet he was equally conscious that she would reject it.

When the boat reached the Alameda wharf she slipped away with the other passengers. He wandered about the hotel garden and the main street in the hope of meeting her again, although he was instinctively conscious that she would not follow the lines of the usual Sunday sight-seers, but had her own destination. He penetrated the depths of the Alameda, and lost himself among its low, trailing oaks, to no purpose. The hope of the morning had died within him; the fire of adventure was quenched, and when the clouds gathered with a rising wind he felt that the promise of that day was gone. He turned to go back to the ferry, but on consulting his watch he found that he had already lost so much time in his devious wanderings that he must run to catch the last boat. The few drops that spattered through the trees presently increased to a shower; he put up his umbrella without lessening his speed, and finally dashed into the main street as the last bell was ringing. But at the same moment a slight, graceful figure slipped out of the woods just ahead of him, with no other protection from the pelting storm than a handkerchief tied over her hat, and ran as swiftly toward the wharf. It needed only one glance for Randolph to recognize Miss Avondale. The moment had come, the opportunity was here, and the next instant he was panting at her side, with the umbrella over her head.

The girl lifted her head quickly, gave a swift look of recognition, a brief smile of gratitude, and continued her pace. She had not taken his arm, but had grasped the handle of the umbrella, which linked them together. Not a word was spoken. Two people cannot be conversational or sentimental flying at the top of their speed beneath a single umbrella, with a crowd of impatient passengers watching and waiting for them. And I grieve to say that, being a happy American crowd, there was some irreverent humor. "Go it, sis! He's gainin' on you!" "Keep it up!" "Steady, sonny! Don't prance!" "No fancy licks! You were nearly over the traces that time!" "Keep up to the pole!" (i. e. the umbrella). "Don't crowd her off the track! Just swing on together; you'll do it."

Randolph had glanced quickly at his companion. She was laughing, yet looking at him shyly as if wondering how HE was taking it. The paddle wheels were beginning to revolve. Another rush, and they were on board as the plank was drawn in.

But they were only on the edge of a packed and seething crowd. Randolph managed, however, to force a way for her to an angle of the paddle box, where they were comparatively alone although still exposed to the rain. She recognized their enforced companionship by dropping her grasp of the umbrella, which she had hitherto been holding over him with a singular kind of mature superiority very like—as Randolph felt—her manner to the boy.

"You have left your little friend?" he said, grasping at the idea for a conversational opening.

"My little cousin? Yes," she said. "I left him with friends. I could not bear to make him run any risk in this weather. But," she hesitated half apologetically, half mischievously, "perhaps I hurried you."

"Oh, no," said Randolph quickly. "This is the last boat, and I must be at the bank to-morrow morning at nine."

"And I must be at the shop at eight," she said. She did not speak bitterly or pointedly, nor yet with the entire familiarity of custom. He noticed that her dress was indeed plainer, and yet she seemed quite concerned over the water-soaked state of that cheap thin silk pelerine and merino skirt. A big lump was in his throat.

"Do you know," he said desperately, yet trying to laugh, "that this is not the first time you have seen me dripping?"

"Yes," she returned, looking at him interestedly; "it was outside of the druggist's in Montgomery Street, about four months ago. You were wetter then even than you are now."

"I was hungry, friendless, and penniless, Miss Avondale." He had spoken thus abruptly in the faint hope that the revelation might equalize their present condition; but somehow his confession, now that it was uttered, seemed exceedingly weak and impotent. Then he blundered in a different direction. "Your eyes were the only kind ones I had seen since I landed." He flushed a little, feeling himself on insecure ground, and ended desperately: "Why, when I left you, I thought of committing suicide."

"Oh, dear, not so bad as that, I hope!" she said quickly, smiling kindly, yet with a certain air of mature toleration, as if she were addressing her little cousin. "You only fancied it. And it isn't very complimentary to my eyes if their kindness drove you to such horrid thoughts. And then what happened?" she pursued smilingly.

"I had a job to carry a man's bag, and it got me a night's lodging and a meal," said Randolph, almost brusquely, feeling the utter collapse of his story.

"And then?" she said encouragingly.

"I got a situation at the bank."

"When?"

"The next day," faltered Randolph, expecting to hear her laugh. But Miss Avondale heaved the faintest sigh.

"You are very lucky," she said.

"Not so very," returned Randolph quickly, "for the next time you saw me you cut me dead."

"I believe I did," she said smilingly.

"Would you mind telling me why?"

"Are you sure you won't be angry?"

"I may be pained," said Randolph prudently.

"I apologize for that beforehand. Well, that first night I saw a young man looking very anxious, very uncomfortable, and very weak. The second time—and not very long after—I saw him well dressed, lounging like any other young man on a Sunday afternoon, and I believed that he took the liberty of bowing to me then because I had once looked at him under a misapprehension."

"Oh, Miss Avondale!"

"Then I took a more charitable view, and came to the conclusion that the first night he had been drinking. But," she added, with a faint smile at Randolph's lugubrious face, "I apologize. And you have had your revenge; for if I cut you on account of your smart clothes, you have tried to do me a kindness on account of my plain ones."

"Oh, Miss Avondale," burst out Randolph, "if you only knew how sorry and indignant I was at the bank—when—you know—the other day"—he stammered. "I wanted to go with you to Mr. Revelstoke, you know, who had been so generous to me, and I know he would have been proud to befriend you until you heard from your friends."

"And I am very glad you did nothing so foolish," said the young lady seriously, "or"—with a smile—"I should have been still more aggravating to you when we met. The bank was quite right. Nor have I any pathetic story like yours. Some years ago my little half-cousin whom you saw lost his mother and was put in my charge by his father, with a certain sum to my credit, to be expended for myself and the child. I lived with an uncle, with whom, for some family reasons, the child's father was not on good terms, and this money and the charge of the child were therefore intrusted entirely to me; perhaps, also, because Bobby and I were fond of each other and I was a friend of his mother. The father was a shipmaster, always away on long voyages, and has been home but once in the three years I have had charge of his son. I have not heard from him since. He is a good-hearted man, but of a restless, roving disposition, with no domestic tastes. Why he should suddenly cease to provide for my little cousin—if he has done so—or if his omission means only some temporary disaster to himself or his fortunes, I do not know. My anxiety was more for the poor boy's sake than for myself, for as long as I live I can provide for him." She said this without the least display of emotion, and with the same mature air of also repressing any emotion on the part of Randolph. But for her size and girlish figure, but for the dripping tangles of her hair and her soft eyes, he would have believed he was talking to a hard, middle-aged matron.

"Then you—he—has no friends here?" asked Randolph.

"No. We are all from Callao, where Bobby was born. My uncle was a merchant there, who came here lately to establish an agency. We lived with him in Sutter Street—where you remember I was so hateful to you," she interpolated, with a mischievous smile—"until his enterprise failed and he was obliged to return; but I stayed here with Bobby, that he might be educated in his father's own tongue. It was unfortunate, perhaps," she said, with a little knitting of her pretty brows, "that the remittances ceased and uncle left about the same time; but, like you, I was lucky, and I managed to get a place in the Emporium."

"The Emporium!" repeated Randolph in surprise. It was a popular "magasin of fashion" in Montgomery Street. To connect this refined girl with its garish display and vulgar attendants seemed impossible.

"The Emporium," reiterated Miss Avondale simply. "You see, we used to dress a good deal in Callao and had the Paris fashions, and that experience was of great service to me. I am now at the head of what they call the 'mantle department,' if you please, and am looked up to as an authority." She made him a mischievous bow, which had the effect of causing a trickle from the umbrella to fall across his budding mustache, and another down her own straight little nose—a diversion that made them laugh together, although Randolph secretly felt that the young girl's quiet heroism was making his own trials appear ridiculous. But her allusion to Callao and the boy's name had again excited his fancy and revived his romantic dream of their common benefactor. As soon as they could get a more perfect shelter and furl the umbrella, he plunged into the full story of the mysterious portmanteau and its missing owner, with the strange discovery that he had made of the similarity of the two handwritings. The young lady listened intently, eagerly, checking herself with what might have been a half smile at his enthusiasm.

"I remember the banker's letter, certainly," she said, "and Captain Dornton—that was the name of Bobby's father—asked me to sign my name in the body of it where HE had also written it with my address. But the likeness of the handwriting to your slip of paper may be only a fancied one. Have you shown it to any one," she said quickly—"I mean," she corrected herself as quickly, "any one who is an expert?"

"Not the two together," said Randolph, explaining how he had shown the paper to Mr. Revelstoke.

But Miss Avondale had recovered herself, and laughed. "That that bit of paper should have been the means of getting you a situation seems to me the more wonderful occurrence. Of course it is quite a coincidence that there should be a child's photograph and a letter signed 'Bobby' in the portmanteau. But"—she stopped suddenly and fixed her dark eyes on his—"you have seen Bobby. Surely you can say if it was his likeness?"

Randolph was embarrassed. The fact was he had always been so absorbed in HER that he had hardly glanced at the child. He ventured to say this, and added a little awkwardly, and coloring, that he had seen Bobby only twice.

"And you still have this remarkable photograph and letter?" she said, perhaps a little too carelessly.

"Yes. Would you like to see them?"

"Very much," she returned quickly; and then added, with a laugh, "you are making me quite curious."

"If you would allow me to see you home," said Randolph, "we have to pass the street where my room is, and," he added timidly, "I could show them to you."

"Certainly," she replied, with sublime unconsciousness of the cause of his hesitation; "that will be very nice?"

Randolph was happy, albeit he could not help thinking that she was treating him like the absent Bobby.

"It's only on Commercial Street, just above Montgomery," he went on. "We go straight up from the wharf"—he stopped short here, for the bulk of a bystander, a roughly clad miner, was pressing him so closely that he was obliged to resist indignantly—partly from discomfort, and partly from a sense that the man was overhearing him. The stranger muttered a kind of apology, and moved away.

"He seems to be perpetually in your way," said Miss Avondale, smiling. "He was right behind you, and you nearly trod on his toes, when you bolted out of the cabin this morning."

"Ah, then you DID see me!" said Randolph, forgetting all else in his delight at the admission.

But Miss Avondale was not disconcerted. "Thanks to your collision, I saw you both."

It was still raining when they disembarked at the wharf, a little behind the other Passengers, who had crowded on the bow of the steamboat. It was only a block or two beyond the place where Randolph had landed that eventful night. He had to pass it now; but with Miss Avondale clinging to his arm, with what different feelings! The rain still fell, the day was fading, but he walked in an enchanted dream, of which the prosaic umbrella was the mystic tent and magic pavilion. He must needs even stop at the corner of the wharf, and show her the exact spot where his unknown benefactor appeared.

"Coming out of the shadow like that man there," she added brightly, pointing to a figure just emerging from the obscurity of an overhanging warehouse. "Why, it's your friend the miner!"

Randolph looked. It was indeed the same man, who had probably reached the wharf by a cross street.

"Let us go on, do!" said Miss Avondale, suddenly tightening her hold of Randolph's arm in some instinctive feminine alarm. "I don't like this place."

But Randolph, with the young girl's arm clinging to his, felt supremely daring. Indeed, I fear he was somewhat disappointed when the stranger peacefully turned into the junk shop at the corner and left them to pursue their way.

They at last stopped before some business offices on a central thoroughfare, where Randolph had a room on the third story. When they had climbed the flight of stairs he unlocked a door and disclosed a good-sized apartment which had been intended for an office, but which was now neatly furnished as a study and bedroom. Miss Avondale smiled at the singular combination.

"I should fancy," she said, "you would never feel as if you had quite left the bank behind you." Yet, with her air of protection and mature experience, she at once began to move one or two articles of furniture into a more tasteful position, while Randolph, nevertheless a little embarrassed at his audacity in asking this goddess into his humble abode, hurriedly unlocked a closet, brought out the portmanteau, and handed her the letter and photograph.

Woman-like, Miss Avondale looked at the picture first. If she experienced any surprise, she repressed it. "It is LIKE Bobby," she said meditatively, "but he was stouter then; and he's changed sadly since he has been in this climate. I don't wonder you didn't recognize him. His father may have had it taken some day when they were alone together. I didn't know of it, though I know the photographer." She then looked at the letter, knit her pretty brows, and with an abstracted air sat down on the edge of Randolph's bed, crossed her little feet, and looked puzzled. But he was unable to detect the least emotion.

"You see," she said, "the handwriting of most children who are learning to write is very much alike, for this is the stage of development when they 'print.' And their composition is the same: they talk only of things that interest all children—pets, toys, and their games. This is only ANY child's letter to ANY father. I couldn't really say it WAS Bobby's. As to the photograph, they have an odd way in South America of selling photographs of anybody, principally of pretty women, by the packet, to any one who wants them. So that it does not follow that the owner of this photograph had any personal interest in it. Now, as to your mysterious patron himself, can you describe him?" She looked at Randolph with a certain feline intensity.

He became embarrassed. "You know I only saw him once, under a street lamp"—he began.

"And I have only seen Captain Dornton—if it were he—twice in three years," she said. "But go on."

Again Randolph was unpleasantly impressed with her cold, dryly practical manner. He had never seen his benefactor but once, but he could not speak of him in that way.

"I think," he went on hesitatingly, "that he had dark, pleasant eyes, a thick beard, and the look of a sailor."

"And there were no other papers in the portmanteau?" she said, with the same intense look.

"None."

"These are mere coincidences," said Miss Avondale, after a pause, "and, after all, they are not as strange as the alternative. For we would have to believe that Captain Dornton arrived here—where he knew his son and I were living—without a word of warning, came ashore for the purpose of going to a hotel and the bank also, and then unaccountably changed his mind and disappeared."

The thought of the rotten wharf, his own escape, and the dead body were all in Randolph's mind; but his reasoning was already staggered by the girl's conclusions, and he felt that it might only pain, without convincing her. And was he convinced himself? She smiled at his blank face and rose. "Thank you all the same. And now I must go."

Randolph rose also. "Would you like to take the photograph and letter to show your cousin?"

"Yes. But I should not place much reliance on his memory." Nevertheless, she took up the photograph and letter, and Randolph, putting the portmanteau back in the closet, locked it, and stood ready to accompany her.

On their way to her house they talked of other things. Randolph learned something of her life in Callao: that she was an orphan like himself, and had been brought from the Eastern States when a child to live with a rich uncle in Callao who was childless; that her aunt had died and her uncle had married again; that the second wife had been at variance with his family, and that it was consequently some relief to Miss Avondale to be independent as the guardian of Bobby, whose mother was a sister of the first wife; that her uncle had objected as strongly as a brother-in-law could to his wife's sister's marriage with Captain Dornton on account of his roving life and unsettled habits, and that consequently there would be little sympathy for her or for Bobby in his mysterious disappearance. The wind blew and the rain fell upon these confidences, yet Randolph, walking again under that umbrella of felicity, parted with her at her own doorstep all too soon, although consoled with the permission to come and see her when the child returned.

He went back to his room a very hopeful, foolish, but happy youth. As he entered he seemed to feel the charm of her presence again in the humble apartment she had sanctified. The furniture she had moved with her own little hands, the bed on which she had sat for a half moment, was glorified to his youthful fancy. And even that magic portmanteau which had brought him all this happiness, that, too,—but he gave a sudden start. The closet door, which he had shut as he went out, was unlocked and open, the portmanteau—his "trust"—gone!

III

Randolph Trent's consternation at the loss of the portmanteau was partly superstitious. For, although it was easy to make up the small sum taken, and the papers were safe in Miss Avondale's possession, yet this displacement of the only link between him and his missing benefactor, and the mystery of its disappearance, raised all his old doubts and suspicions. A vague uneasiness, a still more vague sense of some remissness on his own part, possessed him.

That the portmanteau was taken from his room during his absence with Miss Avondale that afternoon was evident. The door had been opened by a skeleton key, and as the building was deserted on Sunday, there had been no chance of interference with the thief. If mere booty had been his object, the purse would have satisfied him without his burdening himself with a portmanteau which might be identified. Nothing else in the room had been disturbed. The thief must have had some cognizance of its location, and have kept some espionage over Randolph's movements—a circumstance which added to the mystery and his disquiet. He placed a description of his loss with the police authorities, but their only idea of recovering it was by leaving that description with pawnbrokers and second-hand dealers, a proceeding that Randolph instinctively felt was in vain.

A singular but instinctive reluctance to inform Miss Avondale of his loss kept him from calling upon her for the first few days. When he did, she seemed concerned at the news, although far from participating in his superstition or his suspicions.

"You still have the letter and photograph—whatever they may be worth—for identification," she said dryly, "although Bobby cannot remember about the letter. He thinks he went once with his father to a photographer and had a picture taken, but he cannot remember seeing it afterward." She was holding them in her hand, and Randolph almost mechanically took them from her and put them in his pocket. He would not, perhaps, have noticed his own brusqueness had she not looked a little surprised, and, he thought, annoyed. "Are you quite sure you won't lose them?" she said gently. "Perhaps I had better keep them for you."

"I shall seal them up and put them in the bank safe," he said quickly. He could not tell whether his sudden resolution was an instinct or the obstinacy that often comes to an awkward man. "But," he added, coloring, "I shall always regret the loss of the portmanteau, for it was the means of bringing us together."

"I thought it was the umbrella," said Miss Avondale dryly.

She had once before halted him on the perilous edge of sentiment by a similar cynicism, but this time it cut him deeply. For he could not be blind to the fact that she treated him like a mere boy, and in dispelling the illusions of his instincts and beliefs seemed as if intent upon dispelling his illusions of HER; and in her half-smiling abstraction he read only the well-bred toleration of one who is beginning to be bored. He made his excuses early and went home. Nevertheless, although regretting he had not left her the letter and photograph, he deposited them in the bank safe the next day, and tried to feel that he had vindicated his character for grown-up wisdom.

Then, in his conflicting emotions, he punished himself, after the fashion of youth, by avoiding the beloved one's presence for several days. He did this in the belief that it would enable him to make up his mind whether to reveal his real feelings to her, and perhaps there was the more alluring hope that his absence might provoke some manifestations of sentiment on her part. But she made no sign. And then came a reaction in his feelings, with a heightened sense of loyalty to his benefactor. For, freed of any illusion or youthful fancy now, a purely unselfish gratitude to the unknown man filled his heart. In the lapse of his sentiment he clung the more closely to this one honest romance of his life.

One afternoon, at the close of business, he was a little astonished to receive a message from Mr. Dingwall, the deputy manager, that he wished to see him in his private office. He was still more astonished when Mr. Dingwall, after offering him a chair, stood up with his hands under his coat tails before the fireplace, and, with a hesitancy half reserved, half courteous, but wholly English, said,—

"I—er—would be glad, Mr. Trent, if you would—er—give me the pleasure of your company at dinner to-morrow."

Randolph, still amazed, stammered his acceptance.

"There will be—er—a young lady in whom you were—er—interested some time ago. Er—Miss Avondale."

Randolph, feeling he was coloring, and uncertain whether he should speak of having met her since, contented himself with expressing his delight.

"In fact," continued Mr. Dingwall, clearing his throat as if he were also clearing his conscience of a tremendous secret, "she—er—mentioned your name. There is Sir William Dornton coming also. Sir William has recently succeeded his elder brother, who—er—it seems, was the gentleman you were inquiring about when you first came here, and who, it is now ascertained, was drowned in the bay a few months ago. In fact—er—it is probable that you were the last one who saw him alive. I thought I would tell you," continued Mr. Dingwall, settling his chin more comfortably in his checked cravat, "in case Sir William should speak of him to you."

Randolph was staggered. The abrupt revelation of his benefactor's name and fate, casually coupled with an invitation to dinner, shocked and confounded him. Perhaps Mr. Dingwall noticed it and misunderstood the cause, for he added in parenthetical explanation: "Yes, the man whose portmanteau you took charge of is dead; but you did your duty, Mr. Trent, in the matter, although the recovery of the portmanteau was unessential to the case."

"Dead," repeated Randolph, scarcely heeding him. "But is it true? Are they sure?"

Mr. Dingwall elevated his eyebrows. "The large property at stake of course rendered the most satisfactory proofs of it necessary. His father had died only a month previous, and of course they were seeking the presumptive heir, the so-called 'Captain John Dornton'—your man—when they made the discovery of his death."

Randolph thought of the strange body at the wharf, of the coroner's vague verdict, and was unconvinced. "But," he said impulsively, "there was a child." He checked himself as he remembered this was one of Miss Avondale's confidences to him.

"Ah—Miss Avondale has spoken of a child?" said Mr. Dingwall dryly.

"I saw her with one which she said was Captain Dornton's, which had been left in her care after the death of his wife," said Randolph in hurried explanation.

"John Dornton had no WIFE," said Mr. Dingwall severely. "The boy is a natural son. Captain John lived a wild, rough, and—er—an eccentric life."

"I thought—I understood from Miss Avondale that he was married," stammered the young man.

"In your rather slight acquaintance with that young lady I should imagine she would have had some delicacy in telling you otherwise," returned Mr. Dingwall primly.

Randolph felt the truth of this, and was momentarily embarrassed. Yet he lingered.

"Has Miss Avondale known of this discovery long?" he asked.

"About two weeks, I should say," returned Mr. Dingwall. "She was of some service to Sir William in getting up certain proofs he required."

It was three weeks since she had seen Randolph, yet it would have been easy for her to communicate the news to him. In these three weeks his romance of their common interest in his benefactor—even his own dream of ever seeing him again—had been utterly dispelled.

It was in no social humor that he reached Dingwall's house the next evening. Yet he knew the difficulty of taking an aggressive attitude toward his previous idol or of inviting a full explanation from her then.

The guests, with the exception of himself and Miss Avondale, were all English. She, self-possessed and charming in evening dress, nodded to him with her usual mature patronage, but did not evince the least desire to seek him for any confidential aside. He noticed the undoubted resemblance of Sir William Dornton to his missing benefactor, and yet it produced a singular repulsion in him, rather than any sympathetic predilection. At table he found that Miss Avondale was separated from him, being seated beside the distinguished guest, while he was placed next to the young lady he had taken down—a Miss Eversleigh, the cousin of Sir William. She was tall, and Randolph's first impression of her was that she was stiff and constrained—an impression he quickly corrected at the sound of her voice, her frank ingenuousness, and her unmistakable youth. In the habit of being crushed by Miss Avondale's unrelenting superiority, he found himself apparently growing up beside this tall English girl, who had the naivete of a child. After a few commonplaces she suddenly turned her gray eyes on his, and said,—

"Didn't you like Jack? I hope you did. Oh, say you did—do!"

"You mean Captain John Dornton?" said Randolph, a little confused.

"Yes, of course; HIS brother"—glancing toward Sir William. "We always called him Jack, though I was ever so little when he went away. No one thought of calling him anything else but Jack. Say you liked him!"

"I certainly did," returned Randolph impulsively. Then checking himself, he added, "I only saw him once, but I liked his face and manner—and—he was very kind to me."

"Of course he was," said the young girl quickly. "That was only like him, and yet"—lowering her voice slightly—"would you believe that they all say he was wild and wicked and dissipated? And why? Fancy! Just because he didn't care to stay at home and shoot and hunt and race and make debts, as heirs usually do. No, he wanted to see the world and do something for himself. Why, when he was quite young, he could manage a boat like any sailor. Dornton Hall, their place, is on the coast, you know, and they say that, just for adventure's sake, after he went away, he shipped as first mate somewhere over here on the Pacific, and made two or three voyages. You know—don't you?—and how every one was shocked at such conduct in the heir."

Her face was so girlishly animated, with such sparkle of eye and responsive color, that he could hardly reconcile it with her first restraint or with his accepted traditions of her unemotional race, or, indeed, with her relationship to the principal guest. His latent feeling of gratitude to the dead man warmed under the young girl's voice.

"It's so dreadful to think of him as drowned, you know, though even that they put against him," she went on hurriedly, "for they say he was probably drowned in some drunken fit—fell through the wharf or something shocking and awful—worse than suicide. But"—she turned her frank young eyes upon him again—"YOU saw him on the wharf that night, and you could tell how he looked."

"He was as sober as I was," returned Randolph indignantly, as he recalled the incident of the flask and the dead man's caution. From recalling it to repeating it followed naturally, and he presently related the whole story of his meeting with Captain Dornton to the brightly interested eyes beside him. When he had finished, she leaned toward him in girlish confidence, and said:—

"Yes; but EVEN THAT they tell to show how intoxicated he must have been to have given up his portmanteau to an utter stranger like you." She stopped, colored, and yet, reflecting his own half smile, she added: "You know what I mean. For they all agree how nice it was of you not to take any advantage of his condition, and Dingwall said your honesty and faithfulness struck Revelstoke so much that he made a place for you at the bank. Now I think," she continued, with delightful naivete, "it was a proof of poor Jack's

BEING PERFECTLY SOBER, that he knew whom he was trusting, and saw just what you were, at once. There! But I suppose you must not talk to me any longer, but must make yourself agreeable to some one else. But it was very nice of you to tell me all this. I wish you knew my guardian. You'd like him. Do you ever go to England? Do come and see us."

These confidences had not been observed by the others, and Miss Avondale appeared to confine her attentions to Sir William, who seemed to be equally absorbed, except that once he lifted his eyes toward Randolph, as if in answer to some remark from her. It struck Randolph that he was the subject of their conversation, and this did not tend to allay the irritation of a mind already wounded by the contrast of HER lack of sympathy for the dead man who had befriended and trusted her to the simple faith of the girl beside him, who was still loyal to a mere childish recollection.

After the ladies had rustled away, Sir William moved his seat beside Randolph. His manner seemed to combine Mr. Dingwall's restraint with a certain assumption of the man of the world, more notable for its frankness than its tactfulness.

"Sad business this of my brother's, eh," he said, lighting a cigar; "any way you take it, eh? You saw him last, eh?" The interrogating word, however, seemed to be only an exclamation of habit, for he seldom waited for an answer.

"I really don't know," said Randolph, "as I saw him only ONCE, and he left me on the wharf. I know no more where he went to then than where he came from before. Of course you must know all the rest, and how he came to be drowned."

"Yes; it really did not matter much. The whole question was identification and proof of death, you know. Beastly job, eh?"

"Was that his body YOU were helping to get ashore at the wharf one Sunday?" asked Randolph bluntly, now fully recognizing the likeness that had puzzled him in Sir William. "I didn't see any resemblance."

"Precious few would. I didn't—though it's true I hadn't seen him for eight years. Poor old chap been knocked about so he hadn't a feature left, eh? But his shipmate knew him, and there were his traps on the ship."

Then, for the first time, Randolph heard the grim and sordid details of John Dornton's mysterious disappearance. He had arrived the morning before that eventful day on an Australian bark as the principal passenger. The vessel itself had an evil repute, and was believed to have slipped from the hands of the police at Melbourne. John Dornton had evidently amassed a considerable fortune in Australia, although an examination of his papers and effects showed it to be in drafts and letters of credit and shares, and that he had no ready money—a fact borne out by the testimony of his shipmates. The night he arrived was spent in an orgy on board ship, which he did not leave until the early evening of the next day, although, after his erratic fashion, he had ordered a room at a hotel. That evening he took ashore a portmanteau, evidently intending to pass the night at his hotel. He was never seen again, although some of the sailors declared that they had seen him on the wharf WITHOUT THE PORTMANTEAU, and they had drunk together at a low grog shop on the street corner. He had evidently fallen through some hole in the wharf. As he was seen only with the sailors, who also knew he had no ready money on his person, there was no suspicion of foul play.

"For all that, don't you know," continued Sir William, with a forced laugh, which struck Randolph as not only discordant, but as having an insolent significance, "it might have been a deuced bad business for YOU, eh? Last man who was with him, eh? In possession of his portmanteau, eh? Wearing his clothes, eh? Awfully clever of you to go straight to the bank with it. 'Pon my word, my legal man wanted to pounce down on you as 'accessory' until I and Dingwall called him off. But it's all right now."

Randolph's antagonism to the man increased. "The investigation seems to have been peculiar," he said dryly, "for, if I remember rightly, at the coroner's inquest on the body I saw you with, the verdict returned was of the death of an UNKNOWN man."

"Yes; we hadn't clear proof of identity then," he returned coolly, "but we had a reexamination of the body before witnesses afterward, and a verdict according to the facts. That was kept out of the papers in deference to the feelings of the family and friends. I fancy you wouldn't have liked to be cross-examined before a stupid jury about what you were doing with Jack's portmanteau, even if WE were satisfied with it."

"I should have been glad to testify to the kindness of your brother, at any risk," returned Randolph stoutly. "You have heard that the portmanteau was stolen from me, but the amount of money it contained has been placed in Mr. Dingwall's hands for disposal."

"Its contents were known, and all that's been settled," returned Sir William, rising. "But," he continued, with his forced laugh, which to Randolph's fancy masked a certain threatening significance, "I say, it would have been a beastly business, don't you know, if you HAD been called upon to produce it again—ha, ha!—eh?"

Returning to the dining room, Randolph found Miss Avondale alone on a corner of the sofa. She swept her skirts aside as he approached, as an invitation for him to sit beside her. Still sore from his experience, he accepted only in the hope that she was about to confide to him her opinion of this strange story. But, to his chagrin, she looked at him over her fan with a mischievous tolerance. "You seemed more interested in the cousin than the brother of your patron."

Once Randolph might have been flattered at this. But her speech seemed to him only an echo of the general heartlessness. "I found Miss Eversleigh very sympathetic over the fate of the unfortunate man, whom nobody else here seems to care for," said Randolph coldly.

"Yes," returned Miss Avondale composedly; "I believe she was a great friend of Captain Dornton when she was quite a child, and I don't think she can expect much from Sir William, who is very different from his brother. In fact, she was one of the relatives who came over here in quest of the captain, when it was believed he was living and the heir. He was quite a patron of hers."

"But was he not also one of yours?" said Randolph bluntly.

"I think I told you I was the friend of the boy and of poor Paquita, the boy's mother," said Miss Avondale quietly. "I never saw Captain Dornton but twice."

Randolph noticed that she had not said "wife," although in her previous confidences she had so described the mother. But, as Dingwall had said, why should she have exposed the boy's illegitimacy to a comparative stranger; and if she herself had been deceived about it, why should he expect her to tell him? And yet—he was not satisfied.

He was startled by a little laugh. "Well, I declare, you look as if you resented the fact that your benefactor had turned out to be a baronet—just as in some novel—and that you have rendered a service to the English aristocracy. If you are thinking of poor Bobby," she continued, without the slightest show of self-consciousness, "Sir William will provide for him, and thinks of taking him to England to restore his health. Now"—with her smiling, tolerant superiority—"you must go and talk to Miss Eversleigh. I see her looking this way, and I don't think she half likes me as it is."

Randolph, who, however, also saw that Sir William was lounging toward them, here rose formally, as if permitting the latter to take the vacated seat. This partly imposed on him the necessity of seeking Miss Eversleigh, who, having withdrawn to the other end of the room, was turning over the leaves of an album. As Randolph joined her, she said, without looking up, "Is Miss Avondale a friend of yours?"

The question was so pertinent to his reflections at the moment that he answered impulsively, "I really don't know."

"Yes, that's the answer, I think, most of her acquaintances would give, if they were asked the same question and replied honestly," said the young girl, as if musing.

"Even Sir William?" suggested Randolph, half smiling, yet wondering at her unlooked-for serious shrewdness as he glanced toward the sofa.

"Yes; but HE wouldn't care. You see, there would be a pair of them." She stopped with a slight blush, as if she had gone too far, but corrected herself in her former youthful frankness: "You don't mind my saying what I did of her? You're not such a PARTICULAR friend?"

"We both owe a debt of gratitude to your cousin Jack," said Randolph, in some embarrassment.

"Yes, but YOU feel it and she doesn't. So that doesn't make you friends."

"But she has taken good care of Captain Dornton's child," suggested Randolph loyally.

He stopped, however, feeling that he was on dangerous ground. But Miss Eversleigh put her own construction on his reticence, and said,—

"I don't think she cares for it much—or for ANY children."

Randolph remembered his own impression the only time he had ever seen her with the child, and was struck with the young girl's instinct again coinciding with his own. But, possibly because he knew he could never again feel toward Miss Avondale as he had, he was the more anxious to be just, and he was about to utter a protest against this general assumption, when the voice of Sir William broke in upon them. He was taking his leave—and the opportunity of accompanying Miss Avondale to her lodgings on the way to his hotel. He lingered a moment over his handshaking with Randolph.

"Awfully glad to have met you, and I fancy you're awfully glad to get rid of what they call your 'trust.' Must have given you a beastly lot of bother, eh—might have given you more?"

He nodded familiarly to Miss Eversleigh, and turned away with Miss Avondale, who waved her usual smiling patronage to Randolph, even including his companion in that half-amused, half-superior salutation. Perhaps it was this that put a sudden hauteur into the young girl's expression as she stared at Miss Avondale's departing figure.

"If you ever come to England, Mr. Trent," she said, with a pretty dignity in her youthful face, "I hope you will find some people not quite so rude as my cousin and"—

"Miss Avondale, you would say," returned Randolph quietly. "As to HER, I am quite accustomed to her maturer superiority, which, I am afraid, is the effect of my own youth and inexperience; and I believe that, in course of time, your cousin's brusqueness might be as easily understood by me. I dare say," he added, with a laugh, "that I must seem to them a very romantic visionary with my 'trust,' and the foolish importance I have put upon a very trivial occurrence."

"I don't think so," said the girl quickly, "and I consider Bill very rude, and," she added, with a return of her boyish frankness, "I shall tell him so. As for Miss Avondale, she's AT LEAST thirty, I understand; perhaps she can't help showing it in that way, too."

But here Randolph, to evade further personal allusions, continued laughingly: "And as I've LOST my 'trust,' I haven't even that to show in defense. Indeed, when you all are gone I shall have nothing to remind me of my kind benefactor. It will seem like a dream."

Miss Eversleigh was silent for a moment, and then glanced quickly around her. The rest of the company were their elders, and, engaged in conversation at the other end of the apartment, had evidently left the young people to themselves.

"Wait a moment," she said, with a youthful air of mystery and earnestness. Randolph saw that she had slipped an Indian bracelet, profusely hung with small trinkets, from her arm to her wrist, and was evidently selecting one. It proved to be a child's tiny ring with a small pearl setting. "This was given to me by Cousin Jack," said Miss Eversleigh in a low voice, "when I was a child, at some frolic or festival, and I have kept it ever since. I brought it with me when we came here as a kind of memento to show him. You know that is impossible now. You say you have nothing of his to keep. Will you accept this? I know he would be glad to know you had it. You could wear it on your watch chain. Don't say no, but take it."

Protesting, yet filled with a strange joy and pride, Randolph took it from the young girl's hand. The little color which had deepened on her cheek cleared away as he thanked her gratefully, and with a quiet dignity she arose and moved toward the others. Randolph did not linger long after this, and presently took his leave of his host and hostess.

It seemed to him that he walked home that night in the whirling clouds of his dispelled dream. The airy structure he had built up for the last three months had collapsed. The enchanted canopy under which he had stood with Miss Avondale was folded forever. The romance he had evolved from his strange fortune had come to an end, not prosaically, as such romances are apt to do, but with a dramatic termination which, however, was equally fatal to his hopes. At any other time he might have projected the wildest hopes from the fancy that he and Miss Avondale were orphaned of a common benefactor; but it was plain that her interests were apart from his. And there was an indefinable something he did not understand, and did not want to understand, in the story she had told him. How much of it she had withheld, not so much from delicacy or contempt for his understanding as a desire to mislead him, he did not know. His faith in her had gone with his romance. It was not strange that the young English girl's unsophisticated frankness and simple confidences lingered longest in his memory, and that when, a few days later, Mr. Dingwall informed him that Miss Avondale had sailed for England with the Dornton family, he was more conscious of a loss in the stranger girl's departure.

"I suppose Miss Avondale takes charge of—of the boy, sir?" he said quietly.

Mr. Dingwall gave him a quick glance. "Possibly. Sir William has behaved with great—er—consideration," he replied briefly.

IV

Randolph's nature was too hopeful and recuperative to allow him to linger idly in the past. He threw himself into his work at the bank with his old earnestness and a certain simple conscientiousness which, while it often provoked the raillery of his fellow clerks, did not escape the eyes of his employers. He was advanced step by step, and by the end of the year was put in charge of the correspondence with banks and agencies. He had saved some money, and had made one or two profitable investments. He was enabled to take better apartments in the same building he had occupied. He had few of the temptations of youth. His fear of poverty and his natural taste kept him from the speculative and material excesses of the period. A distrust of his romantic weakness kept him from society and meaner entanglements which might have beset his good looks and good nature. He worked in his rooms at night and forbore his old evening rambles.

As the year wore on to the anniversary of his arrival, he thought much of the dead man who had inspired his fortunes, and with it a sense of his old doubts and suspicions revived. His reason had obliged him to accept the loss of the fateful portmanteau as an ordinary theft; his instinct remained unconvinced. There was no superstition connected with his loss. His own prosperity had not been impaired by it. On the contrary, he reflected bitterly that the dead man had apparently died only to benefit others. At such times he recalled, with a pleasure that he knew might become perilous, the tall English girl who had defended Dornton's memory and echoed his own sympathy. But that was all over now.

One stormy night, not unlike that eventful one of his past experience, Randolph sought his rooms in the teeth of a southwest gale. As he buffeted his way along the rain-washed pavement of Montgomery Street, it was not strange that his thoughts reverted to that night and the memory of his dead protector. But reaching his apartment, he sternly banished them with the vanished romance they revived, and lighting his lamp, laid out his papers in the prospect of an evening of uninterrupted work. He was surprised, however, after a little interval, by the sound of uncertain and shuffling steps on the half-lighted passage outside, the noise of some heavy article set down on the floor, and then a tentative knock at his door. A little impatiently he called, "Come in."

The door opened slowly, and out of the half obscurity of the passage a thickset figure lurched toward him into the full light of the room. Randolph half rose, and then sank back into his chair, awed, spellbound, and motionless. He saw the figure standing plainly before him; he saw distinctly the familiar furniture of his room, the storm-twinkling lights in the windows opposite, the flash of passing carriage lamps in the street below. But the figure before him was none other than the dead man of whom he had just been thinking.

The figure looked at him intently, and then burst into a fit of unmistakable laughter. It was neither loud nor unpleasant, and yet it provoked a disagreeable recollection. Nevertheless, it dissipated Randolph's superstitious tremor, for he had never before heard of a ghost who laughed heartily.

"You don't remember me," said the man. "Belay there, and I'll freshen your memory." He stepped back to the door, opened it, put his arm out into the hall, and brought in a portmanteau, closed the door, and appeared before Randolph again with the portmanteau in his hand. It was the one that had been stolen. "There!" he said.

"Captain Dornton," murmured Randolph.

The man laughed again and flung down the portmanteau. "You've got my name pat enough, lad, I see; but I reckoned you'd have spotted ME without that portmanteau."

"I see you've got it back," stammered Randolph in his embarrassment. "It was—stolen from me."

Captain Dornton laughed again, dropped into a chair, rubbed his hands on his knees, and turned his face toward Randolph. "Yes; I stole it—or had it stolen—the same thing, for I'm responsible."

"But I would have given it up to YOU at once," said Randolph reproachfully, clinging to the only idea he could understand in his utter bewilderment. "I have religiously and faithfully kept it for you, with all its contents, ever since—you disappeared."

"I know it, lad," said Captain Dornton, rising, and extending a brown, weather-beaten hand which closed heartily on the young man's; "no need to say that. And you've kept it even better than you know. Look here!"

He lifted the portmanteau to his lap and disclosed BEHIND the usual small pouch or pocket in the lid a slit in the lining. "Between the lining and the outer leather," he went on grimly, "I had two or three bank notes that came to about a thousand dollars, and some papers, lad, that, reckoning by and large, might be worth to me a million. When I got that portmanteau back they were all there, gummed in, just as I had left them. I didn't show up and come for them myself, for I was lying low at the time, and—no offense, lad—I didn't know how you stood with a party who was no particular friend of mine. An old shipmate whom I set to watch that party quite accidentally run across your bows in the ferry boat, and heard enough to make him follow in your wake here, where he got the portmanteau. It's all right," he said, with a laugh, waving aside with his brown hand Randolph's protesting gesture. "The old bag's only got back to its rightful owner. It mayn't have been got in shipshape 'Frisco style, but when a man's life is at stake, at least, when it's a question of his being considered dead or alive, he's got to take things as he finds 'em, and I found 'em d—— bad."

In a flash of recollection Randolph remembered the obtruding miner on the ferry boat, the same figure on the wharf corner, and the advantage taken of his absence with Miss Avondale. And Miss Avondale was the "party" this man's shipmate was watching! He felt his face crimsoning, yet he dared not question him further, nor yet defend her. Captain Dornton noticed it, and with a friendly tact, which Randolph had not expected of him, rising again, laid his hand gently on the young man's shoulder.

"Look here, lad," he said, with his pleasant smile; "don't you worry your head about the ways or doings of the Dornton family, or any of their friends. They're a queer lot—including your humble servant. You've done the square thing accordin' to your lights. You've ridden straight from start to finish, with no jockeying, and I shan't forget it. There are only two men who haven't failed me when I trusted them. One was you when I gave you my portmanteau; the other was Jack Redhill when he stole it from you."

He dropped back in his chair again, and laughed silently.

"Then you did not fall overboard as they supposed," stammered Randolph at last.

"Not much! But the next thing to it. It wasn't the water that I took in that knocked me out, my lad, but something stronger. I was shanghaied."

"Shanghaied?" repeated Randolph vacantly.

"Yes, shanghaied! Hocused! Drugged at that gin mill on the wharf by a lot of crimps, who, mistaking me for a better man, shoved me, blind drunk and helpless, down the steps into a boat, and out to a short-handed brig in the stream. When I came to I was outside the Heads, pointed for Guayaquil. When they found they'd captured, not a poor Jack, but a man who'd trod a quarterdeck, who knew, and was known at every port on the trading line, and who could make it hot for them, they were glad to compromise and set me ashore at Acapulco, and six weeks later I landed in 'Frisco."

"Safe and sound, thank Heaven!" said Randolph joyously.

"Not exactly, lad," said Captain Dornton grimly, "but dead and sat upon by the coroner, and my body comfortably boxed up and on its way to England."

"But that was nine months ago. What have you been doing since? Why didn't you declare yourself then?" said Randolph impatiently, a little irritated by the man's extreme indifference. He really talked like an amused spectator of his own misfortunes.

"Steady, lad. I know what you're going to say. I know all that happened. But the first thing I found when I got back was that the shanghai business had saved my life; that but for that I would have really been occupying that box on its way to England, instead of the poor devil who was taken for me."

A cold tremor passed over Randolph. Captain Dornton, however, was tolerantly smiling.

"I don't understand," said Randolph breathlessly.

Captain Dornton rose and, walking to the door, looked out into the passage; then he shut the door carefully and returned, glancing about the room and at the storm-washed windows. "I thought I heard some one outside. I'm lying low just now, and only go out at night, for I don't want this thing blown before I'm ready. Got anything to drink here?"

Randolph replied by taking a decanter of whiskey and glasses from a cupboard. The captain filled his glass, and continued with the same gentle but exasperating nonchalance, "Mind my smoking?"

"Not at all," said Randolph, pushing a cigar toward him. But the captain put it aside, drew from his pocket a short black clay pipe, stuffed it with black "Cavendish plug," which he had first chipped off in the palm of his hand with a large clasp knife, lighted it, and took a few meditative whiffs. Then, glancing at Randolph's papers, he said, "I'm not keeping you from your work, lad?" and receiving a reply in the negative, puffed at his pipe and once more settled himself comfortably in his chair, with his dark, bearded profile toward Randolph.

"You were saying just now you didn't understand," he went on slowly, without looking up; "so you must take your own bearings from what I'm telling you. When I met you that night I had just arrived from Melbourne. I had been lucky in some trading speculations I had out there, and I had some bills with me, but no money except what I had tucked in the skin of that portmanteau and a few papers connected with my family at home. When a man lives the roving kind of life I have, he learns to keep all that he cares for under his own hat, and isn't apt to blab to friends. But it got out in some way on the voyage that I had money, and as there was a mixed lot of 'Sydney ducks' and 'ticket of leave men' on board, it seems they hatched a nice little plot to waylay me on the wharf on landing, rob me, and drop me into deep water. To make it seem less suspicious, they associated themselves with a lot of crimps who were on the lookout for our sailors, who were going ashore that night too. I'd my suspicions that a couple of those men might be waiting for me at the end of the wharf. I left the ship just a minute or two before the sailors did. Then I met you. That meeting, my lad, was my first step toward salvation. For the two men let you pass with my portmanteau, which they didn't recognize, as I knew they would ME, and supposed you were a stranger, and lay low, waiting for me. I, who went into the gin-mill with the other sailors, was foolish enough to drink, and was drugged and crimped as they were. I hadn't thought of that. A poor devil of a ticket of leave man, about my size, was knocked down for me, and," he added, suppressing a laugh, "will be buried, deeply lamented, in the chancel of Dornton Church. While the row was going on, the skipper, fearing to lose other men, warped out into the stream, and so knew nothing of what happened to me. When they found what they thought was my body, he was willing to identify it in the hope that the crime might be charged to the crimps, and so did the other sailor witnesses. But my brother Bill, who had just arrived here from Callao, where he had been hunting for me, hushed it up to prevent a scandal. All the same, Bill might have known the body wasn't mine, even though he hadn't seen me for years."

"But it was frightfully disfigured, so that even I, who saw you only once, could not have sworn it was NOT you," said Randolph quickly.

"Humph!" said Captain Dornton musingly. "Bill may have acted on the square—though he was in a d———d hurry."

"But," said Randolph eagerly, "you will put an end to all this now. You will assert yourself. You have witnesses to prove your identity."

"Steady, lad," said the captain, waving his pipe gently. "Of course I have. But"—he stopped, laid down his pipe, and put his hands doggedly in his pockets—"IS IT WORTH IT?" Seeing the look of amazement in Randolph's face, he laughed his low laugh, and settled himself back in his chair again. "No," he said quietly, "if it wasn't for my son, and what's due him as my heir, I suppose—I reckon I'd just chuck the whole d——d thing."

"What!" said Randolph. "Give up the property, the title, the family honor, the wrong done to your reputation, the punishment"—He hesitated, fearing he had gone too far.

Captain Dornton withdrew his pipe from his mouth with a gesture of caution, and holding it up, said: "Steady, lad. We'll come to THAT by and by. As to the property and title, I cut and run from THEM ten years ago. To me they meant only the old thing—the life of a country gentleman, the hunting, the shooting, the whole beastly business that the land, over there, hangs like a millstone round your neck. They meant all this to me, who loved adventure and the sea from my cradle. I cut the property, for I hated it, and I hate it still. If I went back I should hear the sea calling me day and night; I should feel the breath of the southwest trades in every wind that blew over that tight little island yonder; I should be always scenting the old trail, lad, the trail that leads straight out of the Gate to swoop down to the South Seas. Do you think a man who has felt his ship's bows heave and plunge under him in the long Pacific swell—just ahead of him a reef breaking white into the lagoon, and beyond a fence of feathery palms—cares to follow hounds over gray hedges under a gray November sky? And the society? A man who's got a speaking acquaintance in every port from Acapulco to Melbourne, who knows every den and every longshoreman in it from a South American tienda to a Samoan beach-comber's hut,—what does he want with society?" He paused as Randolph's eyes were fixed wonderingly on the first sign of emotion on his weather-beaten face, which seemed for a moment to glow with the strength and freshness of the sea, and then said, with a laugh: "You stare, lad. Well, for all the Dorntons are rather proud of their family, like as not there was some beastly old Danish pirate among them long ago, and I've got a taste of his blood in me. But I'm not quite as bad as that yet."

He laughed, and carelessly went on: "As to the family honor, I don't see that it will be helped by my ripping up the whole thing and perhaps showing that Bill was a little too previous in identifying me. As to my reputation, that was gone after I left home, and if I hadn't been the legal heir they wouldn't have bothered their heads about me. My father had given me up long ago, and there isn't a man, woman, or child that wouldn't now welcome Bill in my place."

"There is one who wouldn't," said Randolph impulsively.

"You mean Caroline Avondale?" said Captain Dornton dryly.

Randolph colored. "No; I mean Miss Eversleigh, who was with your brother."

Captain Dornton reflected. "To be sure! Sibyl Eversleigh! I haven't seen her since she was so high. I used to call her my little sweetheart. So Sybby remembered Cousin Jack and came to find him? But when did you meet her?" he asked suddenly, as if this was the only detail of the past which had escaped him, fixing his frank eyes upon Randolph.

The young man recounted at some length the dinner party at Dingwall's, his conversation with Miss Eversleigh, and his interview with Sir William, but spoke little of Miss Avondale. To his surprise, the captain listened smilingly, and only said: "That was like Billy to take a rise out of you by pretending you were suspected. That's his way—a little rough when you don't know him and he's got a little grog amidships. All the same, I'd have given something to have heard him 'running' you, when all the while you had the biggest bulge on him, only neither of you knew it." He laughed again, until Randolph, amazed at his levity and indifference, lost his patience.

"Do you know," he said bluntly, "that they don't believe you were legally married?"

But Captain Dornton only continued to laugh, until, seeing his companion's horrified face, he became demure. "I suppose Bill didn't, for Bill had sense enough to know that otherwise he would have to take a back seat to Bobby."

"But did Miss Avondale know you were legally married, and that your son was the heir?" asked Randolph bluntly.

"She had no reason to suspect otherwise, although we were married secretly. She was an old friend of my wife, not particularly of mine."

Randolph sat back amazed and horrified. Those were HER own words. Or was this man deceiving him as the others had?

But the captain, eying him curiously, but still amusedly, added: "I even thought of bringing her as one of my witnesses, until"—

"Until what?" asked Randolph quickly, as he saw the captain had hesitated.

"Until I found she wasn't to be trusted; until I found she was too thick with Bill," said the captain bluntly. "And now she's gone to England with him and the boy, I suppose she'll make him come to terms."

"Come to terms?" echoed Randolph. "I don't understand." Yet he had an instinctive fear that he did.

"Well," said the captain slowly, "suppose she might prefer the chance of being the wife of a grown-up baronet to being the governess of one who was only a minor? She's a cute girl," he added dryly.

"But," said Randolph indignantly, "you have other witnesses, I hope."

"Of course I have. I've got the Spanish records now from the Callao priest, and they're put in a safe place should anything happen to me—if anything could happen to a dead man!" he added grimly. "These proofs were all I was waiting for before I made up my mind whether I should blow the whole thing, or let it slide."

Randolph looked again with amazement at this strange man who seemed so indifferent to the claims of wealth, position, and even to revenge. It seemed inconceivable, and yet he could not help being impressed with his perfect sincerity. He was relieved, however, when Captain Dornton rose with apparent reluctance and put away his pipe.

"Now look here, my lad, I'm right glad to have overhauled you again, whatever happened or is going to happen, and there's my hand upon it! Now, to come to business. I'm going over to England on this job, and I want you to come and help me."

Randolph's heart leaped. The appeal revived all his old boyish enthusiasm, with his secret loyalty to the man before him. But he suddenly remembered his past illusions, and for an instant he hesitated.

"But the bank," he stammered, scarce knowing what to say.

The captain smiled. "I will pay you better than the bank; and at the end of four months, in whatever way this job turns out, if you still wish to return here, I will see that you are secured from any loss. Perhaps you may be able to get a leave of absence. But your real object must be kept a secret from every one. Not a word of my existence or my purpose must be blown before I am ready. You and Jack Redhill are all that know it now."

"But you have a lawyer?" said the surprised Randolph.

"Not yet. I'm my own lawyer in this matter until I get fairly under way. I've studied the law enough to know that as soon as I prove that I'm alive the case must go on on account of my heir, whether I choose to cry quits or not. And it's just THAT that holds my hand."

Randolph stared at the extraordinary man before him. For a moment, as the strange story of his miraculous escape and his still more wonderful indifference to it all recurred to his mind, he felt a doubt of the narrator's truthfulness or his sanity. But another glance at the sailor's frank eyes dispelled that momentary suspicion. He held out his hand as frankly, and grasping Captain Dornton's, said, "I will go."

V

Randolph's request for a four months' leave of absence was granted with little objection and no curiosity. He had acquired the confidence of his employers, and beyond Mr. Revelstoke's curt surprise that a young fellow on the road to fortune should sacrifice so much time to irrelevant travel, and the remark, "But you know your own business best," there was no comment. It struck the young man, however, that Mr. Dingwall's slight coolness on receiving the news might be attributed to a suspicion that he was following Miss Avondale, whom he had fancied Dingwall disliked, and he quickly made certain inquiries in regard to Miss Eversleigh and the possibility of his meeting her. As, without intending it, and to his own surprise, he achieved a blush in so doing, which Dingwall noted, he received a gracious reply, and the suggestion that it was "quite proper" for him, on arriving, to send the young lady his card.

Captain Dornton, under the alias of "Captain Johns," was ready to catch the next steamer to the Isthmus, and in two days they sailed. The voyage was uneventful, and if Randolph had expected any enthusiasm on the part of the captain in the mission on which he was now fairly launched, he would have been disappointed. Although his frankness was unchanged, he volunteered no confidences. It was evident he was fully acquainted with the legal strength of his claim, yet he, as evidently, deferred making any plan of redress until he reached England. Of Miss Eversleigh he was more communicative. "You would have liked her better, my lad, it you hadn't been bewitched by the Avondale woman, for she is the whitest of the Dorntons." In vain Randolph protested truthfully, yet with an even more convincing color, that it had made no difference, and he HAD liked her. The captain laughed. "Ay, lad! But she's a poor orphan, with scarcely a hundred pounds a year, who lives with her guardian, an old clergyman. And yet," he added grimly, "there are only three lives between her and the property—mine, Bobby's, and Bill's—unless HE should marry and have an heir."

"The more reason why you should assert yourself and do what you can for her now," said Randolph eagerly.

"Ay," returned the captain, with his usual laugh, "when she was a child I used to call her my little sweetheart, and gave her a ring, and I reckon I promised to marry her, too, when she grew up."

The truthful Randolph would have told him of Miss Evereleigh's gift, but unfortunately he felt himself again blushing, and fearful lest the captain would misconstrue his confusion, he said nothing.

Except on this occasion, the captain talked with Randolph chiefly of his later past,—of voyages he had made, of places they were passing, and ports they visited. He spent much of the time with the officers, and even the crew, over whom he seemed to exercise a singular power, and with whom he exhibited an odd freemasonry. To Randolph's eyes he appeared to grow in strength and stature in the salt breath of the sea, and although he was uniformly kind, even affectionate, to him, he was brusque to the other passengers, and at times even with his friends the sailors. Randolph sometimes wondered how he would treat a crew of his own. He found some answer to that question in the captain's manner to Jack Redhill, the abstractor of the portmanteau, and his old shipmate, who was accompanying the captain in some dependent capacity, but who received his master's confidences and orders with respectful devotion.

It was a cold, foggy morning, nearly two months later, that they landed at Plymouth. The English coast had been a vague blank all night, only pierced, long hours apart, by dim star-points or weird yellow beacon flashes against the horizon. And this vagueness and unreality increased on landing, until it seemed to Randolph that they had slipped into a land of dreams. The illusion was kept up as they walked in the weird shadows through half-lit streets into a murky railway station throbbing with steam and sudden angry flashes in the darkness, and then drew away into what ought to have been the open country, but was only gray plains of mist against a lost horizon. Sometimes even the vague outlook was obliterated by passing trains coming from nowhere and slipping into nothingness. As they crept along with the day, without, however, any lightening of the opaque vault overhead to mark its meridian, there came at times a thinning of the gray wall on either side of the track, showing the vague bulk of a distant hill, the battlemented sky line of an old-time hall, or the spires of a cathedral, but always melting back into the mist again as in a dream. Then vague stretches of gloom again, foggy stations obscured by nebulous light and blurred and moving figures, and the black relief of a tunnel. Only once the captain, catching sight of Randolph's awed face under the lamp of the smoking carriage, gave way to his long, low laugh. "Jolly place, England—so very 'Merrie.'" And then they came to a comparatively lighter, broader, and more brilliantly signaled tunnel filled with people, and as they remained in it, Randolph was told it was London. With the sensation of being only half awake, he was guided and put into a cab by his companion, and seemed to be completely roused only at the hotel.

It had been arranged that Randolph should first go down to Chillingworth rectory and call on Miss Eversleigh, and, without disclosing his secret, gather the latest news from Dornton Hall, only a few miles from Chillingworth. For this purpose he had telegraphed to her that evening, and had received a cordial response. The next morning he arose early, and, in spite of the gloom, in the glow of his youthful optimism entered the bedroom of the sleeping Captain Dornton, and shook him by the shoulder in lieu of the accolade, saying: "Rise, Sir John Dornton!"

The captain, a light sleeper, awoke quickly. "Thank you, my lad, all the same, though I don't know that I'm quite ready yet to tumble up to that kind of piping. There's a rotten old saying in the family that only once in a hundred years the eldest son succeeds. That's why Bill was so cocksure, I reckon. Well?"

"In an hour I'm off to Chillingworth to begin the campaign," said Randolph cheerily.

"Luck to you, my boy, whatever happens. Clap a stopper on your jaws, though, now and then. I'm glad you like Sybby, but I don't want you to like her so much as to forget yourself and give me away."

Half an hour out of London the fog grew thinner, breaking into lace-like shreds in the woods as the train sped by, or expanding into lustrous tenuity above him. Although the trees were leafless, there was some recompense in the glimpses their bare boughs afforded of clustering chimneys and gables nestling in ivy. An infinite repose had been laid upon the landscape with the withdrawal of the fog, as of a veil lifted from the face of a sleeper. All his boyish dreams of the mother country came back to him in the books he had read, and re-peopled the vast silence. Even the rotting leaves that lay thick in the crypt-like woods seemed to him the dead laurels of its past heroes and sages. Quaint old-time villages, thatched roofs, the ever-recurring square towers of church or hall, the trim, ordered parks, tiny streams crossed by heavy stone bridges much too large for them—all these were only pages of those books whose leaves he seemed to be turning over. Two hours of this fancy, and then the train stopped at a station within a mile or two of a bleak headland, a beacon, and the gray wash of a pewter-colored sea, where a hilly village street climbed to a Norman church tower and the ivied gables of a rectory.

Miss Eversleigh, dignifiedly tall, but youthfully frank, as he remembered her, was waiting to drive him in a pony trap to the rectory. A little pink, with suppressed consciousness and the responsibilities of presenting a stranger guest to her guardian, she seemed to Randolph more charming than ever.

But her first word of news shocked and held him breathless. Bobby, the little orphan, a frail exotic, had succumbed to the Northern winter. A cold caught in New York had developed into pneumonia, and he died on the passage. Miss Avondale, although she had received marked attention from Sir William, returned to America in the same ship.

"I really don't think she was quite as devoted to the poor child as all that, you know," she continued with innocent frankness, "and Cousin Bill was certainly most kind to them both, yet there really seemed to be some coolness between them after the child's death. But," she added suddenly, for the first time observing her companion's evident distress, and coloring in confusion, "I beg your pardon—I've been horribly rude and heartless. I dare say the poor boy was very dear to you, and of course Miss Avondale was your friend. Please forgive me!"

Randolph, intent only on that catastrophe which seemed to wreck all Captain Dornton's hopes and blunt his only purpose for declaring himself, hurriedly reassured her, yet was not sorry his agitation had been misunderstood. And what was to be done? There was no train back to London for four hours. He dare not telegraph, and if he did, could he trust to his strange patron's wise conduct under the first shock of this news to his present vacillating purpose? He could only wait.

Luckily for his ungallant abstraction, they were speedily at the rectory, where a warm welcome from Mr. Brunton, Sibyl's guardian, and his family forced him to recover himself, and showed him that the story of his devotion to John Dornton had suffered nothing from Miss Eversleigh's recital. Distraught and anxious as he was, he could not resist the young girl's offer after luncheon to show him the church with the vault of the Dorntons and the tablet erected to John Dornton, and, later, the Hall, only two miles distant. But here Randolph hesitated.

"I would rather not call on Sir William to-day," he said.

"You need not. He is over at the horse show at Fern Dyke, and won't be back till late. And if he has been forgathering with his boon companions he won't be very pleasant company."

"Sibyl!" said the rector in good-humored protest.

"Oh, Mr. Trent has had a little of Cousin Bill's convivial manners before now," said the young girl vivaciously, "and isn't shocked. But we can see the Hall from the park on our way to the station."

Even in his anxious preoccupation he could see that the church itself was a quaint and wonderful preservation of the past. For four centuries it had been sacred to the tombs of the Dorntons and their effigies in brass and marble, yet, as Randolph glanced at the stately sarcophagus of the unknown ticket of leave man, its complacent absurdity, combined with his nervousness, made him almost hysterical. Yet again, it seemed to him that something of the mystery and inviolability of the past now invested that degraded dust, and it would be an equal impiety to disturb it. Miss Eversleigh, again believing his agitation caused by the memory of his old patron, tactfully hurried him away.

Yet it was a more bitter thought, I fear, that not only were his lips sealed to his charming companion on the subject in which they could sympathize, but his anxiety prevented him from availing himself of that interview to exchange the lighter confidences he had eagerly looked forward to. It seemed cruel that he was debarred this chance of knitting their friendship closer by another of those accidents that had brought them together. And he was aware that his gloomy abstraction was noticed by her. At first she drew herself up in a certain proud reserve, and then, perhaps, his own nervousness infecting her in turn, he was at last terrified to observe that, as she stood before the tomb, her clear gray eyes filled with tears.

"Oh, please don't do that—THERE, Miss Eversleigh," he burst out impulsively.

"I was thinking of Cousin Jack," she said, a little startled at his abruptness. "Sometimes it seems so strange that he is dead—I scarcely can believe it."

"I meant," stammered Randolph, "that he is much happier—you know"—he grew almost hysterical again as he thought of the captain lying cheerfully in his bed at the hotel—"much happier than you or I," he added bitterly; "that is—I mean, it grieves me so to see YOU grieve, you know."

Miss Eversleigh did NOT know, but there was enough sincerity and real feeling in the young fellow's voice and eyes to make her color slightly and hurry him away to a locality less fraught with emotions. In a few moments they entered the park, and the old Hall rose before them. It was a great Tudor house of mullioned windows, traceries, and battlements; of stately towers, moss-grown balustrades, and statues darkening with the fog that was already hiding the angles and wings of its huge bulk. A peacock spread its ostentatious tail on the broad stone steps before the portal; a flight of rooks from the leafless elms rose above its stacked and twisted chimneys. After all, how little had this stately incarnation of the vested rights and sacred tenures of the past in common with the laughing rover he had left in London that morning! And thinking of the destinies that the captain held so lightly in his hand, and perhaps not a little of the absurdity of his own position to the confiding young girl beside him, for a moment he half hated him.

The fog deepened as they reached the station, and, as it seemed to Randolph, made their parting still more vague and indefinite, and it was with difficulty that he could respond to the young girl's frank hope that he would soon return to them. Yet he half resolved that he would not until he could tell her all.

Nevertheless, as the train crept more and more slowly, with halting signals, toward London, he buoyed himself up with the hope that Captain Dornton would still try conclusions for his patrimony, or at least come to some compromise by which he might be restored to his rank and name. But upon these hopes the vision of that great house settled firmly upon its lands, held there in perpetuity by the dead and stretched-out hands of those that lay beneath its soil, always obtruded itself. Then the fog deepened, and the crawling train came to a dead stop at the next station. The whole line was blocked. Four precious hours were hopelessly lost.

Yet despite his impatience, he reentered London with the same dazed semi-consciousness of feeling as on the night he had first arrived. There seemed to have been no interim; his visit to the rectory and Hall, and even his fateful news, were only a dream. He drove through the same shadow to the hotel, was received by the same halo-encircled lights that had never been put out. After glancing through the halls and reading room he hurriedly made his way to his companion's room. The captain was not there. He quickly summoned the waiter. The gentleman? Yes; Captain Dornton had left with his servant, Redhill, a few hours after Mr. Trent went away. He had left no message.

Again condemned to wait in inactivity, Randolph tried to resist a certain uneasiness that was creeping over him, by attributing the captain's absence to some unexpected legal consultation or the gathering of evidence, his prolonged detention being due to the same fog that had delayed his own train. But he was somewhat surprised to find that the captain had ordered his luggage into the porter's care in the hall below before leaving, and that nothing remained in his room but a few toilet articles and the fateful portmanteau. The hours passed slowly. Owing to that perpetual twilight in which he had passed the day, there seemed no perceptible flight of time, and at eleven o'clock, the captain not arriving, he determined to wait in the latter's room so as to be sure not to miss him. Twelve o'clock boomed from an adjacent invisible steeple, but still he came not. Overcome by the fatigue and excitement of the day, Randolph concluded to lie down in his clothes on the captain's bed, not without a superstitious and uncomfortable recollection of that night, about a year before, when he had awaited him vainly at the San Francisco hotel. Even the fateful portmanteau was there to assist his gloomy fancy. Nevertheless, with the boom of one o'clock in his drowsy ears as his last coherent recollection, he sank into a dreamless sleep.

He was awakened by a tapping at his door, and jumped up to realize by his watch and the still burning gaslight that it was nine o'clock. But the intruder was only a waiter with a letter which he had brought to Randolph's room in obedience to the instructions the latter had given overnight. Not doubting it was from the captain, although the handwriting of the address was unfamiliar, he eagerly broke the seal. But he was surprised to read as follows:—

DEAR MR. TRENT,—We had such sad news from the Hall after you left. Sir William was seized with a kind of fit. It appears that he had just returned from the horse show, and had given his mare to the groom while he walked to the garden entrance. The groom saw him turn at the yew hedge, and was driving to the stables when he heard a queer kind of cry, and turning back to the garden front, found poor Sir William lying on the ground in convulsions. The doctor was sent for, and Mr. Brunton and I went over to the Hall. The doctor thinks it was something like a stroke, but he is not certain, and Sir William is quite delirious, and doesn't recognize anybody. I gathered from the groom that he had been DRINKING HEAVILY. Perhaps it was well that you did not see him, but I thought you ought to know what had happened in case you came down again. It's all very dreadful, and I wonder if that is why I was so nervous all the afternoon. It may have been a kind of presentiment. Don't you think so?

Yours faithfully,

SIBYL EVERSLEIGH.

I am afraid Randolph thought more of the simple-minded girl who, in the midst of her excitement, turned to him half unconsciously, than he did of Sir William. Had it not been for the necessity of seeing the captain, he would probably have taken the next train to the rectory. Perhaps he might later. He thought little of Sir William's illness, and was inclined to accept the young girl's naive suggestion of its cause. He read and reread the letter, staring at the large, grave, childlike handwriting—so like herself—and obeying a sudden impulse, raised the signature, as gravely as if it had been her hand, to his lips.

Still the day advanced and the captain came not. Randolph found the inactivity insupportable. He knew not where to seek him; he had no more clue to his resorts or his friends—if, indeed, he had any in London—than he had after their memorable first meeting in San Francisco. He might, indeed, be the dupe of an impostor, who, at the eleventh hour, had turned craven and fled. He might be, in the captain's indifference, a mere instrument set aside at his pleasure. Yet he could take advantage of Miss Eversleigh's letter and seek her, and confess everything, and ask her advice. It was a great and at the moment it seemed to him an overwhelming temptation. But only for the moment. He had given his word to the captain—more, he had given his youthful FAITH. And, to his credit, he never swerved again. It seemed to him, too, in his youthful superstition, as he looked at the abandoned portmanteau, that he had again to take up his burden—his "trust."

It was nearly four o'clock when the spell was broken. A large packet, bearing the printed address of a London and American bank, was brought to him by a special messenger; but the written direction was in the captain's hand.

Randolph tore it open. It contained one or two inclosures, which he hastily put aside for the letter, two pages of foolscap, which he read breathlessly:—

DEAR TRENT,—Don't worry your head if I have slipped my cable without telling you. I'm all right, only I got the news you are bringing me, JUST AFTER YOU LEFT, by Jack Redhill, whom I had sent to Dornton Hall to see how the land lay the night before. It was not that I didn't trust YOU, but HE had ways of getting news that you wouldn't stoop to. You can guess, from what I have told you already, that, now Bobby is gone, there's nothing to keep me here, and I'm following my own idea of letting the whole blasted thing slide. I only worked this racket for the sake of him. I'm sorry for him, but I suppose the poor little beggar couldn't stand these sunless, God-forsaken longitudes any more than I could. Besides that, as I didn't want to trust any lawyer with my secret, I myself had hunted up some books on the matter, and found that, by the law of entail, I'd have to rip up the whole blessed thing, and Bill would have had to pay back every blessed cent of what rents he had collected since he took hold—not to ME, but the ESTATE—with interest, and that no arrangement I could make with HIM would be legal on account of the boy. At least, that's the way the thing seemed to pan out to me. So that when I heard of Bobby's death I was glad to jump the rest, and that's what I made up my mind to do.

But, like a blasted lubber, now that I COULD do it and cut right away, I must needs think that I'd like first to see Bill on the sly, without letting on to any one else, and tell him what I was going to do. I'd no fear that he'd object, or that he'd hesitate a minute to fall in with my plan of dropping my name and my game, and giving him full swing, while I stood out to sea and the South Pacific, and dropped out of his mess for the rest of my life. Perhaps I wanted to set his mind at rest, if he'd ever had any doubts; perhaps I wanted to have a little fun out of him for his d———d previousness; perhaps, lad, I had a hankering to see the old place for the last time. At any rate, I allowed to go to Dornton Hall. I timed myself to get there about the hour you left, to keep out of sight until I knew he was returning from the horse show, and to waylay him ALONE and have our little talk without witnesses. I daren't go to the Hall, for some of the old servants might recognize me.

I went down there with Jack Redhill, and we separated at the station. I hung around in the fog. I even saw you pass with Sibyl in the dogcart, but you didn't see me. I knew the place, and just where to hide where I could have the chance of seeing him alone. But it was a beastly job waiting there. I felt like a d———d thief instead of a man who was simply visiting his own. Yet, you mayn't believe me, lad, but I hated the place and all it meant more than ever. Then, by and by, I heard him coming. I had arranged it all with myself to get into the yew hedge, and step out as he came to the garden entrance, and as soon as he recognized me to get him round the terrace into the summer house, where we could speak without danger.

I heard the groom drive away to the stable with the cart, and, sure enough, in a minute he came lurching along toward the garden door. He was mighty unsteady on his pins, and I reckon he was more than half full, which was a bad lookout for our confab. But I calculated that the sight of me, when I slipped out, would sober him. And, by ——, it did! For his eyes bulged out of his head and got fixed there; his jaw dropped; he tried to strike at me with a hunting crop he was carrying, and then he uttered an ungodly yell you might have heard at the station, and dropped down in his tracks. I had just time to slip back into the hedge again before the groom came driving back, and then all hands were piped, and they took him into the house.

And of course the game was up, and I lost my only chance. I was thankful enough to get clean away without discovering myself, and I have to trust now to the fact of Bill's being drunk, and thinking it was my ghost that he saw, in a touch of the jimjams! And I'm not sorry to have given him that start, for there was that in his eye, and that in the stroke he made, my lad, that showed a guilty conscience I hadn't reckoned on. And it cured me of my wish to set his mind at ease. He's welcome to all the rest.

And that's why I'm going away—never to return. I'm sorry I couldn't take you with me, but it's better that I shouldn't see you again, and that you didn't even know WHERE I was gone. When you get this I shall be on blue water and heading for the sunshine. You'll find two letters inclosed. One you need not open unless you hear that my secret was blown, and you are ever called upon to explain your relations with me. The other is my thanks, my lad, in a letter of credit on the bank, for the way you have kept your trust, and I believe will continue to keep it, to

JOHN DORNTON.

P.S. I hope you dropped a tear over my swell tomb at Dornton Church. All the same, I don't begrudge it to the poor devil who lost his life instead of me.

J. D.

As Randolph read, he seemed to hear the captain's voice throughout the letter, and even his low, characteristic laugh in the postscript. Then he suddenly remembered the luggage which the porter had said the captain had ordered to be taken below; but on asking that functionary he was told a conveyance for the Victoria Docks had called with an order, and taken it away at daybreak. It was evident that the captain had intended the letter should be his only farewell. Depressed and a little hurt at his patron's abruptness, Randolph returned to his room. Opening the letter of credit, he found it was for a thousand pounds—a munificent beneficence, as it seemed to Randolph, for his dubious services, and a proof of his patron's frequent declarations that he had money enough without touching the Dornton estates.

For a long time he sat with these sole evidences of the reality of his experience in his hands, a prey to a thousand surmises and conflicting thoughts. Was he the self-deceived disciple of a visionary, a generous, unselfish, but weak man, whose eccentricity passed even the bounds of reason? Who would believe the captain's story or the captain's motives? Who comprehend his strange quest and its stranger and almost ridiculous termination? Even if the seal of secrecy were removed in after years, what had he, Randolph, to show in corroboration of his patron's claim?

Then it occurred to him that there was no reason why he should not go down to the rectory and see Miss Eversleigh again under pretense of inquiring after the luckless baronet, whose title and fortune had, nevertheless, been so strangely preserved. He began at once his preparations for the journey, and was nearly ready when a servant entered with a telegram. Randolph's heart leaped. The captain had sent him news—perhaps had changed his mind! He tore off the yellow cover, and read,—

Sir William died at twelve o'clock without recovering consciousness.

S. EVERSLEIGH. VI

For a moment Randolph gazed at the dispatch with a half-hysterical laugh, and then became as suddenly sane and cool. One thought alone was uppermost in his mind: the captain could not have heard this news yet, and if he was still within reach, or accessible by any means whatever, however determined his purpose, he must know it at once. The only clue to his whereabouts was the Victoria Docks. But that was something. In another moment Randolph was in the lower hall, had learned the quickest way of reaching the docks, and plunged into the street.

The fog here swooped down, and to the embarrassment of his mind was added the obscurity of light and distance, which halted him after a few hurried steps, in utter perplexity. Indistinct figures were here and there approaching him out of nothingness and melting away again into the greenish gray chaos. He was in a busy thoroughfare; he could hear the slow trample of hoofs, the dull crawling of vehicles, and the warning outcries of a traffic he could not see. Trusting rather to his own speed than that of a halting conveyance, he blundered on until he reached the railway station. A short but exasperating journey of impulses and hesitations, of detonating signals and warning whistles, and he at last stood on the docks, beyond him a vague bulk or two, and a soft, opaque flowing wall—the river!

But one steamer had left that day—the Dom Pedro, for the River Plate—two hours before, but until the fog thickened, a quarter of an hour ago, she could be seen, so his informant said, still lying, with steam up, in midstream. Yes, it was still possible to board her. But even as the boatman spoke, and was leading the way toward the landing steps, the fog suddenly lightened; a soft salt breath stole in from the distant sea, and a veil seemed to be lifted from the face of the gray waters. The outlines of the two shores came back; the spars of nearer vessels showed distinctly, but the space where the huge hulk had rested was empty and void. There was a trail of something darker and more opaque than fog itself lying near the surface of the water, but the Dom Pedro was a mere speck in the broadening distance.

A bright sun and a keen easterly wind were revealing the curling ridges of the sea beyond the headland when Randolph again passed the gates of Dornton Hall on his way to the rectory. Now, for the first time, he was able to see clearly the outlines of that spot which had seemed to him only a misty dream, and even in his preoccupation he was struck by its grave beauty. The leafless limes and elms in the park grouped themselves as part of the picturesque details of the Hall they encompassed, and the evergreen slope of firs and larches rose as a background to the gray battlements, covered with dark green ivy, whose rich shadows were brought out by the unwonted sunshine. With a half-repugnant curiosity he had tried to identify the garden entrance and the fateful yew hedge the captain had spoken of as he passed. But as quickly he fell back upon the resolution he had taken in coming there—to dissociate his secret, his experience, and his responsibility to his patron from his relations to Sibyl Eversleigh; to enjoy her companionship without an obtruding thought of the strange circumstances that had brought them together at first, or the stranger fortune that had later renewed their acquaintance. He had resolved to think of her as if she had merely passed into his life in the casual ways of society, with only her personal charms to set her apart from others. Why should his exclusive possession of a secret—which, even if confided to her, would only give her needless and hopeless anxiety—debar them from an exchange of those other confidences of youth and sympathy? Why could he not love her and yet withhold from her the knowledge of her cousin's existence? So he had determined to make the most of his opportunity during his brief holiday; to avail himself of her naive invitation, and even of what he dared sometimes to think was her predilection for his companionship. And if, before he left, he had acquired a right to look forward to a time when her future and his should be one—but here his glowing fancy was abruptly checked by his arrival at the rectory door.

Mr. Brunton received him cordially, yet with a slight business preoccupation and a certain air of importance that struck him as peculiar. Sibyl, he informed him, was engaged at that moment with some friends who had come over from the Hall. Mr. Trent would understand that there was a great deal for her to do—in her present position. Wondering why SHE should be selected to do it instead of older and more experienced persons, Randolph, however, contented himself with inquiries regarding the details of Sir William's seizure and death. He learned, as he expected, that nothing whatever was known of the captain's visit, nor was there the least suspicion that the baronet's attack was the result of any predisposing emotion. Indeed, it seemed more possible that his medical attendants, knowing something of his late excesses and their effect upon his constitution, preferred, for the sake of avoiding scandal, to attribute the attack to long-standing organic disease.

Randolph, who had already determined, as a forlorn hope, to write a cautious letter to the captain (informing him briefly of the news without betraying his secret, and directed to the care of the consignees of the Dom Pedro in Brazil, by the next post), was glad to be able to add this medical opinion to relieve his patron's mind of any fear of having hastened his brother's death by his innocent appearance. But here the entrance of Sibyl Eversleigh with her friends drove all else from his mind.

She looked so tall and graceful in her black dress, which set off her dazzling skin, and, with her youthful gravity, gave to her figure the charming maturity of a young widow, that he was for a moment awed and embarrassed. But he experienced a relief when she came eagerly toward him in all her old girlish frankness, and with even something of yearning expectation in her gray eyes.

"It was so good of you to come," she said. "I thought you would imagine how I was feeling"—She stopped, as if she were conscious, as Randolph was, of a certain chill of unresponsiveness in the company, and said in an undertone, "Wait until we are alone." Then, turning with a slight color and a pretty dignity toward her friends, she continued: "Lady Ashbrook, this is Mr. Trent, an old friend of both my cousins when they were in America."

In spite of the gracious response of the ladies, Randolph was aware of their critical scrutiny of both himself and Miss Eversleigh, of the exchange of significant glances, and a certain stiffness in her guardian's manner. It was quite enough to affect Randolph's sensitiveness and bring out his own reserve.

Fancying, however, that his reticence disturbed Miss Eversleigh, he forced himself to converse with Lady Ashbrook—avoiding many of her pointed queries as to himself, his acquaintance with Sibyl, and the length of time he expected to stay in England—and even accompanied her to her carriage. And here he was rewarded by Sibyl running out with a crape veil twisted round her throat and head, and the usual femininely forgotten final message to her visitor. As the carriage drove away, she turned to Randolph, and said quickly,—

"Let us go in by way of the garden."

It was a slight detour, but it gave them a few moments alone.

"It was so awful and sudden," she said, looking gravely at Randolph, "and to think that only an hour before I had been saying unkind things of him! Of course," she added naively, "they were true, and the groom admitted to me that the mare was overdriven and Sir William could hardly stand. And only to think of it! he never recovered complete consciousness, but muttered incoherently all the time. I was with him to the last, and he never said a word I could understand—only once."

"What did he say?" asked Randolph uneasily.

"I don't like to say—it was TOO dreadful!"

Randolph did not press her. Yet, after a pause, she said in a low voice, with a naivete impossible to describe, "It was, 'Jack, damn you!'"

He did not dare to look at her, even with this grim mingling of farce and tragedy which seemed to invest every scene of that sordid drama. Miss Eversleigh continued gravely: "The groom's name was Robert, but Jack might have been the name of one of his boon companions."

Convinced that she suspected nothing, yet in the hope of changing the subject, Randolph said quietly: "I thought your guardian perhaps a little less frank and communicative to-day."

"Yes," said the young girl suddenly, with a certain impatience, and yet in half apology to her companion, "of course. He—THEY—all and everybody—are much more concerned and anxious about my new position than I am. It's perfectly dreadful—this thinking of it all the time, arranging everything, criticising everything in reference to it, and the poor man who is the cause of it all not yet at rest in his grave! The whole thing is inhuman and unchristian!"

"I don't understand," stammered Randolph vaguely. "What IS your new position? What do you mean?"

The girl looked up in his face with surprise. "Why, didn't you know? I'm the next of kin—I'm the heiress—and will succeed to the property in six months, when I am of age."

In a flash of recollection Randolph suddenly recalled the captain's words, "There are only three lives between her and the property." Their meaning had barely touched his comprehension before. She was the heiress. Yes, save for the captain!

She saw the change, the wonder, even the dismay, in his face, and her own brightened frankly. "It's so good to find one who never thought of it, who hadn't it before him as the chief end for which I was born! Yes, I was the next of kin after dear Jack died and Bill succeeded, but there was every chance that he would marry and have an heir. And yet the moment he was taken ill that idea was uppermost in my guardian's mind, good man as he is, and even forced upon me. If this—this property had come from poor Cousin Jack, whom I loved, there would have been something dear in it as a memory or a gift, but from HIM, whom I couldn't bear—I know it's wicked to talk that way, but it's simply dreadful!"

"And yet," said Randolph, with a sudden seriousness he could not control, "I honestly believe that Captain Dornton would be perfectly happy—yes, rejoiced!—if he knew the property had come to YOU."

There was such an air of conviction, and, it seemed to the simple girl, even of spiritual insight, in his manner that her clear, handsome eyes rested wonderingly on his.

"Do you really think so?" she said thoughtfully. "And yet HE knows that I am like him. Yes," she continued, answering Randolph's look of surprise, "I am just like HIM in that. I loathe and despise the life that this thing would condemn me to; I hate all that it means, and all that it binds me to, as he used to; and if I could, I would cut and run from it as HE did."

She spoke with a determined earnestness and warmth, so unlike her usual grave naivete that he was astonished. There was a flush on her cheek and a frank fire in her eye that reminded him strangely of the captain; and yet she had emphasized her words with a little stamp of her narrow foot and a gesture of her hand that was so untrained and girlish that he smiled, and said, with perhaps the least touch of bitterness in his tone, "But you will get over that when you come into the property."

"I suppose I shall," she returned, with an odd lapse to her former gravity and submissiveness. "That's what they all tell me."

"You will be independent and your own mistress," he added.

"Independent," she repeated impatiently, "with Dornton Hall and twenty thousand a year! Independent, with every duty marked out for me! Independent, with every one to criticise my smallest actions—every one who would never have given a thought to the orphan who was contented and made her own friends on a hundred a year! Of course you, who are a stranger, don't understand; yet I thought that you"—she hesitated,—"would have thought differently."

"Why?"

"Why, with your belief that one should make one's own fortune," she said.

"That would do for a man, and in that I respected Captain Dornton's convictions, as you told them to me. But for a girl, how could she be independent, except with money?"

She shook her head as if unconvinced, but did not reply. They were nearing the garden porch, when she looked up, and said: "And as YOU'RE a man, you will be making your way in the world. Mr. Dingwall said you would."

There was something so childishly trustful and confident in her assurance that he smiled. "Mr. Dingwall is too sanguine, but it gives me hope to hear YOU say so."

She colored slightly, and said gravely: "We must go in now." Yet she lingered for a moment before the door. For a long time afterward he had a very vivid recollection of her charming face, in its childlike gravity and its quaint frame of black crape, standing out against the sunset-warmed wall of the rectory. "Promise me you will not mind what these people say or do," she said suddenly.

"I promise," he returned, with a smile, "to mind only what YOU say or do."

"But I might not be always quite right, you know," she said naively.

"I'll risk that."

"Then, when we go in now, don't talk much to me, but make yourself agreeable to all the others, and then go straight home to the inn, and don't come here until after the funeral."

The faintest evasive glint of mischievousness in her withdrawn eyes at this moment mitigated the austerity of her command as they both passed in.

Randolph had intended not to return to London until after the funeral, two days later, and spent the interesting day at the neighboring town, whence he dispatched his exploring and perhaps hopeless letter to the captain. The funeral was a large and imposing one, and impressed Randolph for the first time with the local importance and solid standing of the Dorntons. All the magnates and old county families were represented. The inn yard and the streets of the little village were filled with their quaint liveries, crested paneled carriages, and silver-cipher caparisoned horses, with a sprinkling of fashion from London. He could not close his ears to the gossip of the villagers regarding the suddenness of the late baronet's death, the extinction of the title, the accession of the orphaned girl to the property, and even, to his greater exasperation, speculations upon her future and probable marriage. "Some o' they gay chaps from Lunnon will be lordin' it over the Hall afore long," was the comment of the hostler.

It was with some little bitterness that Randolph took his seat in the crowded church. But this feeling, and even his attempts to discover Miss Eversleigh's face in the stately family pew fenced off from the chancel, presently passed away. And then his mind began to be filled with strange and weird fancies. What grim and ghostly revelations might pass between this dead scion of the Dorntons lying on the trestles before them and the obscure, nameless ticket of leave man awaiting his entrance in the vault below! The incongruity of this thought, with the smug complacency of the worldly minded congregation sitting around him, and the probable smiling carelessness of the reckless rover—the cause of all—even now idly pacing the deck on the distant sea, touched him with horror. And when added to this was the consciousness that Sibyl Eversleigh was forced to become an innocent actor in this hideous comedy, it seemed as much as he could bear. Again he questioned himself, Was he right to withhold his secret from her? In vain he tried to satisfy his conscience that she was happier in her ignorance. The resolve he had made to keep his relations with her apart from his secret, he knew now, was impossible. But one thing was left to him. Until he could disclose his whole story—until his lips were unsealed by Captain Dornton—he must never see her again. And the grim sanctity of the edifice seemed to make that resolution a vow.

He did not dare to raise his eyes again toward her pew, lest a sight of her sweet, grave face might shake his resolution, and he slipped away first among the departing congregation. He sent her a brief note from the inn saying that he was recalled to London by an earlier train, and that he would be obliged to return to California at once, but hoping that if he could be of any further assistance to her she would write to him to the care of the bank. It was a formal letter, and yet he had never written otherwise than formally to her. That night he reached London. On the following night he sailed from Liverpool for America.

Six months had passed. It was difficult, at first, for Randolph to pick up his old life again; but his habitual earnestness and singleness of purpose stood him in good stead, and a vague rumor that he had made some powerful friends abroad, with the nearer fact that he had a letter of credit for a thousand pounds, did not lessen his reputation. He was reinstalled and advanced at the bank. Mr. Dingwall was exceptionally gracious, and minute in his inquiries regarding Miss Eversleigh's succession to the Dornton property, with an occasional shrewdness of eye in his interrogations which recalled to Randolph the questioning of Miss Eversleigh's friends, and which he responded to as cautiously. For the young fellow remained faithful to his vow even in thinking of her, and seemed to be absorbed entirely in his business. Yet there was a vague ambition of purpose in this absorption that would probably have startled the more conservative Englishman had he known it.

He had not heard from Miss Eversleigh since he left, nor had he received any response from the captain. Indeed, he had indulged in little hopes of either. But he kept stolidly at work, perhaps with a larger trust than he knew. And then, one day, he received a letter addressed in a handwriting that made his heart leap, though he had seen it but once, when it conveyed the news of Sir William Dornton's sudden illness. It was from Miss Eversleigh, but the postmark was Callao! He tore open the envelope, and for the next few moments forgot everything—his business devotion, his lofty purpose, even his solemn vow.

It read as follows:—

DEAR MR. TRENT,—I should not be writing to you now if I did not believe that I NOW understand why you left us so abruptly on the day of the funeral, and why you were at times so strange. You might have been a little less hard and cold even if you knew all that you did know. But I must write now, for I shall be in San Francisco a few days after this reaches you, and I MUST see you and have YOUR help, for I can have no other, as you know. You are wondering what this means, and why I am here. I know ALL and EVERYTHING. I know HE is alive and never was dead. I know I have no right to what I have, and never had, and I have come here to seek him and make him take it back. I could do no other. I could not live and do anything but that, and YOU might have known it. But I have not found him here as I hoped I should, though perhaps it was a foolish hope of mine, and I am coming to you to help me seek him, for he MUST BE FOUND. You know I want to keep his and your secret, and therefore the only one I can turn to for assistance and counsel is YOU.

You are wondering how I know what I do. Two months ago I GOT A LETTER FROM HIM—the strangest, quaintest, and yet THE KINDEST LETTER—exactly like himself and the way he used to talk! He had just heard of his brother's death, and congratulated me on coming into the property, and said he was now perfectly happy, and should KEEP DEAD, and never, never come to life again; that he never thought things would turn out as splendidly as they had—for Sir William MIGHT have had an heir—and that now he should REALLY DIE HAPPY. He said something about everything being legally right, and that I could do what I liked with the property. As if THAT would satisfy me! Yet it was all so sweet and kind, and so like dear old Jack, that I cried all night. And then I resolved to come here, where his letter was dated from. Luckily I was of age now, and could do as I liked, and I said I wanted to travel in South America and California; and I suppose they didn't think it very strange that I should use my liberty in that way. Some said it was quite like a Dornton! I knew something of Callao from your friend Miss Avondale, and could talk about it, which impressed them. So I started off with only a maid—my old nurse. I was a little frightened at first, when I came to think what I was doing, but everybody was very kind, and I really feel quite independent now. So, you see, a girl may be INDEPENDENT, after all! Of course I shall see Mr. Dingwall in San Francisco, but he need not know anything more than that I am traveling for pleasure. And I may go to the Sandwich Islands or Sydney, if I think HE is there. Of course I have had to use some money—some of HIS rents—but it shall be paid back. I will tell you everything about my plans when I see you.

Yours faithfully,

SIBYL EVERSLEIGH.

P. S. Why did you let me cry over that man's tomb in the church?

Randolph looked again at the date, and then hurriedly consulted the shipping list. She was due in ten days. Yet, delighted as he was with that prospect, and touched as he had been with her courage and naive determination, after his first joy he laid the letter down with a sigh. For whatever was his ultimate ambition, he was still a mere salaried clerk; whatever was her self-sacrificing purpose, she was still the rich heiress. The seal of secrecy had been broken, yet the situation remained unchanged; their association must still be dominated by it. And he shrank from the thought of making her girlish appeal to him for help an opportunity for revealing his real feelings.

This instinct was strengthened by the somewhat formal manner in which Mr. Dingwall announced her approaching visit. "Miss Eversleigh will stay with Mrs. Dingwall while she is here, on account of her—er—position, and the fact that she is without a chaperon. Mrs. Dingwall will, of course, be glad to receive any friends Miss Eversleigh would like to see."

Randolph frankly returned that Miss Eversleigh had written to him, and that he would be glad to present himself. Nothing more was said, but as the days passed he could not help noticing that, in proportion as Mr. Dingwall's manner became more stiff and ceremonious, Mr. Revelstoke's usually crisp, good-humored suggestions grew more deliberate, and Randolph found himself once or twice the subject of the president's penetrating but smiling scrutiny. And the day before Miss Eversleigh's arrival his natural excitement was a little heightened by a summons to Mr. Revelstoke's private office.

As he entered, the president laid aside his pen and closed the door.

"I have never made it my business, Trent," he said, with good-humored brusqueness, "to interfere in my employees' private affairs, unless they affect their relations to the bank, and I haven't had the least occasion to do so with you. Neither has Mr. Dingwall, although it is on HIS behalf that I am now speaking." As Randolph listened with a contracted brow, he went on with a grim smile: "But he is an Englishman, you know, and has certain ideas of the importance of 'position,' particularly among his own people. He wishes me, therefore, to warn you of what HE calls the 'disparity' of your position and that of a young English lady—Miss Eversleigh—with whom you have some acquaintance, and in whom," he added with a still grimmer satisfaction, "he fears you are too deeply interested."

Randolph blazed. "If Mr. Dingwall had asked ME, sir," he said hotly, "I would have told him that I have never yet had to be reminded that Miss Eversleigh is a rich heiress and I only a poor clerk, but as to his using her name in such a connection, or dictating to me the manner of"—

"Hold hard," said Revelstoke, lifting his hand deprecatingly, yet with his unchanged smile. "I don't agree with Mr. Dingwall, and I have every reason to know the value of YOUR services, yet I admit something is due to HIS prejudices. And in this matter, Trent, the Bank of Eureka, while I am its president, doesn't take a back seat. I have concluded to make you manager of the branch bank at Marysville, an independent position with its salary and commissions. And if that doesn't suit Dingwall, why," he added, rising from his desk with a short laugh, "he has a bigger idea of the value of property than the bank has."

"One moment, sir, I implore you," burst out Randolph breathlessly, "if your kind offer is based upon the mistaken belief that I have the least claim upon Miss Eversleigh's consideration more than that of simple friendship—if anybody has dared to give you the idea that I have aspired by word or deed to more, or that the young lady has ever countenanced or even suspected such aspirations, it is utterly false, and grateful as I am for your kindness, I could not accept it."

"Look here, Trent," returned Revelstoke curtly, yet laying his hand on the young man's shoulder not unkindly. "All that is YOUR private affair, which, as I told you, I don't interfere with. The other is a question between Mr. Dingwall and myself of your comparative value. It won't hurt you with ANYBODY to know how high we've assessed it. Don't spoil a good thing!"

Grateful even in his uncertainty, Randolph could only thank him and withdraw. Yet this fateful forcing of his hand in a delicate question gave him a new courage. It was with a certain confidence now in his capacity as HER friend and qualified to advise HER that he called at Mr. Dingwall's the evening she arrived. It struck him that in the Dingwalls' reception of him there was mingled with their formality a certain respect.

Thanks to this, perhaps, he found her alone. She seemed to him more beautiful than his recollection had painted her, in the development that maturity, freedom from restraint, and time had given her. For a moment his new, fresh courage was staggered. But she had retained her youthful simplicity, and came toward him with the same naive and innocent yearning in her clear eyes that he remembered at their last meeting. Their first words were, naturally, of their great secret, and Randolph told her the whole story of his unexpected and startling meeting with the captain, and the captain's strange narrative, of his undertaking the journey with him to recover his claim, establish his identity, and, as Randolph had hoped, restore to her that member of the family whom she had most cared for. He recounted the captain's hesitation on arriving; his own journey to the rectory; the news she had given him; the reason of his singular behavior; his return to London; and the second disappearance of the captain. He read to her the letter he had received from him, and told her of his hopeless chase to the docks only to find him gone. She listened to him breathlessly, with varying color, with an occasional outburst of pity, or a strange shining of the eyes, that sometimes became clouded and misty, and at the conclusion with a calm and grave paleness.

"But," she said, "you should have told me all."

"It was not my secret," he pleaded.

"You should have trusted me."

"But the captain had trusted ME."

She looked at him with grave wonder, and then said with her old directness: "But if I had been told such a secret affecting you, I should have told you." She stopped suddenly, seeing his eyes fixed on her, and dropped her own lids with a slight color. "I mean," she said hesitatingly, "of course you have acted nobly, generously, kindly, wisely—but I hate secrets! Oh, why cannot one be always frank?"

A wild idea seized Randolph. "But I have another secret—you have not guessed—and I have not dared to tell you. Do you wish me to be frank now?"

"Why not?" she said simply, but she did not look up.

Then he told her! But, strangest of all, in spite of his fears and convictions, it flowed easily and naturally as a part of his other secret, with an eloquence he had not dreamed of before. But when he told her of his late position and his prospects, she raised her eyes to his for the first time, yet without withdrawing her hand from his, and said reproachfully,—

"Yet but for THAT you would never have told me."

"How could I?" he returned eagerly. "For but for THAT how could I help you to carry out YOUR trust? How could I devote myself to your plans, and enable you to carry them out without touching a dollar of that inheritance which you believe to be wrongfully yours?"

Then, with his old boyish enthusiasm, he sketched a glowing picture of their future: how they would keep the Dornton property intact until the captain was found and communicated with; and how they would cautiously collect all the information accessible to find him until such time as Randolph's fortunes would enable them both to go on a voyage of discovery after him. And in the midst of this prophetic forecast, which brought them so closely together that she was enabled to examine his watch chain, she said,—

"I see you have kept Cousin Jack's ring. Did he ever see it?"

"He told me he had given it to you as his little sweetheart, and that he"—

There was a singular pause here.

"He never did THAT—at least, not in that way!" said Sybil Eversleigh.

And, strangely enough, the optimistic Randolph's prophecies came true. He was married a month later to Sibyl Eversleigh, Mr. Dingwall giving away the bride. He and his wife were able to keep their trust in regard to the property, for, without investing a dollar of it in the bank, the mere reputation of his wife's wealth brought him a flood of other investors and a confidence which at once secured his success. In two years he was able to take his wife on a six months' holiday to Europe via Australia, but of the details of that holiday no one knew. It is, however, on record that ten or twelve years ago Dornton Hall, which had been leased or unoccupied for a long time, was refitted for the heiress, her husband, and their children during a brief occupancy, and that in that period extensive repairs were made to the interior of the old Norman church, and much attention given to the redecoration and restoration of its ancient tombs.

# MR. MACGLOWRIE'S WIDOW

Very little was known of her late husband, yet that little was of a sufficiently awe-inspiring character to satisfy the curiosity of Laurel Spring. A man of unswerving animosity and candid belligerency, untempered by any human weakness, he had been actively engaged as survivor in two or three blood feuds in Kentucky, and some desultory dueling, only to succumb, through the irony of fate, to an attack of fever and ague in San Francisco. Gifted with a fine sense of humor, he is said, in his last moments, to have called the simple-minded clergyman to his bedside to assist him in putting on his boots. The kindly divine, although pointing out to him that he was too weak to rise, much less walk, could not resist the request of a dying man. When it was fulfilled, Mr. MacGlowrie crawled back into bed with the remark that his race had always "died with their boots on," and so passed smilingly and tranquilly away.

It is probable that this story was invented to soften the ignominy of MacGlowrie's peaceful end. The widow herself was also reported to be endowed with relations of equally homicidal eccentricities. Her two brothers, Stephen and Hector Boompointer, had Western reputations that were quite as lurid and remote. Her own experiences of a frontier life had been rude and startling, and her scalp—a singularly beautiful one of blond hair—had been in peril from Indians on several occasions. A pair of scissors, with which she had once pinned the intruding hand of a marauder to her cabin doorpost, was to be seen in her sitting room at Laurel Spring. A fair-faced woman with eyes the color of pale sherry, a complexion sallowed by innutritious food, slight and tall figure, she gave little suggestion of this Amazonian feat. But that it exercised a wholesome restraint over the many who would like to have induced her to reenter the married state, there is little reason to doubt. Laurel Spring was a peaceful agricultural settlement. Few of its citizens dared to aspire to the dangerous eminence of succeeding the defunct MacGlowrie; few could hope that the sister of living Boompointers would accept an obvious mesalliance with them. However sincere their affection, life was still sweet to the rude inhabitants of Laurel Spring, and the preservation of the usual quantity of limbs necessary to them in their avocations. With their devotion thus chastened by caution, it would seem as if the charming mistress of Laurel Spring House was secure from disturbing attentions.

It was a pleasant summer afternoon, and the sun was beginning to strike under the laurels around the hotel into the little office where the widow sat with the housekeeper—a stout spinster of a coarser Western type. Mrs. MacGlowrie was looking wearily over some accounts on the desk before her, and absently putting back some tumbled sheaves from the stack of her heavy hair. For the widow had a certain indolent Southern negligence, which in a less pretty woman would have been untidiness, and a characteristic hook and eyeless freedom of attire which on less graceful limbs would have been slovenly. One sleeve cuff was unbuttoned, but it showed the blue veins of her delicate wrist; the neck of her dress had lost a hook, but the glimpse of a bit of edging round the white throat made amends. Of all which, however, it should be said that the widow, in her limp abstraction, was really unconscious.

"I reckon we kin put the new preacher in Kernel Starbottle's room," said Miss Morvin, the housekeeper. "The kernel's going to-night."

"Oh," said the widow in a tone of relief, but whether at the early departure of the gallant colonel or at the successful solution of the problem of lodging the preacher, Miss Morvin could not determine. But she went on tentatively:—

"The kernel was talkin' in the bar room, and kind o' wonderin' why you hadn't got married agin. Said you'd make a stir in Sacramento—but you was jest berried HERE."

"I suppose he's heard of my husband?" said the widow indifferently.

"Yes—but he said he couldn't PLACE YOU," returned Miss Morvin.

The widow looked up. "Couldn't place ME?" she repeated.

"Yes—hadn't heard o' MacGlowrie's wife and disremembered your brothers."

"The colonel doesn't know everybody, even if he is a fighting man," said Mrs. MacGlowrie with languid scorn.

"That's just what Dick Blair said," returned Miss Morvin. "And though he's only a doctor, he jest stuck up agin' the kernel, and told that story about your jabbin' that man with your scissors—beautiful; and how you once fought off a bear with a red-hot iron, so that you'd have admired to hear him. He's awfully gone on you!"

The widow took that opportunity to button her cuff.

"And how long does the preacher calculate to stay?" she added, returning to business details.

"Only a day. They'll have his house fixed up and ready for him to-morrow. They're spendin' a heap o' money on it. He ought to be the pow'ful preacher they say he is—to be worth it."

But here Mrs. MacGlowrie's interest in the conversation ceased, and it dropped.

In her anxiety to further the suit of Dick Blair, Miss Morvin had scarcely reported the colonel with fairness.

That gentleman, leaning against the bar in the hotel saloon with a cocktail in his hand, had expatiated with his usual gallantry upon Mrs. MacGlowrie's charms, and on his own "personal" responsibility had expressed the opinion that they were thrown away on Laurel Spring. That—blank it all—she reminded him of the blankest beautiful woman he had seen even in Washington—old Major Beveridge's daughter from Kentucky. Were they sure she wasn't from Kentucky? Wasn't her name Beveridge—and not Boompointer? Becoming more reminiscent over his second drink, the colonel could vaguely recall only one Boompointer—a blank skulking hound, sir—a mean white shyster—but, of course, he couldn't have been of the same breed as such a blank fine woman as the widow! It was here that Dick Blair interrupted with a heightened color and a glowing eulogy of the widow's relations and herself, which, however, only increased the chivalry of the colonel—who would be the last man, sir, to detract from—or suffer any detraction of—a lady's reputation. It was needless to say that all this was intensely diverting to the bystanders, and proportionally discomposing to Blair, who already experienced some slight jealousy of the colonel as a man whose fighting reputation might possibly attract the affections of the widow of the belligerent MacGlowrie. He had cursed his folly and relapsed into gloomy silence until the colonel left.

For Dick Blair loved the widow with the unselfishness of a generous nature and a first passion. He had admired her from the first day his lot was cast in Laurel Spring, where coming from a rude frontier practice he had succeeded the district doctor in a more peaceful and domestic ministration. A skillful and gentle surgeon rather than a general household practitioner, he was at first coldly welcomed by the gloomy dyspeptics and ague-haunted settlers from riparian lowlands. The few bucolic idlers who had relieved the monotony of their lives by the stimulus of patent medicines and the exaltation of stomach bitters, also looked askance at him. A common-sense way of dealing with their ailments did not naturally commend itself to the shopkeepers who vended these nostrums, and he was made to feel the opposition of trade. But he was gentle to women and children and animals, and, oddly enough, it was to this latter dilection that he owed the widow's interest in him—an interest that eventually made him popular elsewhere.

The widow had a pet dog—a beautiful spaniel, who, however, had assimilated her graceful languor to his own native love of ease to such an extent that he failed in a short leap between a balcony and a window, and fell to the ground with a fractured thigh. The dog was supposed to be crippled for life even if that life were worth preserving—when Dr. Blair came to the rescue, set the fractured limb, put it in splints and plaster after an ingenious design of his own, visited him daily, and eventually restored him to his mistress's lap sound in wind and limb. How far this daily ministration and the necessary exchange of sympathy between the widow and himself heightened his zeal was not known. There were those who believed that the whole thing was an unmanly trick to get the better of his rivals in the widow's good graces; there were others who averred that his treatment of a brute beast like a human being was sinful and unchristian. "He couldn't have done more for a regularly baptized child," said the postmistress. "And what mo' would a regularly baptized child have wanted?" returned Mrs. MacGlowrie, with the drawling Southern intonation she fell back upon when most contemptuous.

But Dr. Blair's increasing practice and the widow's preoccupation presently ended their brief intimacy. It was well known that she encouraged no suitors at the hotel, and his shyness and sensitiveness shrank from ostentatious advances. There seemed to be no chance of her becoming, herself, his patient; her sane mind, indolent nerves, and calm circulation kept her from feminine "vapors" of feminine excesses. She retained the teeth and digestion of a child in her thirty odd years, and abused neither. Riding and the cultivation of her little garden gave her sufficient exercise. And yet the unexpected occurred! The day after Starbottle left, Dr. Blair was summoned hastily to the hotel. Mrs. MacGlowrie had been found lying senseless in a dead faint in the passage outside the dining room. In his hurried flight thither with the messenger he could learn only that she had seemed to be in her usual health that morning, and that no one could assign any cause for her fainting.

He could find out little more when he arrived and examined her as she lay pale and unconscious on the sofa of her sitting room. It had not been thought necessary to loosen her already loose dress, and indeed he could find no organic disturbance. The case was one of sudden nervous shock—but this, with his knowledge of her indolent temperament, seemed almost absurd. They could tell him nothing but that she was evidently on the point of entering the dining room when she fell unconscious. Had she been frightened by anything? A snake or a rat? Miss Morvin was indignant! The widow of MacGlowrie—the repeller of grizzlies—frightened at "sich"! Had she been upset by any previous excitement, passion, or the receipt of bad news? No!—she "wasn't that kind," as the doctor knew. And even as they were speaking he felt the widow's healthy life returning to the pulse he was holding, and giving a faint tinge to her lips. Her blue-veined eyelids quivered slightly and then opened with languid wonder on the doctor and her surroundings. Suddenly a quick, startled look contracted the yellow brown pupils of her eyes, she lifted herself to a sitting posture with a hurried glance around the room and at the door beyond. Catching the quick, observant eyes of Dr.

Blair, she collected herself with an effort, which Dr. Blair felt in her pulse, and drew away her wrist.

"What is it? What happened?" she said weakly.

"You had a slight attack of faintness," said the doctor cheerily, "and they called me in as I was passing, but you're all right now."

"How pow'ful foolish," she said, with returning color, but her eyes still glancing at the door, "slumping off like a green gyrl at nothin'."

"Perhaps you were startled?" said the doctor.

Mrs. MacGlowrie glanced up quickly and looked away. "No!—Let me see! I was just passing through the hall, going into the dining room, when—everything seemed to waltz round me—and I was off! Where did they find me?" she said, turning to Miss Morvin.

"I picked you up just outside the door," replied the housekeeper.

"Then they did not see me?" said Mrs. MacGlowrie.

"Who's they?" responded the housekeeper with more directness than grammatical accuracy.

"The people in the dining room. I was just opening the door—and I felt this coming on—and—I reckon I had just sense enough to shut the door again before I went off."

"Then that accounts for what Jim Slocum said," uttered Miss Morvin triumphantly. "He was in the dining room talkin' with the new preacher, when he allowed he heard the door open and shut behind him. Then he heard a kind of slump outside and opened the door again just to find you lyin' there, and to rush off and get me. And that's why he was so mad at the preacher!—for he says he just skurried away without offerin' to help. He allows the preacher may be a pow'ful exhorter—but he ain't worth much at 'works.'"

"Some men can't bear to be around when a woman's up to that sort of foolishness," said the widow, with a faint attempt at a smile, but a return of her paleness.

"Hadn't you better lie down again?" said the doctor solicitously.

"I'm all right now," returned Mrs. MacGlowrie, struggling to her feet; "Morvin will look after me till the shakiness goes. But it was mighty touching and neighborly to come in, Doctor," she continued, succeeding at last in bringing up a faint but adorable smile, which stirred Blair's pulses. "If I were my own dog—you couldn't have treated me better!"

With no further excuse for staying longer, Blair was obliged to depart—yet reluctantly, both as lover and physician. He was by no means satisfied with her condition. He called to inquire the next day—but she was engaged and sent word to say she was "better."

In the excitement attending the advent of the new preacher the slight illness of the charming widow was forgotten. He had taken the settlement by storm. His first sermon at Laurel Spring exceeded even the extravagant reputation that had preceded him. Known as the "Inspired Cowboy," a common unlettered frontiersman, he was said to have developed wonderful powers of exhortatory eloquence among the Indians, and scarcely less savage border communities where he had lived, half outcast, half missionary. He had just come up from the Southern agricultural districts, where he had been, despite his rude antecedents, singularly effective with women and young people. The moody dyspeptics and lazy rustics of Laurel Spring were stirred as with a new patent medicine. Dr. Blair went to the first "revival" meeting. Without undervaluing the man's influence, he was instinctively repelled by his appearance and methods. The young physician's trained powers of observation not only saw an overwrought emotionalism in the speaker's eloquence, but detected the ring of insincerity in his more lucid speech and acts. Nevertheless, the hysteria of the preacher was communicated to the congregation, who wept and shouted with him. Tired and discontented housewives found their vague sorrows and vaguer longings were only the result of their "unregenerate" state; the lazy country youths felt that the frustration of their small ambitions lay in their not being "convicted of sin." The mourners' bench was crowded with wildly emulating sinners. Dr. Blair turned away with mingled feelings of amusement and contempt. At the door Jim Slocum tapped him on the shoulder: "Fetches the wimmin folk every time, don't he, Doctor?" said Jim.

"So it seems," said Blair dryly.

"You're one o' them scientific fellers that look inter things—what do YOU allow it is?"

The young doctor restrained the crushing answer that rose to his lips. He had learned caution in that neighborhood. "I couldn't say," he said indifferently.

"'Tain't no religion," said Slocum emphatically; "it's jest pure fas'nation. Did ye look at his eye? It's like a rattlesnake's, and them wimmin are like birds. They're frightened of him—but they hev to do jest what he 'wills' 'em. That's how he skeert the widder the other day."

The doctor was alert and on fire at once. "Scared the widow?" he repeated indignantly.

"Yes. You know how she swooned away. Well, sir, me and that preacher, Brown, was the only one in that dinin' room at the time. The widder opened the door behind me and sorter peeked in, and that thar preacher give a start and looked up; and then, that sort of queer light come in his eyes, and she shut the door, and kinder fluttered and flopped down in the passage outside, like a bird! And he crawled away like a snake, and never said a word! My belief is that either he hadn't time to turn on the hull influence, or else she, bein' smart, got the door shut betwixt her and it in time! Otherwise, sure as you're born, she'd hev been floppin' and crawlin' and sobbin' arter him—jist like them critters we've left."

"Better not let the brethren hear you talk like that, or they'll lynch you," said the doctor, with a laugh. "Mrs. MacGlowrie simply had an attack of faintness from some overexertion, that's all."

Nevertheless, he was uneasy as he walked away. Mrs. MacGlowrie had evidently received a shock which was still unexplained, and, in spite of Slocum's exaggerated fancy, there might be some foundation in his story. He did not share the man's superstition, although he was not a skeptic regarding magnetism. Yet even then, the widow's action was one of repulsion, and as long as she was strong enough not to come to these meetings, she was not in danger. A day or two later, as he was passing the garden of the hotel on horseback, he saw her lithe, graceful, languid figure bending over one of her favorite flower beds. The high fence partially concealed him from view, and she evidently believed herself alone. Perhaps that was why she suddenly raised herself from her task, put back her straying hair with a weary, abstracted look, remained for a moment quite still staring at the vacant sky, and then, with a little catching of her breath, resumed her occupation in a dull, mechanical way. In that brief glimpse of her charming face, Blair was shocked at the change; she was pale, the corners of her pretty mouth were drawn, there were deeper shades in the orbits of her eyes, and in spite of her broad garden hat with its blue ribbon, her light flowered frock and frilled apron, she looked as he fancied she might have looked in the first crushing grief of her widowhood. Yet he would have passed on, respecting her privacy of sorrow, had not her little spaniel detected him with her keener senses. And Fluffy being truthful—as dogs are—and recognizing a dear friend in the intruder, barked joyously.

The widow looked up, her eyes met Blair's, and she reddened. But he was too acute a lover to misinterpret what he knew, alas! was only confusion at her abstraction being discovered. Nevertheless, there was something else in her brown eyes he had never seen before. A momentary lighting up of RELIEF—of even hopefulness—in his presence. It was enough for Blair; he shook off his old shyness like the dust of his ride, and galloped around to the front door.

But she met him in the hall with only her usual languid good humor. Nevertheless, Blair was not abashed.

"I can't put you in splints and plaster like Fluffy, Mrs. MacGlowrie," he said, "but I can forbid you to go into the garden unless you're looking better. It's a positive reflection on my professional skill, and Laurel Spring will be shocked, and hold me responsible."

Mrs. MacGlowrie had recovered enough of her old spirit to reply that she thought Laurel Spring could be in better business than looking at her over her garden fence.

"But your dog, who knows you're not well, and doesn't think me quite a fool, had the good sense to call me. You heard him."

But the widow protested that she was as strong as a horse, and that Fluffy was like all puppies, conceited to the last degree.

"Well," said Blair cheerfully, "suppose I admit you are all right, physically, you'll confess you have some trouble on your mind, won't you? If I can't make you SHOW me your tongue, you'll let me hear you USE it to tell me what worries you. If," he added more earnestly, "you won't confide in your physician—you will perhaps—to—to—a—FRIEND."

But Mrs. MacGlowrie, evading his earnest eyes as well as his appeal, was wondering what good it would do either a doctor, or—a—a—she herself seemed to hesitate over the word—"a FRIEND, to hear the worriments of a silly, nervous old thing—who had only stuck a little too closely to her business."

"You are neither nervous nor old, Mrs. MacGlowrie," said the doctor promptly, "though I begin to think you HAVE been too closely confined here. You want more diversion, or—excitement. You might even go to hear this preacher"—he stopped, for the word had slipped from his mouth unawares.

But a swift look of scorn swept her pale face. "And you'd like me to follow those skinny old frumps and leggy, limp chits, that slobber and cry over that man!" she said contemptuously. "No! I reckon I only want a change—and I'll go away, or get out of this for a while."

The poor doctor had not thought of this possible alternative. His heart sank, but he was brave. "Yes, perhaps you are right," he said sadly, "though it would be a dreadful loss—to Laurel Spring—to us all—if you went."

"Do I look so VERY bad, doctor?" she said, with a half-mischievous, half-pathetic smile.

The doctor thought her upturned face very adorable, but restrained his feelings heroically, and contented himself with replying to the pathetic half of her smile. "You look as if you had been suffering," he said gravely, "and I never saw you look so before. You seem as if you had experienced some great shock. Do you know," he went on, in a lower tone and with a half-embarrassed smile, "that when I saw you just now in the garden, you looked as I imagined you might have looked in the first days of your widowhood—when your husband's death was fresh in your heart."

A strange expression crossed her face. Her eyelids dropped instantly, and with both hands she caught up her frilled apron as if to meet them and covered her face. A little shudder seemed to pass over her shoulders, and then a cry that ended in an uncontrollable and half-hysterical laugh followed from the depths of that apron, until shaking her sides, and with her head still enveloped in its covering, she fairly ran into the inner room and closed the door behind her.

Amazed, shocked, and at first indignant, Dr. Blair remained fixed to the spot. Then his indignation gave way to a burning mortification as he recalled his speech. He had made a frightful faux pas! He had been fool enough to try to recall the most sacred memories of that dead husband he was trying to succeed—and her quick woman's wit had detected his ridiculous stupidity. Her laugh was hysterical—but that was only natural in her mixed emotions. He mounted his horse in confusion and rode away.

For a few days he avoided the house. But when he next saw her she had a charming smile of greeting and an air of entire obliviousness of his past blunder. She said she was better. She had taken his advice and was giving herself some relaxation from business. She had been riding again—oh, so far! Alone?—of course; she was always alone—else what would Laurel Spring say?

"True," said Blair smilingly; "besides, I forgot that you are quite able to take care of yourself in an emergency. And yet," he added, admiringly looking at her lithe figure and indolent grace, "do you know I never can associate you with the dreadful scenes they say you have gone through."

"Then please don't!" she said quickly; "really, I'd rather you wouldn't. I'm sick and tired of hearing of it!" She was half laughing and yet half in earnest, with a slight color on her cheek.

Blair was a little embarrassed. "Of course, I don't mean your heroism—like that story of the intruder and the scissors," he stammered.

"Oh, THAT'S the worst of all! It's too foolish—it's sickening!" she went on almost angrily. "I don't know who started that stuff." She paused, and then added shyly, "I really am an awful coward and horribly nervous—as you know."

He would have combated this—but she looked really disturbed, and he had no desire to commit another imprudence. And he thought, too, that he again had seen in her eyes the same hopeful, wistful light he had once seen before, and was happy.

This led him, I fear, to indulge in wilder dreams. His practice, although increasing, barely supported him, and the widow was rich. Her business had been profitable, and she had repaid the advances made her when she first took the hotel. But this disparity in their fortunes which had frightened him before now had no fears for him. He felt that if he succeeded in winning her affections she could afford to wait for him, despite other suitors, until his talents had won an equal position. His rivals had always felt as secure in his poverty as they had in his peaceful profession. How could a poor, simple doctor aspire to the hand of the rich widow of the redoubtable MacGlowrie?

It was late one afternoon, and the low sun was beginning to strike athwart the stark columns and down the long aisles of the redwoods on the High Ridge. The doctor, returning from a patient at the loggers' camp in its depths, had just sighted the smaller groves of Laurel Springs, two miles away. He was riding fast, with his thoughts filled with the widow, when he heard a joyous bark in the underbrush, and Fluffy came bounding towards him. Blair dismounted to caress him, as was his wont, and then, wisely conceiving that his mistress was not far away, sauntered forward exploringly, leading his horse, the dog hounding before him and barking, as if bent upon both leading and announcing him. But the latter he effected first, for as Blair turned from the trail into the deeper woods, he saw the figures of a man and woman walking together suddenly separate at the dog's warning. The woman was Mrs. MacGlowrie—the man was the revival preacher!

Amazed, mystified, and indignant, Blair nevertheless obeyed his first instinct, which was that of a gentleman. He turned leisurely aside as if not recognizing them, led his horse a few paces further, mounted him, and galloped away without turning his head. But his heart was filled with bitterness and disgust. This woman—who but a few days before had voluntarily declared her scorn and contempt for that man and his admirers—had just been giving him a clandestine meeting like one of the most infatuated of his devotees! The story of the widow's fainting, the coarse surmises and comments of Slocum, came back to him with overwhelming significance. But even then his reason forbade him to believe that she had fallen under the preacher's influence—she, with her sane mind and indolent temperament. Yet, whatever her excuse or purpose was, she had deceived him wantonly and cruelly! His abrupt avoidance of her had prevented him from knowing if she, on her part, had recognized him as he rode away. If she HAD, she would understand why he had avoided her, and any explanation must come from her.

Then followed a few days of uncertainty, when his thoughts again reverted to the preacher with returning jealousy. Was she, after all, like other women, and had her gratuitous outburst of scorn of THEIR infatuation been prompted by unsuccessful rivalry? He was too proud to question Slocum again or breathe a word of his fears. Yet he was not strong enough to keep from again seeking the High Ridge, to discover any repetition of that rendezvous. But he saw her neither there, nor elsewhere, during his daily rounds. And one night his feverish anxiety getting the better of him, he entered the great "Gospel Tent" of the revival preacher.

It chanced to be an extraordinary meeting, and the usual enthusiastic audience was reinforced by some sight-seers from the neighboring county town—the district judge and officials from the court in session, among them Colonel Starbottle. The impassioned revivalist—his eyes ablaze with fever, his lank hair wet with perspiration, hanging beside his heavy but weak jaws—was concluding a fervent exhortation to his auditors to confess their sins, "accept conviction," and regenerate then and there, without delay. They must put off "the old Adam," and put on the flesh of righteousness at once! They were to let no false shame or worldly pride keep them from avowing their guilty past before their brethren. Sobs and groans followed the preacher's appeals; his own agitation and convulsive efforts seemed to spread in surging waves through the congregation, until a dozen men and women arose, staggering like drunkards blindly, or led or dragged forward by sobbing sympathizers towards the mourners' bench. And prominent among them, but stepping jauntily and airily forward, was the redoubtable and worldly Colonel Starbottle!

At this proof of the orator's power the crowd shouted—but stopped suddenly, as the colonel halted before the preacher, and ascended the rostrum beside him. Then taking a slight pose with his gold-headed cane in one hand and the other thrust in the breast of his buttoned coat, he said in his blandest, forensic voice:—

"If I mistake not, sir, you are advising these ladies and gentlemen to a free and public confession of their sins and a—er—denunciation of their past life—previous to their conversion. If I am mistaken I—er—ask your pardon, and theirs and—er—hold myself responsible—er—personally responsible!"

The preacher glanced uneasily at the colonel, but replied, still in the hysterical intonation of his exordium:—

"Yes! a complete searching of hearts—a casting out of the seven Devils of Pride, Vain Glory"—

"Thank you—that is sufficient," said the colonel blandly. "But might I—er—be permitted to suggest that you—er—er—SET THEM THE EXAMPLE! The statement of the circumstances attending your own past life and conversion would be singularly interesting and exemplary."

The preacher turned suddenly and glanced at the colonel with furious eyes set in an ashy face.

"If this is the flouting and jeering of the Ungodly and Dissolute," he screamed, "woe to you! I say—woe to you! What have such as YOU to do with my previous state of unregeneracy?"

"Nothing," said the colonel blandly, "unless that state were also the STATE OF ARKANSAS! Then, sir, as a former member of the Arkansas BAR—I might be able to assist your memory—and—er—even corroborate your confession."

But here the enthusiastic adherents of the preacher, vaguely conscious of some danger to their idol, gathered threateningly round the platform from which he had promptly leaped into their midst, leaving the colonel alone, to face the sea of angry upturned faces. But that gallant warrior never altered his characteristic pose. Behind him loomed the reputation of the dozen duels he had fought, the gold-headed stick on which he leaned was believed to contain eighteen inches of shining steel—and the people of Laurel Spring had discretion.

He smiled suavely, stepped jauntily down, and made his way to the entrance without molestation.

But here he was met by Blair and Slocum, and a dozen eager questions:—

"What was it?" "What had he done?" "WHO was he?"

"A blank shyster, who had swindled the widows and orphans in Arkansas and escaped from jail."

"And his name isn't Brown?"

"No," said the colonel curtly.

"What is it?"

"That is a matter which concerns only myself and him, sir," said the colonel loftily; "but for which I am—er—personally responsible."

A wild idea took possession of Blair.

"And you say he was a noted desperado?" he said with nervous hesitation.

The colonel glared.

"Desperado, sir! Never! Blank it all!—a mean, psalm-singing, crawling, sneak thief!"

And Blair felt relieved without knowing exactly why.

The next day it was known that the preacher, Gabriel Brown, had left Laurel Spring on an urgent "Gospel call" elsewhere.

Colonel Starbottle returned that night with his friends to the county town. Strange to say, a majority of the audience had not grasped the full significance of the colonel's unseemly interruption, and those who had, as partisans, kept it quiet. Blair, tortured by doubt, had a new delicacy added to his hesitation, which left him helpless until the widow should take the initiative in explanation.

A sudden summons from his patient at the loggers' camp the next day brought him again to the fateful redwoods. But he was vexed and mystified to find, on arriving at the camp, that he had been made the victim of some stupid blunder, and that no message had been sent from there. He was returning abstractedly through the woods when he was amazed at seeing at a little distance before him the flutter of Mrs. MacGlowrie's well-known dark green riding habit and the figure of the lady herself. Her dog was not with her, neither was the revival preacher—or he might have thought the whole vision a trick of his memory. But she slackened her pace, and he was obliged to rein up abreast of her in some confusion.

"I hope I won't shock you again by riding alone through the woods with a man," she said with a light laugh.

Nevertheless, she was quite pale as he answered, somewhat coldly, that he had no right to be shocked at anything she might choose to do.

"But you WERE shocked, for you rode away the last time without speaking," she said; "and yet"—she looked up suddenly into his eyes with a smileless face—"that man you saw me with once had a better right to ride alone with me than any other man. He was"—

"Your lover?" said Blair with brutal brevity.

"My husband!" returned Mrs. MacGlowrie slowly.

"Then you are NOT a widow," gasped Blair.

"No. I am only a divorced woman. That is why I have had to live a lie here. That man—that hypocrite—whose secret was only half exposed the other night, was my husband—divorced from me by the law, when, an escaped convict, he fled with another woman from the State three years ago." Her face flushed and whitened again; she put up her hand blindly to her straying hair, and for an instant seemed to sway in the saddle.

But Blair as quickly leaped from his horse, and was beside her. "Let me help you down," he said quickly, "and rest yourself until you are better." Before she could reply, he lifted her tenderly to the ground and placed her on a mossy stump a little distance from the trail. Her color and a faint smile returned to her troubled face.

"Had we not better go on?" she said, looking around. "I never went so far as to sit down in the woods with HIM that day."

"Forgive me," he said pleadingly, "but, of course, I knew nothing. I disliked the man from instinct—I thought he had some power over you."

"He has none—except the secret that would also have exposed himself."

"But others knew it. Colonel Starbottle must have known his name? And yet"—as he remembered he stammered—"he refused to tell me."

"Yes, but not because he knew he was my husband, but because he knew he bore the same name. He thinks, as every one does, that my husband died in San Francisco. The man who died there was my husband's cousin—a desperate man and a noted duelist."

"And YOU assumed to be HIS widow?" said the astounded Blair.

"Yes, but don't blame me too much," she said pathetically. "It was a wild, a silly deceit, but it was partly forced upon me. For when I first arrived across the plains, at the frontier, I was still bearing my husband's name, and although I was alone and helpless, I found myself strangely welcomed and respected by those rude frontiersmen. It was not long before I saw it was because I was presumed to be the widow of ALLEN MacGlowrie—who had just died in San Francisco. I let them think so, for I knew—what they did not—that Allen's wife had separated from him and married again, and that my taking his name could do no harm. I accepted their kindness; they gave me my first start in business, which brought me here. It was not much of a deceit," she continued, with a slight tremble of her pretty lip, "to prefer to pass as the widow of a dead desperado than to be known as the divorced wife of a living convict. It has hurt no one, and it has saved me just now."

"You were right! No one could blame you," said Blair eagerly, seizing her hand.

But she disengaged it gently, and went on:—

"And now you wonder why I gave him a meeting here?"

"I wonder at nothing but your courage and patience in all this suffering!" said Blair fervently; "and at your forgiving me for so cruelly misunderstanding you."

"But you must learn all. When I first saw MacGlowrie under his assumed name, I fainted, for I was terrified and believed he knew I was here and had come to expose me even at his own risk. That was why I hesitated between going away or openly defying him. But it appears he was more frightened than I at finding me here—he had supposed I had changed my name after the divorce, and that Mrs. MacGlowrie, Laurel Spring, was his cousin's widow. When he found out who I was he was eager to see me and agree upon a mutual silence while he was here. He thought only of himself," she added scornfully, "and Colonel Starbottle's recognition of him that night as the convicted swindler was enough to put him to flight."

"And the colonel never suspected that you were his wife?" said Blair.

"Never! He supposed from the name that he was some relation of my husband, and that was why he refused to tell it—for my sake. The colonel is an old fogy—and pompous—but a gentleman—as good as they make them!"

A slightly jealous uneasiness and a greater sense of shame came over Blair.

"I seem to have been the only one who suspected and did not aid you," he said sadly, "and yet God knows"—

The widow had put up her slim hand in half-smiling, half-pathetic interruption.

"Wait! I have not told you everything. When I took over the responsibility of being Allen MacGlowrie's widow, I had to take over HER relations and HER history as I gathered it from the frontiersmen. I never frightened any grizzly—I never jabbed anybody with the scissors; it was SHE who did it. I never was among the Injins—I never had any fighting relations; my paw was a plain farmer. I was only a peaceful Blue Grass girl—there! I never thought there was any harm in it; it seemed to keep the men off, and leave me free—until I knew you! And you know I didn't want you to believe it—don't you?"

She hid her flushed face and dimples in her handkerchief.

"But did you never think there might be another way to keep the men off, and sink the name of MacGlowrie forever?" said Blair in a lower voice.

"I think we must be going back now," said the widow timidly, withdrawing her hand, which Blair had again mysteriously got possession of in her confusion.

"But wait just a few minutes longer to keep me company," said Blair pleadingly. "I came here to see a patient, and as there must have been some mistake in the message—I must try to discover it."

"Oh! Is that all?" said the widow quickly. "Why?"—she flushed again and laughed faintly—"Well! I am that patient! I wanted to see you alone to explain everything, and I could think of no other way. I'm afraid I've got into the habit of thinking nothing of being somebody else."

"I wish you would let me select who you should be," said the doctor boldly.

"We really must go back—to the horses," said the widow.

"Agreed—if we will ride home together."

They did. And before the year was over, although they both remained, the name of MacGlowrie had passed out of Laurel Spring.

# A WARD OF COLONEL STARBOTTLE'S

"The kernel seems a little off color to-day," said the barkeeper as he replaced the whiskey decanter, and gazed reflectively after the departing figure of Colonel Starbottle.

"I didn't notice anything," said a bystander; "he passed the time o' day civil enough to me."

"Oh, he's allus polite enough to strangers and wimmin folk even when he is that way; it's only his old chums, or them ez like to be thought so, that he's peppery with. Why, ez to that, after he'd had that quo'll with his old partner, Judge Pratt, in one o' them spells, I saw him the next minit go half a block out of his way to direct an entire stranger; and ez for wimmin!—well, I reckon if he'd just got a head drawn on a man, and a woman spoke to him, he'd drop his battery and take off his hat to her. No—ye can't judge by that!"

And perhaps in his larger experience the barkeeper was right. He might have added, too, that the colonel, in his general outward bearing and jauntiness, gave no indication of his internal irritation. Yet he was undoubtedly in one of his "spells," suffering from a moody cynicism which made him as susceptible of affront as he was dangerous in resentment.

Luckily, on this particular morning he reached his office and entered his private room without any serious rencontre. Here he opened his desk, and arranging his papers, he at once set to work with grim persistency. He had not been occupied for many minutes before the door opened to Mr. Pyecroft—one of a firm of attorneys who undertook the colonel's office work.

"I see you are early to work, Colonel," said Mr. Pyecroft cheerfully.

"You see, sir," said the colonel, correcting him with a slow deliberation that boded no good—"you see a Southern gentleman—blank it!—who has stood at the head of his profession for thirty-five years, obliged to work like a blank nigger, sir, in the dirty squabbles of psalm-singing Yankee traders, instead of—er—attending to the affairs of—er—legislation!"

"But you manage to get pretty good fees out of it—Colonel?" continued Pyecroft, with a laugh.

"Fees, sir! Filthy shekels! and barely enough to satisfy a debt of honor with one hand, and wipe out a tavern score for the entertainment of—er—a few lady friends with the other!"

This allusion to his losses at poker, as well as an oyster supper given to the two principal actresses of the "North Star Troupe," then performing in the town, convinced Mr. Pyecroft that the colonel was in one of his "moods," and he changed the subject.

"That reminds me of a little joke that happened in Sacramento last week. You remember Dick Stannard, who died a year ago—one of your friends?"

"I have yet to learn," interrupted the colonel, with the same deadly deliberation, "what right HE—or ANYBODY—had to intimate that he held such a relationship with me. Am I to understand, sir, that he—er—publicly boasted of it?"

"Don't know!" resumed Pyecroft hastily; "but it don't matter, for if he wasn't a friend it only makes the joke bigger. Well, his widow didn't survive him long, but died in the States t'other day, leavin' the property in Sacramento—worth about three thousand dollars—to her little girl, who is at school at Santa Clara. The question of guardianship came up, and it appears that the widow—who only knew you through her husband—had, some time before her death, mentioned YOUR name in that connection! He! he!"

"What!" said Colonel Starbottle, starting up.

"Hold on!" said Pyecroft hilariously. "That isn't all! Neither the executors nor the probate judge knew you from Adam, and the Sacramento bar, scenting a good joke, lay low and said nothing. Then the old fool judge said that 'as you appeared to be a lawyer, a man of mature years, and a friend of the family, you were an eminently fit person, and ought to be communicated with'—you know his hifalutin' style. Nobody says anything. So that the next thing you'll know you'll get a letter from that executor asking you to look after that kid. Ha! ha! The boys said they could fancy they saw you trotting around with a ten year old girl holding on to your hand, and the Senorita Dolores or Miss Bellamont looking on! Or your being called away from a poker deal some night by the infant, singing, 'Gardy, dear gardy, come home with me now, the clock in the steeple strikes one!' And think of that old fool judge not knowing you! Ha! ha!"

A study of Colonel Starbottle's face during this speech would have puzzled a better physiognomist than Mr. Pyecroft. His first look of astonishment gave way to an empurpled confusion, from which a single short Silenus-like chuckle escaped, but this quickly changed again into a dull coppery indignation, and, as Pyecroft's laugh continued, faded out into a sallow rigidity in which his murky eyes alone seemed to keep what was left of his previous high color. But what was more singular, in spite of his enforced calm, something of his habitual old-fashioned loftiness and oratorical exaltation appeared to be returning to him as he placed his hand on his inflated breast and faced Pyceroft.

"The ignorance of the executor of Mrs. Stannard and the—er—probate judge," he began slowly, "may be pardonable, Mr. Pyecroft, since his Honor would imply that, although unknown to HIM personally, I am at least amicus curiae in this question of—er—guardianship. But I am grieved—indeed I may say shocked—Mr. Pyecroft, that the—er—last sacred trust of a dying widow—perhaps the holiest trust that can be conceived by man—the care and welfare of her helpless orphaned girl—should be made the subject of mirth, sir, by yourself and the members of the Sacramento bar! I shall not allude, sir, to my own feelings in regard to Dick Stannard, one of my most cherished friends," continued the colonel, in a voice charged with emotion, "but I can conceive of no nobler trust laid upon the altar of friendship than the care and guidance of his orphaned girl! And if, as you tell me, the utterly inadequate sum of three thousand dollars is all that is left for her maintenance through life, the selection of a guardian sufficiently devoted to the family to be willing to augment that pittance out of his own means from time to time would seem to be most important."

Before the astounded Pyecroft could recover himself, Colonel Starbottle leaned back in his chair, half closing his eyes, and abandoned himself, quite after his old manner, to one of his dreamy reminiscences.

"Poor Dick Stannard! I have a vivid recollection, sir, of driving out with him on the Shell Road at New Orleans in '54, and of his saying, 'Star'—the only man, sir, who ever abbreviated my name—'Star, if anything happens to me or her, look after our child! It was during that very drive, sir, that, through his incautious neglect to fortify himself against the swampy malaria by a glass of straight Bourbon with a pinch of bark in it, he caught that fever which undermined his constitution. Thank you, Mr. Pyecroft, for—er—recalling the circumstance. I shall," continued the colonel, suddenly abandoning reminiscence, sitting up, and arranging his papers, "look forward with great interest to—er—letter from the executor."

The next day it was universally understood that Colonel Starbottle had been appointed guardian of Pansy Stannard by the probate judge of Sacramento.

There are of record two distinct accounts of Colonel Starbottle's first meeting with his ward after his appointment as her guardian. One, given by himself, varying slightly at times, but always bearing unvarying compliment to the grace, beauty, and singular accomplishments of this apparently gifted child, was nevertheless characterized more by vague, dreamy reminiscences of the departed parents than by any personal experience of the daughter.

"I found the young lady, sir," he remarked to Mr. Pyecroft, "recalling my cherished friend Stannard in—er—form and features, and—although—er—personally unacquainted with her deceased mother—who belonged, sir, to one of the first families of Virginia—I am told that she is—er—remarkably like her. Miss Stannard is at present a pupil in one of the best educational establishments in Santa Clara, where she is receiving tuition in—er—the English classics, foreign belles lettres, embroidery, the harp, and—er—the use of the—er—globes, and—er—blackboard—under the most fastidious care, and my own personal supervision. The principal of the school, Miss Eudoxia Tish—associated with—er—er—Miss Prinkwell—is—er—remarkably gifted woman; and as I was present at one of the school exercises, I had the opportunity of testifying to her excellence in—er—short address I made to the young ladies." From such glittering but unsatisfying generalities as these I prefer to turn to the real interview, gathered from contemporary witnesses.

It was the usual cloudless, dazzling, Californian summer day, tempered with the asperity of the northwest trades that Miss Tish, looking through her window towards the rose-embowered gateway of the seminary, saw an extraordinary figure advancing up the avenue. It was that of a man slightly past middle age, yet erect and jaunty, whose costume recalled the early water-color portraits of her own youthful days. His tightly buttoned blue frock coat with gilt buttons was opened far enough across the chest to allow the expanding of a frilled shirt, black stock, and nankeen waistcoat, and his immaculate white trousers were smartly strapped over his smart varnished boots. A white bell-crowned hat, carried in his hand to permit the wiping of his forehead with a silk handkerchief, and a gold-headed walking stick hooked over his arm, completed this singular equipment. He was followed, a few paces in the rear, by a negro carrying an enormous bouquet, and a number of small boxes and parcels tied up with ribbons. As the figure paused before the door, Miss Tish gasped, and cast a quick restraining glance around the classroom. But it was too late; a dozen pairs of blue, black, round, inquiring, or mischievous eyes were already dancing and gloating over the bizarre stranger through the window.

"A cirkiss—or nigger minstrels—sure as you're born!" said Mary Frost, aged nine, in a fierce whisper.

"No!—a agent from 'The Emporium,' with samples," returned Miss Briggs, aged fourteen.

"Young ladies, attend to your studies," said Miss Tish, as the servant brought in a card. Miss Tish glanced at it with some nervousness, and read to herself, "Colonel Culpeper Starbottle," engraved in script, and below it in pencil, "To see Miss Pansy Stannard, under favor of Miss Tish." Rising with some perturbation, Miss Tish hurriedly intrusted the class to an assistant, and descended to the reception room. She had never seen Pansy's guardian before (the executor had brought the child); and this extraordinary creature, whose visit she could not deny, might be ruinous to school discipline. It was therefore with an extra degree of frigidity of demeanor that she threw open the door of the reception room, and entered majestically. But to her utter astonishment, the colonel met her with a bow so stately, so ceremonious, and so commanding that she stopped, disarmed and speechless.

"I need not ask if I am addressing Miss Tish," said the colonel loftily, "for without having the pleasure of—er—previous acquaintance, I can at once recognize the—er—Lady Superior and—er—chatelaine of this—er—establishment." Miss Tish here gave way to a slight cough and an embarrassed curtsy, as the colonel, with a wave of his white hand towards the burden carried by his follower, resumed more lightly: "I have brought—er—few trifles and gewgaws for my ward—subject, of course, to your rules and discretion. They include some—er—dainties, free from any deleterious substance, as I am informed—a sash—a ribbon or two for the hair, gloves, mittens, and a nosegay—from which, I trust, it will be HER pleasure, as it is my own, to invite you to cull such blossoms as may suit your taste. Boy, you may set them down and retire!"

"At the present moment," stammered Miss Tish, "Miss Stannard is engaged on her lessons. But"—She stopped again, hopelessly.

"I see," said the colonel, with an air of playful, poetical reminiscence—"her lessons! Certainly!

*'We will—er—go to our places,*

*With smiles on our faces,*

*And say all our lessons distinctly and slow.'*

Certainly! Not for worlds would I interrupt them; until they are done, we will—er—walk through the classrooms and inspect"—

"No! no!" interrupted the horrified, principal, with a dreadful presentiment of the appalling effect of the colonel's entry upon the class. "No!—that is—I mean—our rules exclude—except on days of public examination"—

"Say no more, my dear madam," said the colonel politely. "Until she is free I will stroll outside, through—er—the groves of the Academus"—

But Miss Tish, equally alarmed at the diversion this would create at the classroom windows, recalled herself with an effort. "Please wait here a moment," she said hurriedly; "I will bring her down;" and before the colonel could politely open the door for her, she had fled.

Happily unconscious of the sensation he had caused, Colonel Starbottle seated himself on the sofa, his white hands resting easily on the gold-headed cane. Once or twice the door behind him opened and closed quietly, scarcely disturbing him; or again opened more ostentatiously to the words, "Oh, excuse, please," and the brief glimpse of a flaxen braid, or a black curly head—to all of which the colonel nodded politely—even rising later to the apparition of a taller, demure young lady—and her more affected "Really, I beg your pardon!" The only result of this evident curiosity was slightly to change the colonel's attitude, so as to enable him to put his other hand in his breast in his favorite pose. But presently he was conscious of a more active movement in the hall, of the sounds of scuffling, of a high youthful voice saying "I won't" and "I shan't!" of the door opening to a momentary apparition of Miss Tish dragging a small hand and half of a small black-ribboned arm into the room, and her rapid disappearance again, apparently pulled back by the little hand and arm; of another and longer pause, of a whispered conference outside, and then the reappearance of Miss Tish majestically, reinforced and supported by the grim presence of her partner, Miss Prinkwell.

"This—er—unexpected visit," began Miss Tish—"not previously arranged by letter"—

"Which is an invariable rule of our establishment," supplemented Miss Prinkwell—

"And the fact that you are personally unknown to us," continued Miss Tish—

"An ignorance shared by the child, who exhibits a distaste for an interview," interpolated Miss Prinkwell, in a kind of antiphonal response—

"For which we have had no time to prepare her," continued Miss Tish—

"Compels us most reluctantly"—But here she stopped short. Colonel Starbottle, who had risen with a deep bow at their entrance and remained standing, here walked quietly towards them. His usually high color had faded except from his eyes, but his exalted manner was still more pronounced, with a dreadful deliberation superadded.

"I believe—er—I had—the honah—to send up my kyard!" (In his supreme moments the colonel's Southern accent was always in evidence.) "I may—er—be mistaken—but—er—that is my impression." The colonel paused, and placed his right hand statuesquely on his heart.

The two women trembled—Miss Tish fancied the very shirt frill of the colonel was majestically erecting itself—as they stammered in one voice,—

"Ye-e-es!"

"That kyard contained my full name—with a request to see my ward—Miss Stannard," continued the colonel slowly. "I believe that is the fact."

"Certainly! certainly!" gasped the women feebly.

"Then may I—er—point out to you that I AM—er—WAITING?"

Although nothing could exceed the laborious simplicity and husky sweetness of the colonel's utterance, it appeared to demoralize utterly his two hearers—Miss Prinkwell seemed to fade into the pattern of the wall paper, Miss Tish to droop submissively forward like a pink wax candle in the rays of the burning sun.

"We will bring her instantly. A thousand pardons, sir," they uttered in the same breath, backing towards the door.

But here the unexpected intervened. Unnoticed by the three during the colloquy, a little figure in a black dress had peeped through the door, and then glided into the room. It was a girl of about ten, who, in all candor, could scarcely be called pretty, although the awkward change of adolescence had not destroyed the delicate proportions of her hands and feet nor the beauty of her brown eyes. These were, just then, round and wondering, and fixed alternately on the colonel and the two women. But like many other round and wondering eyes, they had taken in the full meaning of the situation, with a quickness the adult mind is not apt to give them credit for. They saw the complete and utter subjugation of the two supreme autocrats of the school, and, I grieve to say, they were filled with a secret and "fearful joy." But the casual spectator saw none of this; the round and wondering eyes, still rimmed with recent and recalcitrant tears, only looked big and innocently shining.

The relief of the two women was sudden and unaffected.

"Oh, here you are, dearest, at last!" said Miss Tish eagerly. "This is your guardian, Colonel Starbottle. Come to him, dear!"

She took the hand of the child, who hung back with an odd mingling of shamefacedness and resentment of the interference, when the voice of Colonel Starbottle, in the same deadly calm deliberation, said,—

"I—er—will speak with her—alone."

The round eyes again saw the complete collapse of authority, as the two women shrank back from the voice, and said hurriedly,—

"Certainly, Colonel Starbottle; perhaps it would be better," and ingloriously quitted the room.

But the colonel's triumph left him helpless. He was alone with a simple child, an unprecedented, unheard-of situation, which left him embarrassed and—speechless. Even his vanity was conscious that his oratorical periods, his methods, his very attitude, were powerless here. The perspiration stood out on his forehead; he looked at her vaguely, and essayed a feeble smile. The child saw his embarrassment, even as she had seen and understood his triumph, and the small woman within her exulted. She put her little hands on her waist, and with the fingers turned downwards and outwards pressed them down her hips to her bended knees until they had forced her skirts into an egregious fullness before and behind, as if she were making a curtsy, and then jumped up and laughed.

"You did it! Hooray!"

"Did what?" said the colonel, pleased yet mystified.

"Frightened 'em!—the two old cats! Frightened 'em outen their slippers! Oh, jiminy! Never, never, NEVER before was they so skeert! Never since school kept did they have to crawl like that! They was skeert enough FIRST when you come, but just now!—Lordy! They wasn't a-goin' to let you see me—but they had to! had to! HAD TO!" and she emphasized each repetition with a skip.

"I believe—er," said the colonel blandly, "that I—er—intimated with some firmness"—

"That's it—just it!" interrupted the child delightedly. "You—you—overdid 'em"

"What?"

"OVERDID 'EM! Don't you know? They're always so high and mighty! Kinder 'Don't tech me. My mother's an angel; my father's a king'—all that sort of thing. They did THIS"—she drew herself up in a presumable imitation of the two women's majestic entrance—"and then," she continued, "you—YOU jest did this"—here she lifted her chin, and puffing out her small chest, strode towards the colonel in evident simulation of his grandest manner.

A short, deep chuckle escaped him—although the next moment his face became serious again. But Pansy in the mean time had taken possession of his coat sleeve and was rubbing her cheek against it like a young colt. At which the colonel succumbed feebly and sat down on the sofa, the child standing beside him, leaning over and transferring her little hands to the lapels of his frock coat, which she essayed to button over his chest as she looked into his murky eyes.

"The other girls said," she began, tugging at the button, "that you was a 'cirkiss'"—another tug—"'a nigger minstrel'"—and a third tug—"'a agent with samples'—but that showed all they knew!"

"Ah," said the colonel with exaggerated blandness, "and—er—what did YOU—er—say?"

The child smiled. "I said you was a Stuffed Donkey—but that was BEFORE I knew you. I was a little skeert too; but NOW"—she succeeded in buttoning the coat and making the colonel quite apoplectic,—"NOW I ain't frightened one bit—no, not one TINY bit! But," she added, after a pause, unbuttoning the coat again and smoothing down the lapels between her fingers, "you're to keep on frightening the old cats—mind! Never mind about the GIRLS. I'll tell them."

The colonel would have given worlds to be able to struggle up into an upright position with suitable oral expression. Not that his vanity was at all wounded by these irresponsible epithets, which only excited an amused wonder, but he was conscious of an embarrassed pleasure in the child's caressing familiarity, and her perfect trustfulness in him touched his extravagant chivalry. He ought to protect her, and yet correct her. In the consciousness of these duties he laid his white hand upon her head. Alas! she lifted her arm and instantly transferred his hand and part of his arm around her neck and shoulders, and comfortably snuggled against him. The colonel gasped. Nevertheless, something must be said, and he began, albeit somewhat crippled in delivery:—

"The—er—use of elegant and precise language by—er—young ladies cannot be too sedulously cultivated"—

But here the child laughed, and snuggling still closer, gurgled: "That's right! Give it to her when she comes down! That's the style!" and the colonel stopped, discomfited. Nevertheless, there was a certain wholesome glow in the contact of this nestling little figure.

Presently he resumed tentativery: "I have—er—brought you a few dainties."

"Yes," said Pansy, "I see; but they're from the wrong shop, you dear old silly! They're from Tomkins's, and we girls just abominate his things. You oughter have gone to Emmons's. Never mind. I'll show you when we go out. We're going out, aren't we?" she said suddenly, lifting her head anxiously. "You know it's allowed, and it's RIGHTS 'to parents and guardians'!"

"Certainly, certainly," said the colonel. He knew he would feel a little less constrained in the open air.

"Then we'll go now," said Pansy, jumping up. "I'll just run upstairs and put on my things. I'll say it's 'orders' from you. And I'll wear my new frock—it's longer." (The colonel was slightly relieved at this; it had seemed to him, as a guardian, that there was perhaps an abnormal display of Pansy's black stockings.) "You wait; I won't be long."

She darted to the door, but reaching it, suddenly stopped, returned to the sofa, where the colonel still sat, imprinted a swift kiss on his mottled cheek, and fled, leaving him invested with a mingled flavor of freshly ironed muslin, wintergreen lozenges, and recent bread and butter. He sat still for some time, staring out of the window. It was very quiet in the room; a bumblebee blundered from the jasmine outside into the open window, and snored loudly at the panes. But the colonel heeded it not, and remained abstracted and silent until the door opened to Miss Tish and Pansy—in her best frock and sash, at which the colonel started and became erect again and courtly.

"I am about to take my ward out," he said deliberately, "to—er—taste the air in the Alameda, and—er—view the shops. We may—er—also—indulge in—er—slight suitable refreshment;—er—seed cake—or—bread and butter—and—a dish of tea."

Miss Tish, now thoroughly subdued, was delighted to grant Miss Stannard the half holiday permitted on such occasions. She begged the colonel to suit his own pleasure, and intrusted "the dear child" to her guardian "with the greatest confidence."

The colonel made a low bow, and Pansy, demurely slipping her hand into his, passed with him into the hall; there was a slight rustle of vanishing skirts, and Pansy pressed his hand significantly. When they were well outside, she said, in a lower voice:—

"Don't look up until we're under the gymnasium windows." The colonel, mystified but obedient, strutted on. "Now!" said Pansy. He looked up, beheld the windows aglow with bright young faces, and bewildering with many handkerchiefs and clapping hands, stopped, and then taking off his hat, acknowledged the salute with a sweeping bow. Pansy was delighted. "I knew they'd be there; I'd already fixed 'em. They're just dyin' to know you."

The colonel felt a certain glow of pleasure, "I—er—had already intimated a—er—willingness to—er—inspect the classes; but—I—er—understood that the rules"—

"They're sick old rules," interrupted the child. "Tish and Prinkwell are the rules! You say just right out that you WILL! Just overdo her!"

The colonel had a vague sense that he ought to correct both the spirit and language of this insurrectionary speech, but Pansy pulled him along, and then swept him quite away with a torrent of prattle of the school, of her friends, of the teachers, of her life and its infinitely small miseries and pleasures. Pansy was voluble; never before had the colonel found himself relegated to the place of a passive listener. Nevertheless, he liked it, and as they passed on, under the shade of the Alameda, with Pansy alternately swinging from his hand and skipping beside him, there was a vague smile of satisfaction on his face. Passers-by turned to look after the strangely assorted pair, or smiled, accepting them, as the colonel fancied, as father and daughter. An odd feeling, half of pain and half of pleasure, gripped at the heart of the empty and childless man.

And now, as they approached the more crowded thoroughfares, the instinct of chivalrous protection was keen in his breast. He piloted her skillfully; he jauntily suited his own to her skipping step; he lifted her with scrupulous politeness over obstacles; strutting beside her on crowded pavements, he made way for her with his swinging stick. All the while, too, he had taken note of the easy carriage of her head and shoulders, and most of all of her small, slim feet and hands, that, to his fastidious taste, betokened her race. "Ged, sir," he muttered to himself, "she's 'Blue Grass' stock, all through." To admiration succeeded pride, with a slight touch of ownership. When they went into a shop, which, thanks to the ingenuous Pansy, they did pretty often, he would introduce her with a wave of the hand and the remark, "I am—er—seeking nothing to-day, but if you will kindly—er—serve my WARD—Miss Stannard!" Later, when they went into the confectioner's for refreshment, and Pansy frankly declared for "ice cream and cream cakes," instead of the "dish of tea and bread and butter" he had ordered in pursuance of his promise, he heroically took it himself—to satisfy his honor. Indeed, I know of no more sublime figure than Colonel Starbottle—rising superior to a long-withstood craving for a "cocktail," morbidly conscious also of the ridiculousness of his appearance to any of his old associates who might see him—drinking luke-warm tea and pecking feebly at his bread and butter at a small table, beside his little tyrant.

And this domination of the helpless continued on their way home. Although Miss Pansy no longer talked of herself, she was equally voluble in inquiry as to the colonel's habits, ways of life, friends and acquaintances, happily restricting her interrogations, in regard to those of her own sex, to "any LITTLE girls that he knew." Saved by this exonerating adjective, the colonel saw here a chance to indulge his postponed monitorial duty, as well as his vivid imagination. He accordingly drew elaborate pictures of impossible children he had known—creatures precise in language and dress, abstinent of play and confectionery, devoted to lessons and duties, and otherwise, in Pansy's own words, "loathsome to the last degree!" As "daughters of oldest and most cherished friends," they might perhaps have excited Pansy's childish jealousy but for the singular fact that they had all long ago been rewarded by marriage with senators, judges, and generals—also associates of the colonel. This remoteness of presence somewhat marred their effect as an example, and the colonel was mortified, though not entirely displeased, to observe that their surprising virtues did not destroy Pansy's voracity for sweets, the recklessness of her skipping, nor the freedom of her language. The colonel was remorseful—but happy.

When they reached the seminary again, Pansy retired with her various purchases, but reappeared after an interval with Miss Tish.

"I remember," hesitated that lady, trembling under the fascination of the colonel's profound bow, "that you were anxious to look over the school, and although it was not possible then, I shall be glad to show you now through one of the classrooms."

The colonel, glancing at Pansy, was momentarily shocked by a distortion of one side of her face, which seemed, however, to end in a wink of her innocent brown eyes, but recovering himself, gallantly expressed his gratitude. The next moment he was ascending the stairs, side by side with Miss Tish, and had a distinct impression that he had been pinched in the calf by Pansy, who was following close behind.

It was recess, but the large classroom was quite filled with pupils, many of them older and prettier girls, inveigled there, as it afterwards appeared, by Pansy, in some precocious presentiment of her guardian's taste. The colonel's apologetic yet gallant bow on entering, and his erect, old-fashioned elegance, instantly took their delighted attention. Indeed, all would have gone well had not Miss Prinkwell, with the view of impressing the colonel as well as her pupils, majestically introduced him as "a distinguished jurist deeply interested in the cause of education, as well as guardian of their fellow pupil." That opportunity was not thrown away on Colonel Starbottle.

Stepping up to the desk of the astounded principal, he laid the points of his fingers delicately upon it, and, with a preparatory inclination of his head towards her, placed his other hand in his breast, and with an invocatory glance at the ceiling, began.

It was the colonel's habit at such moments to state at first, with great care and precision, the things that he "would not say," that he "NEED not say," and apparently that it was absolutely unnecessary even to allude to. It was therefore, not strange that the colonel informed them that he need not say that he counted his present privilege among the highest that had been granted him; for besides the privilege of beholding the galaxy of youthful talent and excellence before him, besides the privilege of being surrounded by a garland of the blossoms of the school in all their freshness and beauty, it was well understood that he had the greater privilege of—er—standing in loco parentis to one of these blossoms. It was not for him to allude to the high trust imposed upon him by—er—deceased and cherished friend, and daughter of one of the first families of Virginia, by the side of one who must feel that she was the recipient of trusts equally supreme (here the colonel paused, and statuesquely regarded the alarmed Miss Prinkwell as if he were in doubt of it), but he would say that it should be HIS devoted mission to champion the rights of the orphaned and innocent whenever and wherever the occasion arose, against all odds, and even in the face of misguided authority. (Having left the impression that Miss Prinkwell contemplated an invasion of those rights, the colonel became more lenient and genial.) He fully recognized her high and noble office; he saw in her the worthy successor of those two famous instructresses of Athens—those Greek ladies—er—whose names had escaped his memory, but which—er—no doubt Miss Prinkwell would be glad to recall to her pupils, with some account of their lives. (Miss Prinkwell colored; she had never heard of them before, and even the delight of the class in the colonel's triumph was a little dampened by this prospect of hearing more about them.) But the colonel was only too content with seeing before him these bright and beautiful faces, destined, as he firmly believed, in after years to lend their charm and effulgence to the highest places as the happy helpmeets of the greatest in the land. He was—er—leaving a—er—slight testimonial of his regard in the form of some—er—innocent refreshments in the hands of his ward, who would—er—act as—er—his proxy in their distribution; and the colonel sat down to the flutter of handkerchiefs, an applause only half restrained, and the utter demoralization of Miss Prinkwell.

But the time of his departure had come by this time, and he was too experienced a public man to risk the possibility of an anticlimax by protracting his leave-taking. And in an ominous shining of Pansy's big eyes as the time approached he felt an embarrassment as perplexing as the odd presentiment of loneliness that was creeping over him. But with an elaborate caution as to the dangers of self-indulgence, and the private bestowal of a large gold piece slipped into her hand, a promise to come again soon, and an exaction that she would write to him often, the colonel received in return a wet kiss, a great deal of wet cheek pressed against his own, and a momentary tender clinging, like that which attends the pulling up of some small flower, as he passed out into the porch. In the hall, on the landing above him, there was a close packing of brief skirts against the railing, and a voice, apparently proceeding from a pair of very small mottled legs protruding through the balusters, said distinctly, "Free cheers for Ternel Tarbottle!" And to this benediction the colonel, hat in hand, passed out of this Eden into the world again.

The colonel's next visit to the seminary did not produce the same sensation as the first, although it was accompanied with equal disturbance to the fair principals. Had he been a less conceited man he might have noticed that their antagonism, although held in restraint by their wholesome fear of him, was in danger of becoming more a conviction than a mere suspicion. He was made aware of it through Pansy's resentment towards them, and her revelation of a certain inquisition that she had been subjected to in regard to his occupation, habits, and acquaintances. Naturally of these things Pansy knew very little, but this had not prevented her from saying a great deal. There had been enough in her questioners' manner to make her suspect that her guardian was being attacked, and to his defense she brought the mendacity and imagination of a clever child. What she had really said did not transpire except through her own comments to the colonel: "And of course you've killed people—for you're a kernel, you know?" (Here the colonel admitted, as a point of fact, that he had served in the Mexican war.) "And you kin PREACH, for they heard you do it when you was here before," she added confidently; "and of course you own niggers—for there's 'Jim.'" (The colonel here attempted to explain that Jim, being in a free State, was now a free man, but Pansy swept away such fine distinctions.) "And you're rich, you know, for you gave me that ten-dollar gold piece all for myself. So I jest gave 'em as good as they sent—the old spies and curiosity shops!" The colonel, more pleased at Pansy's devotion than concerned over the incident itself, accepted this interpretation of his character as a munificent, militant priest with a smiling protest. But a later incident caused him to remember it more seriously.

They had taken their usual stroll through the Alameda, and had made the round of the shops, where the colonel had exhibited his usual liberality of purchase and his exalted parental protection, and so had passed on to their usual refreshment at the confectioner's, the usual ices and cakes for Pansy, but this time—a concession also to the tyrant Pansy—a glass of lemon soda and a biscuit for the colonel. He was coughing over his unaccustomed beverage, and Pansy, her equanimity and volubility restored by sweets, was chirruping at his side; the large saloon was filling up with customers—mainly ladies and children, embarrassing to him as the only man present, when suddenly Pansy's attention was diverted by another arrival. It was a good-looking young woman, overdressed, striking, and self-conscious, who, with an air of one who was in the habit of challenging attention, affectedly seated herself with a male companion at an empty table, and began to pull off an overtight glove.

"My!" said Pansy in admiring wonder, "ain't she fine?"

Colonel Starbottle looked up abstractedly, but at the first glance his face flushed redly, deepened to a purple, and then became gray and stern. He had recognized in the garish fair one Miss Flora Montague, the "Western Star of Terpsichore and Song," with whom he had supped a few days before at Sacramento. The lady was "on tour" with her "Combination troupe."

The colonel leaned over and fixed his murky eyes on Pansy. "The room is filling up; the place is stifling; I must—er—request you to—er—hurry."

There was a change in the colonel's manner, which the quick-witted child heeded. But she had not associated it with the entrance of the strangers, and as she obediently gulped down her ice, she went on innocently,—

"That fine lady's smilin' and lookin' over here. Seems to know you; so does the man with her."

"I—er—must request you," said the colonel, with husky precision, "NOT to look that way, but finish your—er—repast."

His tone was so decided that the child's lips pouted, but before she could speak a shadow leaned over their table. It was the companion of the "fine lady."

"Don't seem to see us, Colonel," he said with coarse familiarity, laying his hand on the colonel's shoulder. "Florry wants to know what's up."

The colonel rose at the touch. "Tell her, sir," he said huskily, but with slow deliberation, "that I 'am up' and leaving this place with my ward, Miss Stannard. Good-morning." He lifted Pansy with infinite courtesy from her chair, took her hand, strolled to the counter, threw down a gold piece, and passing the table of the astonished fair one with an inflated breast, swept with Pansy out of the shop. In the street he paused, bidding the child go on; and then, finding he was not followed by the woman's escort, rejoined his little companion.

For a few moments they walked silently side by side. Then Pansy's curiosity, getting the better of her pout, demanded information. She had applied a child's swift logic to the scene. The colonel was angry, and had punished the woman for something. She drew closer to his side, and looking up with her big eyes, said confidentially.

"What had she been a-doing?"

The colonel was amazed, embarrassed, and speechless. He was totally unprepared for the question, and as unable to answer it. His abrupt departure from the shop had been to evade the very truth now demanded of him. Only a supreme effort of mendacity was left him. He wiped his brow with his handkerchief, coughed, and began deliberately:—

"The—er—lady in question is in the habit of using a scent called—er—patchouli, a—er—perfume exceedingly distressing to me. I detected it instantly on her entrance. I wished to avoid it—without further contact. It is—er—singular but accepted fact that some people are—er—peculiarly affected by odors. I had—er—old cherished friend who always—er—fainted at the odor of jasmine; and I was intimately acquainted with General Bludyer, who—er—dropped like a shot on the presentation of a simple violet. The—er—habit of using such perfumes excessively in public," continued the colonel, looking down upon the innocent Pansy, and speaking in tones of deadly deliberation, "cannot be too greatly condemned, as well as the habit of—er—frequenting places of public resort in extravagant costumes, with—er—individuals who—er—intrude upon domestic privacy. I trust you will eschew such perfumes, places, costumes, and—er—companions FOREVER and—ON ALL OCCASIONS!" The colonel had raised his voice to his forensic emphasis, and Pansy, somewhat alarmed, assented. Whether she entirely accepted the colonel's explanation was another matter.

The incident, although not again alluded to, seemed to shadow the rest of their brief afternoon holiday, and the colonel's manner was unmistakably graver. But it seemed to the child more affectionate and thoughtful. He had previously at parting submitted to be kissed by Pansy with stately tolerance and an immediate resumption of his loftiest manner. On this present leave-taking he laid his straight closely shaven lips on the crown of her dark head, and as her small arms clipped his neck, drew her closely to his side. The child uttered a slight cry; the colonel hurriedly put his hand to his breast. Her round cheek had come in contact with his derringer—a small weapon of beauty and precision—which invariably nestled also at his side, in his waistcoat pocket. The child laughed; so did the colonel, but his cheek flushed mightily.

It was four months later, and a turbulent night. The early rains, driven by a strong southwester against the upper windows of the Magnolia Restaurant, sometimes blurred the radiance of the bright lights within, and the roar of the encompassing pines at times drowned the sounds of song and laughter that rose from a private supper room. Even the clattering arrival and departure of the Sacramento stage coach, which disturbed the depths below, did not affect these upper revelers. For Colonel Starbottle, Jack Hamlin, Judge Beeswinger, and Jo Wynyard, assisted by Mesdames Montague, Montmorency, Bellefield, and "Tinky" Clifford, of the "Western Star Combination Troupe," then performing "on tour," were holding "high jinks" in the supper room. The colonel had been of late moody, irritable, and easily upset. In the words of a friend and admirer, "he was kam only at twelve paces."

In a lull in the general tumult a Chinese waiter was seen at the door vainly endeavoring to attract the attention of the colonel by signs and interjections. Mr. Hamlin's quick eye first caught sight of the intruder. "Come in, Confucius," said Jack pleasantly; "you're a trifle late for a regular turn, but any little thing in the way of knife swallowing"—

"Lill missee to see connle! Waitee waitee, bottom side housee," interrupted the Chinaman, dividing his speech between Jack and the colonel.

"What! ANOTHER lady? This is no place for me!" said Jack, rising with finely simulated decorum.

"Ask her up," chirped "Tinky" Clifford.

But at this moment the door opened against the Chinaman, and a small figure in a cloak and hat, dripping with raindrops, glided swiftly in. After a moment's half-frightened, half-admiring glance at the party, she darted forward with a little cry and threw her wet arms round the colonel. The rest of the company, arrested in their festivity, gasped with vague and smiling wonder; the colonel became purple and gasped. But only for a moment. The next instant he was on his legs, holding the child with one hand, while with the other he described a stately sweep of the table.

"My ward—Miss Pansy Stannard," he said with husky brevity. But drawing the child aside, he whispered quickly, "What has happened? Why are you here?"

But Pansy, child-like, already diverted by the lights, the table piled with delicacies, the gayly dressed women, and the air of festivity, answered half abstractedly, and as much, perhaps, to the curious eyes about her as to the colonel's voice,—

"I runned away!"

"Hush!" whispered the colonel, aghast.

But Pansy, responding again to the company rather than her guardian's counsel, and as if appealing to them, went on half poutingly: "Yes! I runned away because they teased me! Because they didn't like you and said horrid things. Because they told awful, dreadful lies! Because they said I wasn't no orphan!—that my name wasn't Stannard, and that you'd made it all up. Because they said I was a liar—and YOU WAS MY FATHER!"

A sudden outbreak of laughter here shook the room, and even drowned the storm outside; again and again it rose, as the colonel staggered gaspingly to his feet. For an instant it seemed as if his struggles to restrain himself would end in an apoplectic fit. Perhaps it was for this reason that Jack Hamlin checked his own light laugh and became alert and grave. Yet the next moment Colonel Starbottle went as suddenly dead white, as leaning over the table he said huskily, but deliberately, "I must request the ladies present to withdraw."

"Don't mind US, Colonel," said Judge Beeswinger, "it's all in the family here, you know! And now I look at the girl—hang it all! she DOES favor you, old man. Ha! ha!"

"And as for the ladies," said Wynyard with a weak, vinous laugh, "unless any of 'em is inclined to take the matter as PERSONAL—eh?"

"Stop!" roared the colonel.

There was no mistaking his voice nor his intent now. The two men, insulted and instantly sobered, were silent. Mr. Hamlin rose, playfully but determinedly tapped his fair companions on the shoulders, saying, "Run away and play, girls," actually bundled them, giggling and protesting, from the room, closed the door, and stood with his back against it. Then it was seen that the colonel, still very white, was holding the child by the hand, as she shrank back wonderingly and a little frightened against him.

"I thank YOU, Mr. Hamlin," said the colonel in a lower voice—yet with a slight touch of his habitual stateliness in it, "for being here to bear witness, in the presence of this child, to my unqualified statement that a more foul, vile, and iniquitous falsehood never was uttered than that which has been poured into her innocent ears!" He paused, walked to the door, still holding her hand, and, as Mr. Hamlin stepped aside, opened it, told her to await him in the public parlor, closed the door again, and once more faced the two men. "And," he continued more deliberately, "for the infamous jests that you, Judge Beeswinger, and you, Mr. Wynyard, have dared to pass in her presence and mine, I shall expect from each of you the fullest satisfaction—personal satisfaction. My seconds will wait on you in the morning!"

The two men stood up sobered—yet belligerent.

"As you like, sir," said Beeswinger, flashing.

"The sooner the better for me," added Wynyard curtly.

They passed the unruffled Jack Hamlin with a smile and a vaguely significant air, as if calling him as a witness to the colonel's madness, and strode out of the room.

As the door closed behind them, Mr. Hamlin lightly settled his white waistcoat, and, with his hands on his hips, lounged towards the colonel. "And THEN?" he said quietly.

"Eh?" said the colonel.

"After you've shot one or both of these men, or one of 'em has knocked you out, what's to become of that child?"

"If—I am—er—spared, sir," said the colonel huskily, "I shall continue to defend her—against calumny and sneers"—

"In this style, eh? After her life has been made a hell by her association with a man of your reputation, you propose to whitewash it by a quarrel with a couple of drunken scallawags like Beeswinger and Wynyard, in the presence of three painted trollops and a d———d scamp like myself! Do you suppose this won't be blown all over California before she can be sent back to school? Do you suppose those cackling hussies in the next room won't give the whole story away to the next man who stands treat?" (A fine contempt for the sex in general was one of Mr. Hamlin's most subtle attractions for them.)

"Nevertheless, sir," stammered the colonel, "the prompt punishment of the man who has dared"—

"Punishment!" interrupted Hamlin, "who's to punish the man who has dared most? The one man who is responsible for the whole thing? Who's to punish YOU?"

"Mr. Hamlin—sir!" gasped the colonel, falling back, as his hand involuntarily rose to the level of his waistcoat pocket and his derringer.

But Mr. Hamlin only put down the wine glass he had lifted from the table and was delicately twirling between his fingers, and looked fixedly at the colonel.

"Look here," he said slowly. "When the boys said that you accepted the guardianship of that child NOT on account of Dick Stannard, but only as a bluff against the joke they'd set up at you, I didn't believe them! When these men and women to-night tumbled to that story of the child being YOURS, I didn't believe that! When it was said by others that you were serious about making her your ward, and giving her your property, because you doted on her like a father, I didn't believe that."

"And—why not THAT?" said the colonel quickly, yet with an odd tremor in his voice.

"Because," said Hamlin, becoming suddenly as grave as the colonel, "I could not believe that any one who cared a picayune for the child could undertake a trust that might bring her into contact with a life and company as rotten as ours. I could not believe that even the most God-forsaken, conceited fool would, for the sake of a little sentimental parade and splurge among people outside his regular walk, allow the prospects of that child to be blasted. I couldn't believe it, even if he thought he was acting like a father. I didn't believe it—but I'm beginning to believe it now!"

There was little to choose between the attitudes and expressions of the two set stern faces now regarding each other, silently, a foot apart. But the colonel was the first to speak:—

"Mr. Hamlin—sir! You said a moment ago that I was—er—ahem—responsible for this evening's affair—but you expressed a doubt as to who could—er—punish me for it. I accept the responsibility you have indicated, sir, and offer you that chance. But as this matter between us must have precedence over—my engagements with that canaille, I shall expect you with your seconds at sunrise on Burnt Ridge. Good-evening, sir."

With head erect the colonel left the room. Mr. Hamlin slightly shrugged his shoulders, turned to the door of the room whither he had just banished the ladies, and in a few minutes his voice was heard melodiously among the gayest.

For all that he managed to get them away early. When he had bundled them into a large carryall, and watched them drive away through the storm, he returned for a minute to the waiting room for his overcoat. He was surprised to hear the sound of the child's voice in the supper room, and the door being ajar, he could see quite distinctly that she was seated at the table, with a plate full of sweets before her, while Colonel Starbottle, with his back to the door, was sitting opposite to her, his shoulders slightly bowed as he eagerly watched her. It seemed to Mr. Hamlin that it was the close of an emotional interview, for Pansy's voice was broken, partly by sobs, and partly, I grieve to say, by the hurried swallowing of the delicacies before her. Yet, above the beating of the storm outside, he could hear her saying,—

"Yes! I promise to be good—(sob)—and to go with Mrs. Pyecroft—(sob)—and to try to like another guardian—(sob)—and not to cry any more—(sob)—and—oh, please, DON'T YOU DO IT EITHER!"

But here Mr. Hamlin slipped out of the room and out of the house, with a rather grave face. An hour later, when the colonel drove up to the Pyecrofts' door with Pansy, he found that Mr. Pyecroft was slightly embarrassed, and a figure, which, in the darkness, seemed to resemble Mr. Hamlin's, had just emerged from the door as he entered.

Yet the sun was not up on Burnt Ridge earlier than Mr. Hamlin. The storm of the night before had blown itself out; a few shreds of mist hung in the valleys from the Ridge, that lay above coldly reddening. Then a breeze swept over it, and out of the dissipating mist fringe Mr. Hamlin saw two black figures, closely buttoned up like himself, emerge, which he recognized as Beeswinger and Wynyard, followed by their seconds. But the colonel came not, Hamlin joined the others in an animated confidential conversation, attended by a watchful outlook for the missing adversary. Five, ten minutes elapsed, and yet the usually prompt colonel was not there. Mr. Hamlin looked grave; Wynyard and Beeswinger exchanged interrogatory glances. Then a buggy was seen driving furiously up the grade, and from it leaped Colonel Starbottle, accompanied by Dick MacKinstry, his second, carrying his pistol case. And then—strangely enough for men who were waiting the coming of an antagonist who was a dead shot—they drew a breath of relief!

MacKinstry slightly preceded his principal, and the others could see that Starbottle, though erect, was walking slowly. They were surprised also to observe that he was haggard and hollow eyed, and seemed, in the few hours that had elapsed since they last saw him, to have aged ten years. MacKinstry, a tall Kentuckian, saluted, and was the first one to speak.

"Colonel Starbottle," he said formally, "desires to express his regrets at this delay, which was unavoidable, as he was obliged to attend his ward, who was leaving by the down coach for Sacramento with Mrs. Pyecroft, this morning." Hamlin, Wynyard, and Beeswinger exchanged glances. "Colonel Starbottle," continued MacKinstry, turning to his principal, "desires to say a word to Mr. Hamlin."

As Mr. Hamlin would have advanced from the group, Colonel Starbottle lifted his hand deprecatingly. "What I have to say must be said before these gentlemen," he began slowly. "Mr. Hamlin—sir! when I solicited the honor of this meeting I was under a grievous misapprehension of the intent and purpose of your comments on my action last evening. I think," he added, slightly inflating his buttoned-up figure, "that the reputation I have always borne in—er—meetings of this kind will prevent any—er—misunderstanding of my present action—which is to—er—ask permission to withdraw my challenge—and to humbly beg your pardon."

The astonishment produced by this unexpected apology, and Mr. Hamlin's prompt grasp of the colonel's hand, had scarcely passed before the colonel drew himself up again, and turning to his second said, "And now I am at the service of Judge Beeswinger and Mr. Wynyard—whichever may elect to honor me first."

But the two men thus addressed looked for a moment strangely foolish and embarrassed. Yet the awkwardness was at last broken by Judge Beeswinger frankly advancing towards the colonel with an outstretched hand. "We came here only to apologize, Colonel Starbottle. Without possessing your reputation and experience in these matters, we still think we can claim, as you have, an equal exemption from any misunderstanding when we say that we deeply regret our foolish and discourteous conduct last evening."

A quick flush mounted to the colonel's haggard cheek as he drew back with a suspicious glance at Hamlin.

"Mr. Hamlin!—gentlemen!—if this is—er—!"

But before he could finish his sentence Hamlin had clapped his hand on the colonel's shoulder. "You'll take my word, colonel, that these gentlemen honestly intended to apologize, and came here for that purpose;—and—SO DID I—only you anticipated me!"

In the laughter that followed Mr. Hamlin's frankness the colonel's features relaxed grimly, and he shook the hands of his late possible antagonists.

"And now," said Mr. Hamlin gayly, "you'll all adjourn to breakfast with me—and try to make up for the supper we left unfinished last night."

It was the only allusion to that interruption and its consequences, for during the breakfast the colonel said nothing in regard to his ward, and the other guests were discreetly reticent. But Mr. Hamlin was not satisfied. He managed to get the colonel's servant, Jim, aside, and extracted from the negro that Colonel Starbottle had taken the child that night to Pyecroft's; that he had had a long interview with Pyecroft; had written letters and "walked de flo'" all night; that he (Jim) was glad the child was gone!

"Why?" asked Hamlin, with affected carelessness.

"She was just makin' de kernel like any o' de low-down No'th'n folks—keerful, and stingy, and mighty 'fraid o' de opinions o' de biggety people. And fo' what? Jess to strut round wid dat child like he was her 'spectable go to meeting fader!"

"And was the child sorry to leave him?" asked Hamlin.

"Wull—no, sah. De mighty curos thing, Marse Jack, about the gals—big and little—is dey just USE de kernel—dat's all! Dey just use de ole man like a pole to bring down deir persimmons—see?"

But Mr. Hamlin did not smile.

Later it was known that Colonel Starbottle had resigned his guardianship with the consent of the court. Whether he ever again saw his late ward was not known, nor if he remained loyal to his memories of her.

Readers of these chronicles may, however, remember that years after, when the colonel married the widow of a certain Mr. Tretherick, both in his courtship and his short married life he was singularly indifferent to the childish graces of Carrie Tretherick, her beloved little daughter, and that his obtuseness in that respect provoked the widow's ire.

# PROSPER'S "OLD MOTHER"

"It's all very well," said Joe Wynbrook, "for us to be sittin' here, slingin' lies easy and comfortable, with the wind whistlin' in the pines outside, and the rain just liftin' the ditches to fill our sluice boxes with gold ez we're smokin' and waitin', but I tell you what, boys—it ain't home! No, sir, it ain't HOME!"

The speaker paused, glanced around the bright, comfortable barroom, the shining array of glasses beyond, and the circle of complacent faces fronting the stove, on which his own boots were cheerfully steaming, lifted a glass of whiskey from the floor under his chair, and in spite of his deprecating remark, took a long draught of the spirits with every symptom of satisfaction.

"If ye mean," returned Cyrus Brewster, "that it ain't the old farmhouse of our boyhood, 'way back in the woods, I'll agree with you; but ye'll just remember that there wasn't any gold placers lying round on the medder on that farm. Not much! Ef thar had been, we wouldn't have left it."

"I don't mean that," said Joe Wynbrook, settling himself comfortably back in his chair; "it's the family hearth I'm talkin' of. The soothin' influence, ye know—the tidiness of the women folks."

"Ez to the soothin' influence," remarked the barkeeper, leaning his elbows meditatively on his counter, "afore I struck these diggin's I had a grocery and bar, 'way back in Mizzoori, where there was five old-fashioned farms jined. Blame my skin ef the men folks weren't a darned sight oftener over in my grocery, sittin' on barrils and histin' in their reg'lar corn-juice, than ever any of you be here—with all these modern improvements."

"Ye don't catch on, any of you," returned Wynbrook impatiently. "Ef it was a mere matter o' buildin' houses and becomin' family men, I reckon that this yer camp is about prosperous enough to do it, and able to get gals enough to marry us, but that would be only borryin' trouble and lettin' loose a lot of jabberin' women to gossip agin' each other and spile all our friendships. No, gentlemen! What we want here—each of us—is a good old mother! Nothin' new-fangled or fancy, but the reg'lar old-fashioned mother we was used to when we was boys!"

The speaker struck a well-worn chord—rather the worse for wear, and one that had jangled falsely ere now, but which still produced its effect. The men were silent. Thus encouraged, Wynbrook proceeded:—

"Think o' comin' home from the gulch a night like this and findin' yer old mother a-waitin' ye! No fumblin' around for the matches ye'd left in the gulch; no high old cussin' because the wood was wet or you forgot to bring it in; no bustlin' around for your dry things and findin' you forgot to dry 'em that mornin'—but everything waitin' for ye and ready. And then, mebbe, she brings ye in some doughnuts she's just cooked for ye—cooked ez only SHE kin cook 'em! Take Prossy Riggs—alongside of me here—for instance! HE'S made the biggest strike yet, and is puttin' up a high-toned house on the hill. Well! he'll hev it finished off and furnished slap-up style, you bet! with a Chinese cook, and a Biddy, and a Mexican vaquero to look after his horse—but he won't have no mother to housekeep! That is," he corrected himself perfunctorily, turning to his companion, "you've never spoke o' your mother, so I reckon you're about fixed up like us."

The young man thus addressed flushed slightly, and then nodded his head with a sheepish smile. He had, however, listened to the conversation with an interest almost childish, and a reverent admiration of his comrades—qualities which, combined with an intellect not particularly brilliant, made him alternately the butt and the favorite of the camp. Indeed, he was supposed to possess that proportion of stupidity and inexperience which, in mining superstition, gives "luck" to its possessor. And this had been singularly proven in the fact that he had made the biggest "strike" of the season.

Joe Wynbrook's sentimentalism, albeit only argumentative and half serious, had unwittingly touched a chord of simple history, and the flush which had risen to his cheek was not entirely bashfulness. The home and relationship of which they spoke so glibly, HE had never known; he was a foundling! As he lay awake that night he remembered the charitable institution which had protected his infancy, the master to whom he had later been apprenticed; that was all he knew of his childhood. In his simple way he had been greatly impressed by the strange value placed by his companions upon the family influence, and he had received their extravagance with perfect credulity. In his absolute ignorance and his lack of humor he had detected no false quality in their sentiment. And a vague sense of his responsibility, as one who had been the luckiest, and who was building the first "house" in the camp, troubled him. He lay staringly wide awake, hearing the mountain wind, and feeling warm puffs of it on his face through the crevices of the log cabin, as he thought of the new house on the hill that was to be lathed and plastered and clapboarded, and yet void and vacant of that mysterious "mother"! And then, out of the solitude and darkness, a tremendous idea struck him that made him sit up in his bunk!

A day or two later "Prossy" Riggs stood on a sand-blown, wind-swept suburb of San Francisco, before a large building whom forbidding exterior proclaimed that it was an institution of formal charity. It was, in fact, a refuge for the various waifs and strays of ill-advised or hopeless immigration. As Prosper paused before the door, certain told recollections of a similar refuge were creeping over him, and, oddly enough, he felt as embarrassed as if he had been seeking relief for himself. The perspiration stood out on his forehead as he entered the room of the manager.

It chanced, however, that this official, besides being a man of shrewd experience of human weakness, was also kindly hearted, and having, after his first official scrutiny of his visitor and his resplendent watch chain, assured himself that he was not seeking personal relief, courteously assisted him in his stammering request.

"If I understand you, you want some one to act as your housekeeper?"

"That's it! Somebody to kinder look arter things—and me—ginrally," returned Prosper, greatly relieved.

"Of what age?" continued the manager, with a cautious glance at the robust youth and good-looking, simple face of Prosper.

"I ain't nowise partickler—ez long ez she's old—ye know. Ye follow me? Old—ez of—betwixt you an' me, she might be my own mother."

The manager smiled inwardly. A certain degree of discretion was noticeable in this rustic youth! "You are quite right," he answered gravely, "as yours is a mining camp where there are no other women, Still, you don't want any one TOO old or decrepit. There is an elderly maiden lady"—But a change was transparently visible on Prosper's simple face, and the manager paused.

"She oughter be kinder married, you know—ter be like a mother," stammered Prosper.

"Oh, ay. I see," returned the manager, again illuminated by Prosper's unexpected wisdom.

He mused for a moment. "There is," he began tentatively, "a lady in reduced circumstances—not an inmate of this house, but who has received some relief from us. She was the wife of a whaling captain who died some years ago, and broke up her home. She was not brought up to work, and this, with her delicate health, has prevented her from seeking active employment. As you don't seem to require that of her, but rather want an overseer, and as your purpose, I gather, is somewhat philanthropical, you might induce her to accept a 'home' with you. Having seen better days, she is rather particular," he added, with a shrewd smile.

Simple Prosper's face was radiant. "She'll have a Chinaman and a Biddy to help her," he said quickly. Then recollecting the tastes of his comrades, he added, half apologetically, half cautiously, "Ef she could, now and then, throw herself into a lemming pie or a pot of doughnuts, jest in a motherly kind o' way, it would please the boys."

"Perhaps you can arrange that, too," returned the manager, "but I shall have to broach the whole subject to her, and you had better call again to-morrow, when I will give you her answer."

"Ye kin say," said Prosper, lightly fingering his massive gold chain and somewhat vaguely recalling the language of advertisement, "that she kin have the comforts of a home and no questions asked, and fifty dollars a month."

Rejoiced at the easy progress of his plan, and half inclined to believe himself a miracle of cautious diplomacy, Prosper, two days later, accompanied the manager to the cottage on Telegraph Hill where the relict of the late Captain Pottinger lamented the loss of her spouse, in full view of the sea he had so often tempted. On their way thither the manager imparted to Prosper how, according to hearsay, that lamented seaman had carried into the domestic circle those severe habits of discipline which had earned for him the prefix of "Bully" and "Belaying-pin" Pottinger during his strenuous life. "They say that though she is very quiet and resigned, she once or twice stood up to the captain; but that's not a bad quality to have, in a rough community, as I presume yours is, and would insure her respect."

Ushered at last into a small tank-like sitting room, whose chief decorations consisted of large abelone shells, dried marine algae, coral, and a swordfish's broken weapon, Prosper's disturbed fancy discovered the widow, sitting, apparently, as if among her husband's remains at the bottom of the sea. She had a dejected yet somewhat ruddy face; her hair was streaked with white, but primly disposed over her ears like lappets, and her garb was cleanly but sombre. There was no doubt but that she was a lugubrious figure, even to Prosper's optimistic and inexperienced mind. He could not imagine her as beaming on his hearth! It was with some alarm that, after the introduction had been completed, he beheld the manager take his leave. As the door closed, the bashful Prosper felt the murky eyes of the widow fixed upon him. A gentle cough, accompanied with the resigned laying of a black mittened hand upon her chest, suggested a genteel prelude to conversation, with possible pulmonary complications.

"I am induced to accept your proposal temporarily," she said, in a voice of querulous precision, "on account of pressing pecuniary circumstances which would not have happened had my claim against the shipowners for my dear husband's loss been properly raised. I hope you fully understand that I am unfitted both by ill health and early education from doing any menial or manual work in your household. I shall simply oversee and direct. I shall expect that the stipend you offer shall be paid monthly in advance. And as my medical man prescribes a certain amount of stimulation for my system, I shall expect to be furnished with such viands—or even"—she coughed slightly—"such beverages as may be necessary. I am far from strong—yet my wants are few."

"Ez far ez I am ketchin' on and followin' ye, ma'am," returned Prosper timidly, "ye'll hev everything ye want—jest like it was yer own home. In fact," he went on, suddenly growing desperate as the difficulties of adjusting this unexpectedly fastidious and superior woman to his plan seemed to increase, "ye'll jest consider me ez yer"—But here her murky eyes were fixed on his and he faltered. Yet he had gone too far to retreat. "Ye see," he stammered, with a hysterical grimness that was intended to be playful—"ye see, this is jest a little secret betwixt and between you and me; there'll be only you and me in the house, and it would kinder seem to the boys more homelike—ef—ef—you and me had—you bein' a widder, you know—a kind of—of"—here his smile became ghastly—"close relationship."

The widow of Captain Pottinger here sat up so suddenly that she seemed to slip through her sombre and precise enwrappings with an exposure of the real Mrs. Pottinger that was almost improper. Her high color deepened; the pupils of her black eyes contracted in the light the innocent Prosper had poured into them. Leaning forward, with her fingers clasped on her bosom, she said: "Did you tell this to the manager?"

"Of course not," said Prosper; "ye see, it's only a matter 'twixt you and me."

Mrs. Pottinger looked at Prosper, drew a deep breath, and then gazed at the abelone shells for moral support. A smile, half querulous, half superior, crossed her face as she said: "This is very abrupt and unusual. There is, of course, a disparity in our ages! You have never seen me before—at least to my knowledge—although you may have heard of me. The Spraggs of Marblehead are well known—perhaps better than the Pottingers. And yet, Mr. Griggs"—

"Riggs," suggested Prosper hurriedly.

"Riggs. Excuse me! I was thinking of young Lieutenant Griggs of the Navy, whom I knew in the days now past. Mr. Riggs, I should say. Then you want me to"—

"To be my old mother, ma'am," said Prosper tremblingly. "That is, to pretend and look ez ef you was! You see, I haven't any, but I thought it would be nice for the boys, and make it more like home in my new house, ef I allowed that my old mother would be comin' to live with me. They don't know I never had a mother to speak of. They'll never find it out! Say ye will, Mrs. Pottinger! Do!"

And here the unexpected occurred. Against all conventional rules and all accepted traditions of fiction, I am obliged to state that Mrs. Pottinger did NOT rise up and order the trembling Prosper to leave the house! She only gripped the arm of her chair a little tighter, leaned forward, and disdaining her usual precision and refinement of speech, said quietly: "It's a bargain. If THAT'S what you're wanting, my son, you can count upon me as becoming your old mother, Cecilia Jane Pottinger Riggs, every time!"

A few days later the sentimentalist Joe Wynbrook walked into the Wild Cat saloon, where his comrades were drinking, and laid a letter down on the bar with every expression of astonishment and disgust. "Look," he said, "if that don't beat all! Ye wouldn't believe it, but here's Prossy Riggs writin' that he came across his mother—his MOTHER, gentlemen—in 'Frisco; she hevin', unbeknownst to him, joined a party visiting the coast! And what does this blamed fool do? Why, he's goin' to bring her—that old woman—HERE! Here—gentlemen—to take charge of that new house—and spoil our fun. And the God-forsaken idiot thinks that we'll LIKE it!"

It was one of those rare mornings in the rainy season when there was a suspicion of spring in the air, and after a night of rainfall the sun broke through fleecy clouds with little islets of blue sky—when Prosper Riggs and his mother drove into Wild Cat camp. An expression of cheerfulness was on the faces of his old comrades. For it had been recognized that, after all, "Prossy" had a perfect right to bring his old mother there—his well-known youth and inexperience preventing this baleful performance from being established as a precedent. For these reasons hats were cheerfully doffed, and some jackets put on, as the buggy swept up the hill to the pretty new cottage, with its green blinds and white veranda, on the crest.

Yet I am afraid that Prosper was not perfectly happy, even in the triumphant consummation of his plans. Mrs. Pottinger's sudden and business-like acquiescence in it, and her singular lapse from her genteel precision, were gratifying but startling to his ingenuousness. And although from the moment she accepted the situation she was fertile in resources and full of precaution against any possibility of detection, he saw, with some uneasiness, that its control had passed out of his hands.

"You say your comrades know nothing of your family history?" she had said to him on the journey thither. "What are you going to tell them?"

"Nothin', 'cept your bein' my old mother," said Prosper hopelessly.

"That's not enough, my son." (Another embarrassment to Prosper was her easy grasp of the maternal epithets.) "Now listen! You were born just six months after your father, Captain Riggs (formerly Pottinger) sailed on his first voyage. You remember very little of him, of course, as he was away so much."

"Hadn't I better know suthin about his looks?" said Prosper submissively.

"A tall dark man, that's enough," responded Mrs. Pottinger sharply.

"Hadn't he better favor me?" said Prosper, with his small cunning recognizing the fact that he himself was a decided blond.

"Ain't at all necessary," said the widow firmly. "You were always wild and ungovernable," she continued, "and ran away from school to join some Western emigration. That accounts for the difference of our styles."

"But," continued Prosper, "I oughter remember suthin about our old times—runnin' arrants for you, and bringin' in the wood o' frosty mornin's, and you givin' me hot doughnuts," suggested Prosper dubiously.

"Nothing of the sort," said Mrs. Pottinger promptly. "We lived in the city, with plenty of servants. Just remember, Prosper dear, your mother wasn't THAT low-down country style."

Glad to be relieved from further invention, Prosper was, nevertheless, somewhat concerned at this shattering of the ideal mother in the very camp that had sung her praises. But he could only trust to her recognizing the situation with her usual sagacity, of which he stood in respectful awe.

Joe Wynbrook and Cyrus Brewster had, as older members of the camp, purposely lingered near the new house to offer any assistance to "Prossy and his mother," and had received a brief and passing introduction to the latter. So deep and unexpected was the impression she made upon them that these two oracles of the camp retired down the hill in awkward silence for some time, neither daring to risk his reputation by comment or oversurprise.

But when they approached the curious crowd below awaiting them, Cyrus Brewster ventured to say, "Struck me ez ef that old gal was rather high-toned for Prossy's mother."

Joe Wynbrook instantly seized the fatal admission to show the advantage of superior insight:—

"Struck YOU! Why, it was no more than I expected all along! What did we know of Prossy? Nothin'! What did he ever tell us'? Nothin'! And why'? 'Cos it was his secret. Lord! a blind mule could see that. All this foolishness and simplicity o' his come o' his bein' cuddled and pampered as a baby. Then, like ez not, he was either kidnapped or led away by some feller—and nearly broke his mother's heart. I'll bet my bottom dollar he has been advertised for afore this—only we didn't see the paper. Like as not they had agents out seekin' him, and he jest ran into their hands in 'Frisco! I had a kind o' presentiment o' this when he left, though I never let on anything."

"I reckon, too, that she's kinder afraid he'll bolt agin. Did ye notice how she kept watchin' him all the time, and how she did the bossin' o' everything? And there's ONE thing sure! He's changed—yes! He don't look as keerless and free and foolish ez he uster."

Here there was an unmistakable chorus of assent from the crowd that had joined them. Every one—even those who had not been introduced to the mother—had noticed his strange restraint and reticence. In the impulsive logic of the camp, conduct such as this, in the face of that superior woman—his mother—could only imply that her presence was distasteful to him; that he was either ashamed of their noticing his inferiority to her, or ashamed of THEM! Wild and hasty as was their deduction, it was, nevertheless, voiced by Joe Wynbrook in a tone of impartial and even reluctant conviction. "Well, gentlemen, some of ye may remember that when I heard that Prossy was bringin' his mother here I kicked—kicked because it only stood to reason that, being HIS mother, she'd be that foolish she'd upset the camp. There wasn't room enough for two such chuckle-heads—and one of 'em being a woman, she couldn't be shut up or sat upon ez we did to HIM. But now, gentlemen, ez we see she ain't that kind, but high-toned and level-headed, and that she's got the grip on Prossy—whether he likes it or not—we ain't goin' to let him go back on her! No, sir! we ain't goin' to let him break her heart the second time! He may think we ain't good enough for her, but ez long ez she's civil to us, we'll stand by her."

In this conscientious way were the shackles of that unhallowed relationship slowly riveted on the unfortunate Prossy. In his intercourse with his comrades during the next two or three days their attitude was shown in frequent and ostentatious praise of his mother, and suggestive advice, such as: "I wouldn't stop at the saloon, Prossy; your old mother is wantin' ye;" or, "Chuck that 'ere tarpolin over your shoulders, Pross, and don't take your wet duds into the house that yer old mother's bin makin' tidy." Oddly enough, much of this advice was quite sincere, and represented—for at least twenty minutes—the honest sentiments of the speaker. Prosper was touched at what seemed a revival of the sentiment under which he had acted, forgot his uneasiness, and became quite himself again—a fact also noticed by his critics. "Ye've only to keep him up to his work and he'll be the widder's joy agin," said Cyrus Brewster. Certainly he was so far encouraged that he had a long conversation with Mrs. Pottinger that night, with the result that the next morning Joe Wynbrook, Cyrus Brewster, Hank Mann, and Kentucky Ike were invited to spend the evening at the new house. As the men, clean shirted and decently jacketed, filed into the neat sitting room with its bright carpet, its cheerful fire, its side table with a snowy cloth on which shining tea and coffee pots were standing, their hearts thrilled with satisfaction. In a large stuffed rocking chair, Prossy's old mother, wrapped up in a shawl and some mysterious ill health which seemed to forbid any exertion, received them with genteel languor and an extended black mitten.

"I cannot," said Mrs. Pottinger, with sad pensiveness, "offer you the hospitality of my own home, gentlemen—you remember, Prosper, dear, the large salon and our staff of servants at Lexington Avenue!—but since my son has persuaded me to take charge of his humble cot, I hope you will make all allowances for its deficiencies—even," she added, casting a look of mild reproach on the astonished Prosper—"even if HE cannot."

"I'm sure he oughter to be thankful to ye, ma'am," said Joe Wynbrook quickly, "for makin' a break to come here to live, jest ez we're thankful—speakin' for the rest of this camp—for yer lightin' us up ez you're doin'! I reckon I'm speakin' for the crowd," he added, looking round him.

Murmurs of "That's so" and "You bet" passed through the company, and one or two cast a half-indignant glance at Prosper.

"It's only natural," continued Mrs. Pottinger resignedly, "that having lived so long alone, my dear Prosper may at first be a little impatient of his old mother's control, and perhaps regret his invitation."

"Oh no, ma'am," said the embarrassed Prosper.

But here the mercurial Wynbrook interposed on behalf of amity and the camp's esprit de corps. "Why, Lord! ma'am, he's jest bin longin' for ye! Times and times agin he's talked about ye; sayin' how ef he could only get ye out of yer Fifth Avenue saloon to share his humble lot with him here, he'd die happy! YOU'VE heard him talk, Brewster?"

"Frequent," replied the accommodating Brewster.

"Part of the simple refreshment I have to offer you," continued Mrs. Pottinger, ignoring further comment, "is a viand the exact quality of which I am not familiar with, but which my son informs me is a great favorite with you. It has been prepared by Li Sing, under my direction. Prosper, dear, see that the—er—doughnuts—are brought in with the coffee."

Satisfaction beamed on the faces of the company, with perhaps the sole exception of Prosper. As a dish containing a number of brown glistening spheres of baked dough was brought in, the men's eyes shone in sympathetic appreciation. Yet that epicurean light was for a moment dulled as each man grasped a sphere, and then sat motionless with it in his hand, as if it was a ball and they were waiting the signal for playing.

"I am told," said Mrs. Pottinger, with a glance of Christian tolerance at Prosper, "that lightness is considered desirable by some—perhaps you gentlemen may find them heavy."

"Thar is two kinds," said the diplomatic Joe cheerfully, as he began to nibble his, sideways, like a squirrel, "light and heavy; some likes 'em one way, and some another."

They were hard and heavy, but the men, assisted by the steaming coffee, finished them with heroic politeness. "And now, gentlemen," said Mrs. Pottinger, leaning back in her chair and calmly surveying the party, "you have my permission to light your pipes while you partake of some whiskey and water."

The guests looked up—gratified but astonished. "Are ye sure, ma'am, you don't mind it?" said Joe politely.

"Not at all," responded Mrs. Pottinger briefly. "In fact, as my physician advises the inhalation of tobacco smoke for my asthmatic difficulties, I will join you." After a moment's fumbling in a beaded bag that hung from her waist, she produced a small black clay pipe, filled it from the same receptacle, and lit it.

A thrill of surprise went round the company, and it was noticed that Prosper seemed equally confounded. Nevertheless, this awkwardness was quickly overcome by the privilege and example given them, and with, a glass of whiskey and water before them, the men were speedily at their ease. Nor did Mrs. Pottinger disdain to mingle in their desultory talk. Sitting there with her black pipe in her mouth, but still precise and superior, she told a thrilling whaling adventure of Prosper's father (drawn evidently from the experience of the lamented Pottinger), which not only deeply interested her hearers, but momentarily exalted Prosper in their minds as the son of that hero. "Now you speak o' that, ma'am," said the ingenuous Wynbrook, "there's a good deal o' Prossy in that yarn o' his father's; same kind o' keerless grit! You remember, boys, that day the dam broke and he stood thar, the water up to his neck, heavin' logs in the break till he stopped it." Briefly, the evening, in spite of its initial culinary failure and its surprises, was a decided social success, and even the bewildered and doubting Prosper went to bed relieved. It was followed by many and more informal gatherings at the house, and Mrs Pottinger so far unbent—if that term could be used of one who never altered her primness of manner—as to join in a game of poker—and even permitted herself to win.

But by the end of six weeks another change in their feelings towards Prosper seemed to creep insidiously over the camp. He had been received into his former fellowship, and even the presence of his mother had become familiar, but he began to be an object of secret commiseration. They still frequented the house, but among themselves afterwards they talked in whispers. There was no doubt to them that Prosper's old mother drank not only what her son had provided, but what she surreptitiously obtained from the saloon. There was the testimony of the barkeeper, himself concerned equally with the camp in the integrity of the Riggs household. And there was an even darker suspicion. But this must be given in Joe Wynbrook's own words:—

"I didn't mind the old woman winnin' and winnin' reg'lar—for poker's an unsartin game;—it ain't the money that we're losin'—for it's all in the camp. But when she's developing a habit o' holdin' FOUR aces when somebody else hez TWO, who don't like to let on because it's Prosper's old mother—it's gettin' rough! And dangerous too, gentlemen, if there happened to be an outsider in, or one of the boys should kick. Why, I saw Bilson grind his teeth—he holdin' a sequence flush—ace high—when the dear old critter laid down her reg'lar four aces and raked in the pile. We had to nearly kick his legs off under the table afore he'd understand—not havin' an old mother himself."

"Some un will hev to tackle her without Prossy knowin' it. For it would jest break his heart, arter all he's gone through to get her here!" said Brewster significantly.

"Onless he DID know it and it was that what made him so sorrowful when they first came. B'gosh! I never thought o' that," said Wynbrook, with one of his characteristic sudden illuminations.

"Well, gentlemen, whether he did or not," said the barkeeper stoutly, "he must never know that WE know it. No, not if the old gal cleans out my bar and takes the last scad in the camp."

And to this noble sentiment they responded as one man.

How far they would have been able to carry out that heroic resolve was never known, for an event occurred which eclipsed its importance. One morning at breakfast Mrs. Pottinger fixed a clouded eye upon Prosper.

"Prosper," she said, with fell deliberation "you ought to know you have a sister."

"Yes, ma'am," returned Prosper, with that meekness with which he usually received these family disclosures.

"A sister," continued the lady, "whom you haven't seen since you were a child; a sister who for family reasons has been living with other relatives; a girl of nineteen."

"Yea, ma'am," said Prosper humbly. "But ef you wouldn't mind writin' all that down on a bit o' paper—ye know my short memory! I would get it by heart to-day in the gulch. I'd have it all pat enough by night, ef," he added, with a short sigh, "ye was kalkilatin' to make any illusions to it when the boys are here."

"Your sister Augusta," continued Mrs. Pottinger, calmly ignoring these details, "will be here to-morrow to make me a visit."

But here the worm Prosper not only turned, but stood up, nearly upsetting the table. "It can't be did, ma'am it MUSTN'T be did!" he said wildly. "It's enough for me to have played this camp with YOU—but now to run in"—

"Can't be did!" repeated Mrs. Pottinger, rising in her turn and fixing upon the unfortunate Prosper a pair of murky piratical eyes that had once quelled the sea-roving Pottinger. "Do you, my adopted son, dare to tell me that I can't have my own flesh and blood beneath my roof?"

"Yes! I'd rather tell the whole story—I'd rather tell the boys I fooled them—than go on again!" burst out the excited Prosper.

But Mrs. Pottinger only set her lips implacably together. "Very well, tell them then," she said rigidly; "tell them how you lured me from my humble dependence in San Francisco with the prospect of a home with you; tell them how you compelled me to deceive their trusting hearts with your wicked falsehoods; tell them how you—a foundling—borrowed me for your mother, my poor dead husband for your father, and made me invent falsehood upon falsehood to tell them while you sat still and listened!"

Prosper gasped.

"Tell them," she went on deliberately, "that when I wanted to bring my helpless child to her only home—THEN, only then—you determined to break your word to me, either because you meanly begrudged her that share of your house, or to keep your misdeeds from her knowledge! Tell them that, Prossy, dear, and see what they'll say!"

Prosper sank back in his chair aghast. In his sudden instinct of revolt he had forgotten the camp! He knew, alas, too well what they would say! He knew that, added to their indignation at having been duped, their chivalry and absurd sentiment would rise in arms against the abandonment of two helpless women!

"P'r'aps ye're right, ma'am," he stammered. "I was only thinkin'," he added feebly, "how SHE'D take it."

"She'll take it as I wish her to take it," said Mrs. Pottinger firmly.

"Supposin', ez the camp don't know her, and I ain't bin talkin' o' havin' any SISTER, you ran her in here as my COUSIN? See? You bein' her aunt?"

Mrs. Pottinger regarded him with compressed lips for some time. Then she said, slowly and half meditatively: "Yes, it might be done! She will probably be willing to sacrifice her nearer relationship to save herself from passing as your sister. It would be less galling to her pride, and she wouldn't have to treat you so familiarly."

"Yes, ma'am," said Prosper, too relieved to notice the uncomplimentary nature of the suggestion. "And ye see I could call her 'Miss Pottinger,' which would come easier to me."

In its high resolve to bear with the weaknesses of Prosper's mother, the camp received the news of the advent of Prosper's cousin solely with reference to its possible effect upon the aunt's habits, and very little other curiosity. Prosper's own reticence, they felt, was probably due to the tender age at which he had separated from his relations. But when it was known that Prosper's mother had driven to the house with a very pretty girl of eighteen, there was a flutter of excitement in that impressionable community. Prosper, with his usual shyness, had evaded an early meeting with her, and was even loitering irresolutely on his way home from work, when, as he approached the house, to his discomfiture the door suddenly opened, the young lady appeared and advanced directly towards him.

She was slim, graceful, and prettily dressed, and at any other moment Prosper might have been impressed by her good looks. But her brows were knit, her dark eyes—in which there was an unmistakable reminiscence of Mrs. Pottinger—were glittering, and although she was apparently anticipating their meeting, it was evidently with no cousinly interest. When within a few feet of him she stopped. Prosper with a feeble smile offered his hand. She sprang back.

"Don't touch me! Don't come a step nearer or I'll scream!"

Prosper, still with smiling inanity, stammered that he was only "goin' to shake hands," and moved sideways towards the house.

"Stop!" she said, with a stamp of her slim foot. "Stay where you are! We must have our talk out HERE. I'm not going to waste words with you in there, before HER."

Prosper stopped.

"What did you do this for?" she said angrily. "How dared you? How could you? Are you a man, or the fool she takes you for?"

"Wot did I do WOT for?" said Prosper sullenly.

"This! Making my mother pretend you were her son! Bringing her here among these men to live a lie!"

"She was willin'," said Prosper gloomily. "I told her what she had to do, and she seemed to like it."

"But couldn't you see she was old and weak, and wasn't responsible for her actions? Or were you only thinking of yourself?"

This last taunt stung him. He looked up. He was not facing a helpless, dependent old woman as he had been the day before, but a handsome, clever girl, in every way his superior—and in the right! In his vague sense of honor it seemed more creditable for him to fight it out with HER. He burst out: "I never thought of myself! I never had an old mother; I never knew what it was to want one—but the men did! And as I couldn't get one for them, I got one for myself—to share and share alike—I thought they'd be happier ef there was one in the camp!"

There was the unmistakable accent of truth in his voice. There came a faint twitching of the young girl's lips and the dawning of a smile. But it only acted as a goad to the unfortunate Prosper. "Ye kin laugh, Miss Pottinger, but it's God's truth! But one thing I didn't do. No! When your mother wanted to bring you in here as my sister, I kicked! I did! And you kin thank me, for all your laughin', that you're standing in this camp in your own name—and ain't nothin' but my cousin."

"I suppose you thought your precious friends didn't want a SISTER too?" said the girl ironically.

"It don't make no matter wot they want now," he said gloomily. "For," he added, with sudden desperation, "it's come to an end! Yes! You and your mother will stay here a spell so that the boys don't suspicion nothin' of either of ye. Then I'll give it out that you're takin' your aunt away on a visit. Then I'll make over to her a thousand dollars for all the trouble I've given her, and you'll take her away. I've bin a fool, Miss Pottinger, mebbe I am one now, but what I'm doin' is on the square, and it's got to be done!"

He looked so simple and so good—so like an honest schoolboy confessing a fault and abiding by his punishment, for all his six feet of altitude and silky mustache—that Miss Pottinger lowered her eyes. But she recovered herself and said sharply:—

"It's all very well to talk of her going away! But she WON'T. You have made her like you—yes! like you better than me—than any of us! She says you're the only one who ever treated her like a mother—as a mother should be treated. She says she never knew what peace and comfort were until she came to you. There! Don't stare like that! Don't you understand? Don't you see? Must I tell you again that she is strange—that—that she was ALWAYS queer and strange—and queerer on account of her unfortunate habits—surely you knew THEM, Mr. Riggs! She quarreled with us all. I went to live with my aunt, and she took herself off to San Francisco with a silly claim against my father's shipowners. Heaven only knows how she managed to live there; but she always impressed people with her manners, and some one always helped her! At last I begged my aunt to let me seek her, and I tracked her here. There! If you've confessed everything to me, you have made me confess everything to you, and about my own mother, too! Now, what is to be done?"

"Whatever is agreeable to you is the same to me, Miss Pottinger," he said formally.

"But you mustn't call me 'Miss Pottinger' so loud. Somebody might hear you," she returned mischievously.

"All right—'cousin,' then," he said, with a prodigious blush. "Supposin' we go in."

In spite of the camp's curiosity, for the next few days they delicately withheld their usual evening visits to Prossy's mother. "They'll be wantin' to talk o' old times, and we don't wanter be too previous," suggested Wynbrook. But their verdict, when they at last met the new cousin, was unanimous, and their praises extravagant. To their inexperienced eyes she seemed to possess all her aunt's gentility and precision of language, with a vivacity and playfulness all her own. In a few days the whole camp was in love with her. Yet she dispensed her favors with such tactful impartiality and with such innocent enjoyment—free from any suspicion of coquetry—that there were no heartburnings, and the unlucky man who nourished a fancied slight would have been laughed at by his fellows. She had a town-bred girl's curiosity and interest in camp life, which she declared was like a "perpetual picnic," and her slim, graceful figure halting beside a ditch where the men were working seemed to them as grateful as the new spring sunshine. The whole camp became tidier; a coat was considered de rigueur at "Prossy's mother" evenings; there was less horseplay in the trails, and less shouting. "It's all very well to talk about 'old mothers,'" said the cynical barkeeper, "but that gal, single handed, has done more in a week to make the camp decent than old Ma'am Riggs has in a month o' Sundays."

Since Prosper's brief conversation with Miss Pottinger before the house, the question "What is to be done?" had singularly lapsed, nor had it been referred to again by either. The young lady had apparently thrown herself into the diversions of the camp with the thoughtless gayety of a brief holiday maker, and it was not for him to remind her—even had he wished to—that her important question had never been answered. He had enjoyed her happiness with the relief of a secret shared by her. Three weeks had passed; the last of the winter's rains had gone. Spring was stirring in underbrush and wildwood, in the pulse of the waters, in the sap of the great pines, in the uplifting of flowers. Small wonder if Prosper's boyish heart had stirred a little too.

In fact, he had been possessed by another luminous idea—a wild idea that to him seemed almost as absurd as the one which had brought him all this trouble. It had come to him like that one—out of a starlit night—and he had risen one morning with a feverish intent to put it into action! It brought him later to take an unprecedented walk alone with Miss Pottinger, to linger under green leaves in unfrequented woods, and at last seemed about to desert him as he stood in a little hollow with her hand in his—their only listener an inquisitive squirrel. Yet this was all the disappointed animal heard him stammer,—

"So you see, dear, it would THEN be no lie—for—don't you see?—she'd be really MY mother as well as YOURS."

The marriage of Prosper Riggs and Miss Pottinger was quietly celebrated at Sacramento, but Prossy's "old mother" did not return with the happy pair.

Of Mrs. Pottinger's later career some idea may be gathered from a letter which Prosper received a year after his marriage. "Circumstances," wrote Mrs. Pottinger, "which had induced me to accept the offer of a widower to take care of his motherless household, have since developed into a more enduring matrimonial position, so that I can always offer my dear Prosper a home with his mother, should he choose to visit this locality, and a second father in Hiram W. Watergates, Esq., her husband."

# THE CONVALESCENCE OF JACK HAMLIN

The habitually quiet, ascetic face of Seth Rivers was somewhat disturbed and his brows were knitted as he climbed the long ascent of Windy Hill to its summit and his own rancho. Perhaps it was the effect of the characteristic wind, which that afternoon seemed to assault him from all points at once and did not cease its battery even at his front door, but hustled him into the passage, blew him into the sitting room, and then celebrated its own exit from the long, rambling house by the banging of doors throughout the halls and the slamming of windows in the remote distance.

Mrs. Rivers looked up from her work at this abrupt onset of her husband, but without changing her own expression of slightly fatigued self-righteousness. Accustomed to these elemental eruptions, she laid her hands from force of habit upon the lifting tablecloth, and then rose submissively to brush together the scattered embers and ashes from the large hearthstone, as she had often done before.

"You're in early, Seth," she said.

"Yes. I stopped at the Cross Roads Post Office. Lucky I did, or you'd hev had kempany on your hands afore you knowed it—this very night! I found this letter from Dr. Duchesne," and he produced a letter from his pocket.

Mrs. Rivers looked up with an expression of worldly interest. Dr. Duchesne had brought her two children into the world with some difficulty, and had skillfully attended her through a long illness consequent upon the inefficient maternity of soulful but fragile American women of her type. The doctor had more than a mere local reputation as a surgeon, and Mrs. Rivers looked up to him as her sole connecting link with a world of thought beyond Windy Hill.

"He's comin' up yer to-night, bringin' a friend of his—a patient that he wants us to board and keep for three weeks until he's well agin," continued Mr. Rivers. "Ye know how the doctor used to rave about the pure air on our hill."

Mrs. Rivers shivered slightly, and drew her shawl over her shoulders, but nodded a patient assent.

"Well, he says it's just what that patient oughter have to cure him. He's had lung fever and other things, and this yer air and gin'ral quiet is bound to set him up. We're to board and keep him without any fuss or feathers, and the doctor sez he'll pay liberal for it. This yer's what he sez," concluded Mr. Rivers, reading from the letter: "'He is now fully convalescent, though weak, and really requires no other medicine than the—ozone'—yes, that's what the doctor calls it—'of Windy Hill, and in fact as little attendance as possible. I will not let him keep even his negro servant with him. He'll give you no trouble, if he can be prevailed upon to stay the whole time of his cure.'"

"There's our spare room—it hasn't been used since Parson Greenwood was here," said Mrs. Rivers reflectively. "Melinda could put it to rights in an hour. At what time will he come?"

"He'd come about nine. They drive over from Hightown depot. But," he added grimly, "here ye are orderin' rooms to be done up and ye don't know who for."

"You said a friend of Dr. Duchesne," returned Mrs. Rivers simply.

"Dr. Duchesne has many friends that you and me mightn't cotton to," said her husband. "This man is Jack Hamlin." As his wife's remote and introspective black eyes returned only vacancy, he added quickly. "The noted gambler!"

"Gambler?" echoed his wife, still vaguely.

"Yes—reg'lar; it's his business."

"Goodness, Seth! He can't expect to do it here."

"No," said Seth quickly, with that sense of fairness to his fellow man which most women find it so difficult to understand. "No—and he probably won't mention the word 'card' while he's here."

"Well?" said Mrs. Rivers interrogatively.

"And," continued Seth, seeing that the objection was not pressed, "he's one of them desprit men! A reg'lar fighter! Killed two or three men in dools!"

Mrs. Rivers stared. "What could Dr. Duchesne have been thinking of? Why, we wouldn't be safe in the house with him!"

Again Seth's sense of equity triumphed. "I never heard of his fightin' anybody but his own kind, and when he was bullyragged. And ez to women he's quite t'other way in fact, and that's why I think ye oughter know it afore you let him come. He don't go round with decent women. In fact"—But here Mr. Rivers, in the sanctity of conjugal confidences and the fullness of Bible reading, used a few strong scriptural substantives happily unnecessary to repeat here.

"Seth!" said Mrs. Rivers suddenly, "you seem to know this man."

The unexpectedness and irrelevancy of this for a moment startled Seth. But that chaste and God-fearing man had no secrets. "Only by hearsay, Jane," he returned quietly; "but if ye say the word I'll stop his comin' now."

"It's too late," said Mrs. Rivers decidedly.

"I reckon not," returned her husband, "and that's why I came straight here. I've only got to meet them at the depot and say this thing can't be done—and that's the end of it. They'll go off quiet to the hotel."

"I don't like to disappoint the doctor, Seth," said Mrs. Rivers. "We might," she added, with a troubled look of inquiry at her husband, "we might take that Mr. Hamlin on trial. Like as not he won't stay, anyway, when he sees what we're like, Seth. What do you think? It would be only our Christian duty, too."

"I was thinkin' o' that as a professin' Christian, Jane," said her husband. "But supposin' that other Christians don't look at it in that light. Thar's Deacon Stubbs and his wife and the parson. Ye remember what he said about 'no covenant with sin'?"

"The Stubbses have no right to dictate who I'll have in my house," said Mrs. Rivers quickly, with a faint flush in her rather sallow cheeks.

"It's your say and nobody else's," assented her husband with grim submissiveness. "You do what you like."

Mrs. Rivers mused. "There's only myself and Melinda here," she said with sublime naivete; "and the children ain't old enough to be corrupted. I am satisfied if you are, Seth," and she again looked at him inquiringly.

"Go ahead, then, and get ready for 'em," said Seth, hurrying away with unaffected relief. "If you have everything fixed by nine o'clock, that'll do."

Mrs. Rivers had everything "fixed" by that hour, including herself presumably, for she had put on a gray dress which she usually wore when shopping in the county town, adding a prim collar and cuffs. A pearl-encircled brooch, the wedding gift of Seth, and a solitaire ring next to her wedding ring, with a locket containing her children's hair, accented her position as a proper wife and mother. At a quarter to nine she had finished tidying the parlor, opening the harmonium so that the light might play upon its polished keyboard, and bringing from the forgotten seclusion of her closet two beautifully bound volumes of Tupper's "Poems" and Pollok's "Course of Time," to impart a literary grace to the centre table. She then drew a chair to the table and sat down before it with a religious magazine in her lap. The wind roared over the deep-throated chimney, the clock ticked monotonously, and then there came the sound of wheels and voices.

But Mrs. Rivers was not destined to see her guest that night. Dr. Duchesne, under the safe lee of the door, explained that Mr. Hamlin had been exhausted by the journey, and, assisted by a mild opiate, was asleep in the carriage; that if Mrs. Rivers did not object, they would carry him at once to his room. In the flaring and guttering of candles, the flashing of lanterns, the flapping of coats and shawls, and the bewildering rush of wind, Mrs. Rivers was only vaguely conscious of a slight figure muffled tightly in a cloak carried past her in the arms of a grizzled negro up the staircase, followed by Dr. Duchesne. With the closing of the front door on the tumultuous world without, a silence fell again on the little parlor.

When the doctor made his reappearance it was to say that his patient was being undressed and put to bed by his negro servant, who, however, would return with the doctor to-night, but that the patient would be left with everything that was necessary, and that he would require no attention from the family until the next day. Indeed, it was better that he should remain undisturbed. As the doctor confined his confidences and instructions entirely to the physical condition of their guest, Mrs. Rivers found it awkward to press other inquiries.

"Of course," she said at last hesitatingly, but with a certain primness of expression, "Mr. Hamlin must expect to find everything here very different from what he is accustomed to—at least from what my husband says are his habits."

"Nobody knows that better than he, Mrs. Rivers," returned the doctor with an equally marked precision of manner, "and you could not have a guest who would be less likely to make you remind him of it."

A little annoyed, yet not exactly knowing why, Mrs. Rivers abandoned the subject, and as the doctor shortly afterwards busied himself in the care of his patient, with whom he remained until the hour of his departure, she had no chance of renewing it. But as he finally shook hands with his host and hostess, it seemed to her that he slightly recurred to it. "I have the greatest hope of the curative effect of this wonderful locality on my patient, but even still more of the beneficial effect of the complete change of his habits, his surroundings, and their influences." Then the door closed on the man of science and the grizzled negro servant, the noise of the carriage wheels was shut out with the song of the wind in the pine tops, and the rancho of Windy Hill possessed Mr. Jack Hamlin in peace. Indeed, the wind was now falling, as was its custom at that hour, and the moon presently arose over a hushed and sleeping landscape.

For the rest of the evening the silent presence in the room above affected the household; the half-curious servants and ranch hands spoke in whispers in the passages, and at evening prayers, in the dining room, Seth Rivers, kneeling before and bowed over a rush-bottomed chair whose legs were clutched by his strong hands, included "the stranger within our gates" in his regular supplications. When the hour for retiring came, Seth, with a candle in his hand, preceded his wife up the staircase, but stopped before the door of their guest's room. "I reckon," he said interrogatively to Mrs. Rivers, "I oughter see ef he's wantin' anythin'?"

"You heard what the doctor said," returned Mrs. Rivers cautiously. At the same time she did not speak decidedly, and the frontiersman's instinct of hospitality prevailed. He knocked lightly; there was no response. He turned the door handle softly. The door opened. A faint clean perfume—an odor of some general personality rather than any particular thing—stole out upon them. The light of Seth's candle struck a few glints from some cut-glass and silver, the contents of the guest's dressing case, which had been carefully laid out upon a small table by his negro servant. There was also a refined neatness in the disposition of his clothes and effects which struck the feminine eye of even the tidy Mrs. Rivers as something new to her experience. Seth drew nearer the bed with his shaded candle, and then, turning, beckoned his wife to approach. Mrs. Rivers hesitated—but for the necessity of silence she would have openly protested—but that protest was shut up in her compressed lips as she came forward.

For an instant that awe with which absolute helplessness invests the sleeping and dead was felt by both husband and wife. Only the upper part of the sleeper's face was visible above the bedclothes, held in position by a thin white nervous hand that was encircled at the wrist by a ruffle. Seth stared. Short brown curls were tumbled over a forehead damp with the dews of sleep and exhaustion. But what appeared more singular, the closed eyes of this vessel of wrath and recklessness were fringed with lashes as long and silky as a woman's. Then Mrs. Rivers gently pulled her husband's sleeve, and they both crept back with a greater sense of intrusion and even more cautiously than they had entered. Nor did they speak until the door was closed softly and they were alone on the landing. Seth looked grimly at his wife.

"Don't look much ez ef he could hurt anybody."

"He looks like a sick man," returned Mrs. Rivers calmly.

The unconscious object of this criticism and attention slept until late; slept through the stir of awakened life within and without, through the challenge of early cocks in the lean-to shed, through the creaking of departing ox teams and the lazy, long-drawn commands of teamsters, through the regular strokes of the morning pump and the splash of water on stones, through the far-off barking of dogs and the half-intelligible shouts of ranchmen; slept through the sunlight on his ceiling, through its slow descent of his wall, and awoke with it in his eyes! He woke, too, with a delicious sense of freedom from pain, and of even drawing a long breath without difficulty—two facts so marvelous and dreamlike that he naturally closed his eyes again lest he should waken to a world of suffering and dyspnoea. Satisfied at last that this relief was real, he again opened his eyes, but upon surroundings so strange, so wildly absurd and improbable, that he again doubted their reality. He was lying in a moderately large room, primly and severely furnished, but his attention was for the moment riveted to a gilt frame upon the wall beside him bearing the text, "God Bless Our Home," and then on another frame on the opposite wall which admonished him to "Watch and Pray." Beside them hung an engraving of the "Raising of Lazarus," and a Hogarthian lithograph of "The Drunkard's Progress." Mr. Hamlin closed his eyes; he was dreaming certainly—not one of those wild, fantastic visions that had so miserably filled the past long nights of pain and suffering, but still a dream! At last, opening one eye stealthily, he caught the flash of the sunlight upon the crystal and silver articles of his dressing case, and that flash at once illuminated his memory. He remembered his long weeks of illness and the devotion of Dr. Duchesne. He remembered how, when the crisis was past, the doctor had urged a complete change and absolute rest, and had told him of a secluded rancho in some remote locality kept by an honest Western pioneer whose family he had attended. He remembered his own reluctant assent, impelled by gratitude to the doctor and the helplessness of a sick man. He now recalled the weary journey thither, his exhaustion and the semi-consciousness of his arrival in a bewildering wind on a shadowy hilltop. And this was the place!

He shivered slightly, and ducked his head under the cover again. But the brightness of the sun and some exhilarating quality in the air tempted him to have another outlook, avoiding as far as possible the grimly decorated walls. If they had only left him his faithful servant he could have relieved himself of that mischievous badinage which always alternately horrified and delighted that devoted negro. But he was alone—absolutely alone—in this conventicle!

Presently he saw the door open slowly. It gave admission to the small round face and yellow ringlets of a little girl, and finally to her whole figure, clasping a doll nearly as large as herself. For a moment she stood there, arrested by the display of Mr. Hamlin's dressing case on the table. Then her glances moved around the room and rested upon the bed. Her blue eyes and Mr. Hamlin's brown ones met and mingled. Without a moment's hesitation she moved to the bedside. Taking her doll's hands in her own, she displayed it before him.

"Isn't it pitty?"

Mr. Hamlin was instantly his old self again. Thrusting his hand comfortably under the pillow, he lay on his side and gazed at it long and affectionately. "I never," he said in a faint voice, but with immovable features, "saw anything so perfectly beautiful. Is it alive?"

"It's a dolly," she returned gravely, smoothing down its frock and straightening its helpless feet. Then seized with a spontaneous idea, like a young animal she suddenly presented it to him with both hands and said,—

"Kiss it."

Mr. Hamlin implanted a chaste salute on its vermilion cheek. "Would you mind letting me hold it for a little?" he said with extreme diffidence.

The child was delighted, as he expected. Mr. Hamlin placed it in a sitting posture on the edge of his bed, and put an ostentatious paternal arm around it.

"But you're alive, ain't you?" he said to the child.

This subtle witticism convulsed her. "I'm a little girl," she gurgled.

"I see; her mother?"

"Ess."

"And who's your mother?"

"Mammy."

"Mrs. Rivers?"

The child nodded until her ringlets were shaken on her cheek. After a moment she began to laugh bashfully and with repression, yet as Mr. Hamlin thought a little mischievously. Then as he looked at her interrogatively she suddenly caught hold of the ruffle of his sleeve.

"Oo's got on mammy's nighty."

Mr. Hamlin started. He saw the child's obvious mistake and actually felt himself blushing. It was unprecedented—it was the sheerest weakness—it must have something to do with the confounded air.

"I grieve to say you are deeply mistaken—it is my very own," he returned with great gravity. Nevertheless, he drew the coverlet close over his shoulder. But here he was again attracted by another face at the half-opened door—a freckled one, belonging to a boy apparently a year or two older than the girl. He was violently telegraphing to her to come away, although it was evident that he was at the same time deeply interested in the guest's toilet articles. Yet as his bright gray eyes and Mr. Hamlin's brown ones met, he succumbed, as the girl had, and walked directly to the bedside. But he did it bashfully—as the girl had not. He even attempted a defensive explanation.

"She hadn't oughter come in here, and mar wouldn't let her, and she knows it," he said with superior virtue.

"But I asked her to come as I'm asking you," said Mr. Hamlin promptly, "and don't you go back on your sister or you'll never be president of the United States." With this he laid his hand on the boy's tow head, and then, lifting himself on his pillow to a half-sitting posture, put an arm around each of the children, drawing them together, with the doll occupying the central post of honor. "Now," continued Mr. Hamlin, albeit in a voice a little faint from the exertion, "now that we're comfortable together I'll tell you the story of the good little boy who became a pirate in order to save his grandmother and little sister from being eaten by a wolf at the door."

But, alas! that interesting record of self-sacrifice never was told. For it chanced that Melinda Bird, Mrs. Rivers's help, following the trail of the missing children, came upon the open door and glanced in. There, to her astonishment, she saw the domestic group already described, and to her eyes dominated by the "most beautiful and perfectly elegant" young man she had ever seen. But let not the incautious reader suppose that she succumbed as weakly as her artless charges to these fascinations. The character and antecedents of that young man had been already delivered to her in the kitchen by the other help. With that single glance she halted; her eyes sought the ceiling in chaste exaltation. Falling back a step, she called in ladylike hauteur and precision, "Mary Emmeline and John Wesley."

Mr. Hamlin glanced at the children. "It's Melindy looking for us," said John Wesley. But they did not move. At which Mr. Hamlin called out faintly but cheerfully, "They're here, all right."

Again the voice arose with still more marked and lofty distinctness, "John Wesley and Mary Em-me-line." It seemed to Mr. Hamlin that human accents could not convey a more significant and elevated ignoring of some implied impropriety in his invitation. He was for a moment crushed.

But he only said to his little friends with a smile, "You'd better go now and we'll have that story later."

"Affer beckus?" suggested Mary Emmeline.

"In the woods," added John Wesley.

Mr. Hamlin nodded blandly. The children trotted to the door. It closed upon them and Miss Bird's parting admonition, loud enough for Mr. Hamlin to hear, "No more freedoms, no more intrudings, you hear."

The older culprit, Hamlin, retreated luxuriously under his blankets, but presently another new sensation came over him—absolutely, hunger. Perhaps it was the child's allusion to "beckus," but he found himself wondering when it would be ready. This anxiety was soon relieved by the appearance of his host himself bearing a tray, possibly in deference to Miss Bird's sense of propriety. It appeared also that Dr. Duchesne had previously given suitable directions for his diet, and Mr. Hamlin found his repast simple but enjoyable. Always playfully or ironically polite to strangers, he thanked his host and said he had slept splendidly.

"It's this yer 'ozone' in the air that Dr. Duchesne talks about," said Seth complacently.

"I am inclined to think it is also those texts," said Mr. Hamlin gravely, as he indicated them on the wall. "You see they reminded me of church and my boyhood's slumbers there. I have never slept so peacefully since." Seth's face brightened so interestedly at what he believed to be a suggestion of his guest's conversion that Mr. Hamlin was fain to change the subject. When his host had withdrawn he proceeded to dress himself, but here became conscious of his weakness and was obliged to sit down. In one of those enforced rests he chanced to be near the window, and for the first time looked on the environs of his place of exile. For a moment he was staggered. Everything seemed to pitch downward from the rocky outcrop on which the rambling house and farm sheds stood. Even the great pines around it swept downward like a green wave, to rise again in enormous billows as far as the eye could reach. He could count a dozen of their tumbled crests following each other on their way to the distant plain. In some vague point of that shimmering horizon of heat and dust was the spot he came from the preceding night. Yet the recollection of it and his feverish past seemed to confuse him, and he turned his eyes gladly away.

Pale, a little tremulous, but immaculate and jaunty in his white flannels and straw hat, he at last made his way downstairs. To his great relief he found the sitting room empty, as he would have willingly deferred his formal acknowledgments to his hostess later. A single glance at the interior determined him not to linger, and he slipped quietly into the open air and sunshine. The day was warm and still, as the wind only came up with the going down of the sun, and the atmosphere was still redolent with the morning spicing of pine and hay and a stronger balm that seemed to fill his breast with sunshine. He walked toward the nearest shade—a cluster of young buckeyes—and having with a certain civic fastidiousness flicked the dust from a stump with his handkerchief he sat down. It was very quiet and calm. The life and animation of early morning had already vanished from the hill, or seemed to be suspended with the sun in the sky. He could see the ranchmen and oxen toiling on the green terraced slopes below, but no sound reached his ears. Even the house he had just quitted seemed empty of life throughout its rambling length. His seclusion was complete. Could he stand it for three weeks? Perhaps it need not be for so long; he was already stronger! He foresaw that the ascetic Seth might become wearisome. He had an intuition that Mrs. Rivers would be equally so; he should certainly quarrel with Melinda, and this would probably debar him from the company of the children—his only hope.

But his seclusion was by no means so complete as he expected. He presently was aware of a camp-meeting hymn hummed somewhat ostentatiously by a deep contralto voice, which he at once recognized as Melinda's, and saw that severe virgin proceeding from the kitchen along the ridge until within a few paces of the buckeyes, when she stopped and, with her hand shading her eyes, apparently began to examine the distant fields. She was a tall, robust girl, not without certain rustic attractions, of which she seemed fully conscious. This latter weakness gave Mr. Hamlin a new idea. He put up the penknife with which he had been paring his nails while wondering why his hands had become so thin, and awaited events. She presently turned, approached the buckeyes, plucked a spike of the blossoms with great girlish lightness, and then apparently discovering Mr. Hamlin, started in deep concern and said with somewhat stentorian politeness: "I BEG your pardon—didn't know I was intruding!"

"Don't mention it," returned Jack promptly, but without moving. "I saw you coming and was prepared; but generally—as I have something the matter with my heart—a sudden joy like this is dangerous."

Somewhat mystified, but struggling between an expression of rigorous decorum and gratified vanity, Miss Melinda stammered, "I was only"—

"I knew it—I saw what you were doing," interrupted Jack gravely, "only I wouldn't do it if I were you. You were looking at one of those young men down the hill. You forgot that if you could see him he could see you looking too, and that would only make him conceited. And a girl with YOUR attractions don't require that."

"Ez if," said Melinda, with lofty but somewhat reddening scorn, "there was a man on this hull rancho that I'd take a second look at."

"It's the first look that does the business," returned Jack simply. "But maybe I was wrong. Would you mind—as you're going straight back to the house" (Miss Melinda had certainly expressed no such intention)—"turning those two little kids loose out here? I've a sort of engagement with them."

"I will speak to their mar," said Melinda primly, yet with a certain sign of relenting, as she turned away.

"You can say to her that I regretted not finding her in the sitting room when I came down," continued Jack tactfully.

Apparently the tact was successful, for he was delighted a few moments later by the joyous onset of John Wesley and Mary Emmeline upon the buckeyes, which he at once converted into a game of hide and seek, permitting himself at last to be shamelessly caught in the open. But here he wisely resolved upon guarding against further grown-up interruption, and consulting with his companions found that on one of the lower terraces there was a large reservoir fed by a mountain rivulet, but they were not allowed to play there.

Thither, however, the reckless Jack hied with his playmates and was presently ensconced under a willow tree, where he dexterously fashioned tiny willow canoes with his penknife and sent them sailing over a submerged expanse of nearly an acre. But half an hour of this ingenious amusement was brought to an abrupt termination. While cutting bark, with his back momentarily turned on his companions, he heard a scream, and turned quickly to see John Wesley struggling in the water, grasping a tree root, and Mary Emmeline—nowhere! In another minute he saw the strings of her pinafore appear on the surface a few yards beyond, and in yet another minute, with a swift rueful glance at his white flannels, he had plunged after her. A disagreeable shock of finding himself out of his depths was, however, followed by contact with the child's clothing, and clutching her firmly, a stroke or two brought him panting to the bank. Here a gasp, a gurgle, and then a roar from Mary Emmeline, followed by a sympathetic howl from John Wesley, satisfied him that the danger was over. Rescuing the boy from the tree root, he laid them both on the grass and contemplated them exercising their lungs with miserable satisfaction. But here he found his own breathing impeded in addition to a slight faintness, and was suddenly obliged to sit down beside them, at which, by some sympathetic intuition, they both stopped crying.

Encouraged by this, Mr. Hamlin got them to laughing again, and then proposed a race home in their wet clothes, which they accepted, Mr. Hamlin, for respiratory reasons, lagging in their rear until he had the satisfaction of seeing them captured by the horrified Melinda in front of the kitchen, while he slipped past her and regained his own room. Here he changed his saturated clothes, tried to rub away a certain chilliness that was creeping over him, and lay down in his dressing gown to miserable reflections. He had nearly drowned the children and overexcited himself, in spite of his promise to the doctor! He would never again be intrusted with the care of the former nor be believed by the latter!

But events are not always logical in sequence. Mr. Hamlin went comfortably to sleep and into a profuse perspiration. He was awakened by a rapping at his door, and opening it, was surprised to find Mrs. Rivers with anxious inquiries as to his condition. "Indeed," she said, with an emotion which even her prim reserve could not conceal, "I did not know until now how serious the accident was, and how but for you and Divine Providence my little girl might have been drowned. It seems Melinda saw it all."

Inwardly objurgating the spying Melinda, but relieved that his playmates hadn't broken their promise of secrecy, Mr. Hamlin laughed.

"I'm afraid that your little girl wouldn't have got into the water at all but for me—and you must give all the credit of getting her out to the other fellow." He stopped at the severe change in Mrs. Rivers's expression, and added quite boyishly and with a sudden drop from his usual levity, "But please don't keep the children away from me for all that, Mrs. Rivers."

Mrs. Rivers did not, and the next day Jack and his companions sought fresh playing fields and some new story-telling pastures. Indeed, it was a fine sight to see this pale, handsome, elegantly dressed young fellow lounging along between a blue-checkered pinafored girl on one side and a barefooted boy on the other. The ranchmen turned and looked after him curiously. One, a rustic prodigal, reduced by dissipation to the swine-husks of ranching, saw fit to accost him familiarly.

"The last time I saw you dealing poker in Sacramento, Mr. Hamlin, I did not reckon to find you up here playing with a couple of kids."

"No!" responded Mr. Hamlin suavely, "and yet I remember I was playing with some country idiots down there, and you were one of them. Well! understand that up here I prefer the kids. Don't let me have to remind you of it."

Nevertheless, Mr. Hamlin could not help noticing that for the next two or three days there were many callers at the ranch and that he was obliged in his walks to avoid the highroad on account of the impertinent curiosity of wayfarers. Some of them were of that sex which he would not have contented himself with simply calling "curious."

"To think," said Melinda confidently to her mistress, "that that thar Mrs. Stubbs, who wouldn't go to the Hightown Hotel because there was a play actress thar, has been snoopin' round here twice since that young feller came."

Of this fact, however, Mr. Hamlin was blissfully unconscious.

Nevertheless, his temper was growing uncertain; the angle of his smart straw hat was becoming aggressive to strangers; his politeness sardonic. And now Sunday morning had come with an atmosphere of starched piety and well-soaped respectability at the rancho, and the children were to be taken with the rest of the family to the day-long service at Hightown. As these Sabbath pilgrimages filled the main road, he was fain to take himself and his loneliness to the trails and byways, and even to invade the haunts of some other elegant outcasts like himself—to wit, a crested hawk, a graceful wild cat beautifully marked, and an eloquently reticent rattlesnake. Mr. Hamlin eyed them without fear, and certainly without reproach. They were not out of their element.

Suddenly he heard his name called in a stentorian contralto. An impatient ejaculation rose to his lips, but died upon them as he turned. It was certainly Melinda, but in his present sensitive loneliness it struck him for the first time that he had never actually seen her before as she really was. Like most men in his profession he was a quick reader of thoughts and faces when he was interested, and although this was the same robust, long-limbed, sunburnt girl he had met, he now seemed to see through her triple incrustation of human vanity, conventional piety, and outrageous Sabbath finery an honest, sympathetic simplicity that commanded his respect.

"You are back early from church," he said.

"Yes. One service is good enough for me when thar ain't no special preacher," she returned, "so I jest sez to Silas, 'as I ain't here to listen to the sisters cackle ye kin put to the buckboard and drive me home ez soon ez you please.'"

"And so his name is Silas," suggested Mr. Hamlin cheerfully.

"Go 'long with you, Mr. Hamlin, and don't pester," she returned, with heifer-like playfulness. "Well, Silas put to, and when we rose the hill here I saw your straw hat passin' in the gulch, and sez to Silas, sez I, 'Ye kin pull up here, for over yar is our new boarder, Jack Hamlin, and I'm goin' to talk with him.' 'All right,' sez he, 'I'd sooner trust ye with that gay young gambolier every day of the week than with them saints down thar on Sunday. He deals ez straight ez he shoots, and is about as nigh onto a gentleman as they make 'em.'"

For one moment or two Miss Bird only saw Jack's long lashes. When his eyes once more lifted they were shining. "And what did you say?" he said, with a short laugh.

"I told him he needn't be Christopher Columbus to have discovered that." She turned with a laugh toward Jack, to be met by the word "shake," and an outstretched thin white hand which grasped her large red one with a frank, fraternal pressure.

"I didn't come to tell ye that," remarked Miss Bird as she sat down on a boulder, took off her yellow hat, and restacked her tawny mane under it, "but this: I reckoned I went to Sunday meetin' as I ought ter. I kalkilated to hear considerable about 'Faith' and 'Works,' and sich, but I didn't reckon to hear all about you from the Lord's Prayer to the Doxology. You were in the special prayers ez a warnin', in the sermon ez a text; they picked out hymns to fit ye! And always a dreful example and a visitation. And the rest o' the tune it was all gabble, gabble by the brothers and sisters about you. I reckon, Mr. Hamlin, that they know everything you ever did since you were knee-high to a grasshopper, and a good deal more than you ever thought of doin'. The women is all dead set on convertin' ye and savin' ye by their own precious selves, and the men is ekally dead set on gettin' rid o' ye on that account."

"And what did Seth and Mrs. Rivers say?" asked Hamlin composedly, but with kindling eyes.

"They stuck up for ye ez far ez they could. But ye see the parson hez got a holt upon Seth, havin' caught him kissin' a convert at camp meeting; and Deacon Turner knows suthin about Mrs. Rivers's sister, who kicked over the pail and jumped the fence years ago, and she's afeard a' him. But what I wanted to tell ye was that they're all comin' up here to take a look at ye— some on 'em to-night. You ain't afeard, are ye?" she added, with a loud laugh.

"Well, it looks rather desperate, doesn't it?" returned Jack, with dancing eyes.

"I'll trust ye for all that," said Melinda. "And now I reckon I'll trot along to the rancho. Ye needn't offer ter see me home," she added, as Jack made a movement to accompany her. "Everybody up here ain't as fair-minded ez Silas and you, and Melinda Bird hez a character to lose! So long!" With this she cantered away, a little heavily, perhaps, adjusting her yellow hat with both hands as she clattered down the steep hill.

That afternoon Mr. Hamlin drew largely on his convalescence to mount a half-broken mustang, and in spite of the rising afternoon wind to gallop along the highroad in quite as mischievous and breezy a fashion. He was wont to allow his mustang's nose to hang over the hind rails of wagons and buggies containing young couples, and to dash ahead of sober carryalls that held elderly "members in good standing."

An accomplished rider, he picked up and brought back the flying parasol of Mrs. Deacon Stubbs without dismounting. He finally came home a little blown, but dangerously composed.

There was the usual Sunday evening gathering at Windy Hill Rancho— neighbors and their wives, deacons and the pastor—but their curiosity was not satisfied by the sight of Mr. Hamlin, who kept his own room and his own counsel. There was some desultory conversation, chiefly on church topics, for it was vaguely felt that a discussion of the advisability or getting rid of the guest of their host was somewhat difficult under this host's roof, with the guest impending at any moment. Then a diversion was created by some of the church choir practicing the harmonium with the singing of certain more or less lugubrious anthems. Mrs. Rivers presently joined in, and in a somewhat faded soprano, which, however, still retained considerable musical taste and expression, sang, "Come, ye disconsolate." The wind moaned over the deep-throated chimney in a weird harmony with the melancholy of that human appeal as Mrs. Rivers sang the first verse:—

*"Come, ye disconsolate, where'er ye languish,*

*Come to the Mercy Seat, fervently kneel;*

> *Here bring your wounded hearts—here tell your anguish,*
>
> *Earth has no sorrow that Heaven cannot heal!"*

A pause followed, and the long-drawn, half-human sigh of the mountain wind over the chimney seemed to mingle with the wail of the harmonium. And then, to their thrilled astonishment, a tenor voice, high, clear, but tenderly passionate, broke like a skylark over their heads in the lines of the second verse:—

> *"Joy of the desolate, Light of the straying,*
>
> *Hope of the penitent—fadeless and pure;*
>
> *Here speaks the Comforter, tenderly saying,*
>
> *Earth has no sorrow that Heaven cannot cure!"*

The hymn was old and familiar enough, Heaven knows. It had been quite popular at funerals, and some who sat there had had its strange melancholy borne upon them in time of loss and tribulations, but never had they felt its full power before. Accustomed as they were to emotional appeal and to respond to it, as the singer's voice died away above them, their very tears flowed and fell with that voice. A few sobbed aloud, and then a voice asked tremulously,—

"Who is it?"

"It's Mr. Hamlin," said Seth quietly. "I've heard him often hummin' things before."

There was another silence, and the voice of Deacon Stubbs broke in harshly,—

"It's rank blasphemy."

"If it's rank blasphemy to sing the praise o' God, not only better than some folks in the choir, but like an angel o' light, I wish you'd do a little o' that blaspheming on Sundays, Mr. Stubbs."

The speaker was Mrs. Stubbs, and as Deacon Stubbs was a notoriously bad singer the shot told.

"If he's sincere, why does he stand aloof? Why does he not join us?" asked the parson.

"He hasn't been asked," said Seth quietly. "If I ain't mistaken this yer gathering this evening was specially to see how to get rid of him."

There was a quick murmur of protest at this. The parson exchanged glances with the deacon and saw that they were hopelessly in the minority.

"I will ask him myself," said Mrs. Rivers suddenly.

"So do, Sister Rivers; so do," was the unmistakable response.

Mrs. Rivers left the room and returned in a few moments with a handsome young man, pale, elegant, composed, even to a grave indifference. What his eyes might have said was another thing; the long lashes were scarcely raised.

"I don't mind playing a little," he said quietly to Mrs. Rivers, as if continuing a conversation, "but you'll have to let me trust my memory."

"Then you—er—play the harmonium?" said the parson, with an attempt at formal courtesy.

"I was for a year or two the organist in the choir of Dr. Todd's church at Sacramento," returned Mr. Hamlin quietly.

The blank amazement on the faces of Deacons Stubbs and Turner and the parson was followed by wreathed smiles from the other auditors and especially from the ladies. Mr. Hamlin sat down to the instrument, and in another moment took possession of it as it had never been held before. He played from memory as he had implied, but it was the memory of a musician. He began with one or two familiar anthems, in which they all joined. A fragment of a mass and a Latin chant followed. An "Ave Maria" from an opera was his first secular departure, but his delighted audience did not detect it. Then he hurried them along in unfamiliar language to "O mio Fernando" and "Spiritu gentil," which they fondly imagined were hymns, until, with crowning audacity, after a few preliminary chords of the "Miserere," he landed them broken-hearted in the Trovatore's donjon tower with "Non te scordar de mi."

Amidst the applause he heard the preacher suavely explain that those Popish masses were always in the Latin language, and rose from the instrument satisfied with his experiment. Excusing himself as an invalid from joining them in a light collation in the dining room, and begging his hostess's permission to retire, he nevertheless lingered a few moments by the door as the ladies filed out of the room, followed by the gentlemen, until Deacon Turner, who was bringing up the rear, was abreast of him. Here Mr. Hamlin became suddenly deeply interested in a framed pencil drawing which hung on the wall. It was evidently a schoolgirl's amateur portrait, done by Mrs. Rivers. Deacon Turner halted quickly by his side as the others passed out—which was exactly what Mr. Hamlin expected.

"Do you know the face?" said the deacon eagerly.

Thanks to the faithful Melinda, Mr. Hamlin did know it perfectly. It was a pencil sketch of Mrs. Rivers's youthfully erring sister. But he only said he thought he recognized a likeness to some one he had seen in Sacramento.

The deacon's eye brightened. "Perhaps the same one—perhaps," he added in a submissive and significant tone "a—er—painful story."

"Rather—to him," observed Hamlin quietly.

"How?—I—er—don't understand," said Deacon Turner.

"Well, the portrait looks like a lady I knew in Sacramento who had been in some trouble when she was a silly girl, but had got over it quietly. She was, however, troubled a good deal by some mean hound who was every now and then raking up the story wherever she went. Well, one of her friends—I might have been among them, I don't exactly remember just now—challenged him, but although he had no conscientious convictions about slandering a woman, he had some about being shot for it, and declined. The consequence was he was cowhided once in the street, and the second time tarred and feathered and ridden on a rail out of town. That, I suppose, was what you meant by your 'painful story.' But is this the woman?"

"No, no," said the deacon hurriedly, with a white face, "you have quite misunderstood."

"But whose is this portrait?" persisted Jack.

"I believe that—I don't know exactly—but I think it is a sister of Mrs. Rivers's," stammered the deacon.

"Then, of course, it isn't the same woman," said Jack in simulated indignation.

"Certainly—of course not," returned the deacon.

"Phew!" said Jack. "That was a mighty close call. Lucky we were alone, wasn't it?"

"Yes," said the deacon, with a feeble smile.

"Seth," continued Jack, with a thoughtful air, "looks like a quiet man, but I shouldn't like to have made that mistake about his sister-in-law before him. These quiet men are apt to shoot straight. Better keep this to ourselves."

Deacon Turner not only kept the revelation to himself but apparently his own sacred person also, as he did not call again at Windy Hill Rancho during Mr. Hamlin's stay. But he was exceedingly polite in his references to Jack, and alluded patronizingly to a "little chat" they had had together. And when the usual reaction took place in Mr. Hamlin's favor and Jack was actually induced to perform on the organ at Hightown Church next Sunday, the deacon's voice was loudest in his praise. Even Parson Greenwood allowed himself to be non-committal as to the truth of the rumor, largely circulated, that one of the most desperate gamblers in the State had been converted through his exhortations.

So, with breezy walks and games with the children, occasional confidences with Melinda and Silas, and the Sabbath "singing of anthems," Mr. Hamlin's three weeks of convalescence drew to a close. He had lately relaxed his habit of seclusion so far as to mingle with the company gathered for more social purposes at the rancho, and once or twice unbent so far as to satisfy their curiosity in regard to certain details of his profession.

"I have no personal knowledge of games of cards," said Parson Greenwood patronizingly, "and think I am right in saying that our brothers and sisters are equally inexperienced. I am—ahem—far from believing, however, that entire ignorance of evil is the best preparation for combating it, and I should be glad if you'd explain to the company the intricacies of various games. There is one that you mentioned, with a—er—scriptural name."

"Faro," said Hamlin, with an unmoved face.

"Pharaoh," repeated the parson gravely; "and one which you call 'poker,' which seems to require great self-control."

"I couldn't make you understand poker without your playing it," said Jack decidedly.

"As long as we don't gamble—that is, play for money—I see no objection," returned the parson.

"And," said Jack musingly, "you could use beans."

It was agreed finally that there would be no falling from grace in their playing among themselves, in an inquiring Christian spirit, under Jack's guidance, he having decided to abstain from card playing during his convalescence, and Jack permitted himself to be persuaded to show them the following evening.

It so chanced, however, that Dr. Duchesne, finding the end of Jack's "cure" approaching, and not hearing from that interesting invalid, resolved to visit him at about this time. Having no chance to apprise Jack of his intention, on coming to Hightown at night he procured a conveyance at the depot to carry him to Windy Hill Rancho. The wind blew with its usual nocturnal rollicking persistency, and at the end of his turbulent drive it seemed almost impossible to make himself heard amongst the roaring of the pines and some astounding preoccupation of the inmates. After vainly knocking, the doctor pushed open the front door and entered. He rapped at the closed sitting room door, but receiving no reply, pushed it open upon the most unexpected and astounding scene he had ever witnessed. Around the centre table several respectable members of the Hightown Church, including the parson, were gathered with intense and eager faces playing poker, and behind the parson, with his hands in his pockets, carelessly lounged the doctor's patient, the picture of health and vigor. A disused pack of cards was scattered on the floor, and before the gentle and precise Mrs. Rivers was heaped a pile of beans that would have filled a quart measure.

When Dr. Duchesne had tactfully retreated before the hurried and stammering apologies of his host and hostess, and was alone with Jack in his rooms, he turned to him with a gravity that was more than half affected and said, "How long, sir, did it take you to effect this corruption?"

"Upon my honor," said Jack simply, "they played last night for the first time. And they forced me to show them. But," added Jack after a significant pause, "I thought it would make the game livelier and be more of a moral lesson if I gave them nearly all good pat hands. So I ran in a cold deck on them—the first time I ever did such a thing in my life. I fixed up a pack of cards so that one had three tens, another three jacks, and another three queens, and so on up to three aces. In a minute they had all tumbled to the game, and you never saw such betting. Every man and woman there believed he or she had struck a sure thing, and staked accordingly. A new panful of beans was brought on, and Seth, your friend, banked for them. And at last the parson raked in the whole pile."

"I suppose you gave him the three aces," said Dr. Duchesne gloomily.

"The parson," said Jack slowly, "HADN'T A SINGLE PAIR IN HIS HAND. It was the stoniest, deadest, neatest BLUFF I ever saw. And when he'd frightened off the last man who held out and laid that measly hand of his face down on that pile of kings, queens, and aces, and looked around the table as he raked in the pile, there was a smile of humble self-righteousness on his face that was worth double the money."

# A PUPIL OF CHESTNUT RIDGE

The schoolmaster of Chestnut Ridge was interrupted in his after-school solitude by the click of hoof and sound of voices on the little bridle path that led to the scant clearing in which his schoolhouse stood. He laid down his pen as the figures of a man and woman on horseback passed the windows and dismounted before the porch. He recognized the complacent, good-humored faces of Mr. and Mrs. Hoover, who owned a neighboring ranch of some importance and who were accounted well to do people by the community. Being a childless couple, however, while they generously contributed to the support of the little school, they had not added to its flock, and it was with some curiosity that the young schoolmaster greeted them and awaited the purport of their visit. This was protracted in delivery through a certain polite dalliance with the real subject characteristic of the Southwestern pioneer.

"Well, Almiry," said Mr. Hoover, turning to his wife after the first greeting with the schoolmaster was over, "this makes me feel like old times, you bet! Why, I ain't bin inside a schoolhouse since I was knee-high to a grasshopper. Thar's the benches, and the desks, and the books and all them 'a b, abs,' jest like the old days. Dear! Dear! But the teacher in those days was ez old and grizzled ez I be—and some o' the scholars—no offense to you, Mr. Brooks—was older and bigger nor you. But times is changed: yet look, Almiry, if thar ain't a hunk o' stale gingerbread in that desk jest as it uster be! Lord! how it all comes back! Ez I was sayin' only t'other day, we can't be too grateful to our parents for givin' us an eddication in our youth;" and Mr. Hoover, with the air of recalling an alma mater of sequestered gloom and cloistered erudition, gazed reverently around the new pine walls.

But Mrs. Hoover here intervened with a gracious appreciation of the schoolmaster's youth after her usual kindly fashion. "And don't you forget it, Hiram Hoover, that these young folks of to-day kin teach the old schoolmasters of 'way back more'n you and I dream of. We've heard of your book larnin', Mr. Brooks, afore this, and we're proud to hev you here, even if the Lord has not pleased to give us the children to send to ye. But we've always paid our share in keeping up the school for others that was more favored, and now it looks as if He had not forgotten us, and ez if"—with a significant, half-shy glance at her husband and a corroborating nod from that gentleman—"ez if, reelly, we might be reckonin' to send you a scholar ourselves."

The young schoolmaster, sympathetic and sensitive, felt somewhat embarrassed. The allusion to his extreme youth, mollified though it was by the salve of praise from the tactful Mrs. Hoover, had annoyed him, and perhaps added to his slight confusion over the information she vouchsafed. He had not heard of any late addition to the Hoover family, he would not have been likely to, in his secluded habits; and although he was accustomed to the naive and direct simplicity of the pioneer, he could scarcely believe that this good lady was announcing a maternal expectation. He smiled vaguely and begged them to be seated.

"Ye see," said Mr. Hoover, dropping upon a low bench, "the way the thing pans out is this. Almiry's brother is a pow'ful preacher down the coast at San Antonio and hez settled down thar with a big Free Will Baptist Church congregation and a heap o' land got from them Mexicans. Thar's a lot o' poor Spanish and Injin trash that belong to the land, and Almiry's brother hez set about convertin' 'em, givin' 'em convickshion and religion, though the most of 'em is Papists and followers of the Scarlet Woman. Thar was an orphan, a little girl that he got outer the hands o' them priests, kinder snatched as a brand from the burnin', and he sent her to us to be brought up in the ways o' the Lord, knowin' that we had no children of our own. But we thought she oughter get the benefit o' schoolin' too, besides our own care, and we reckoned to bring her here reg'lar to school."

Relieved and pleased to help the good-natured couple in the care of the homeless waif, albeit somewhat doubtful of their religious methods, the schoolmaster said he would be delighted to number her among his little flock. Had she already received any tuition?

"Only from them padres, ye know, things about saints, Virgin Marys, visions, and miracles," put in Mrs. Hoover; "and we kinder thought ez you know Spanish you might be able to get rid o' them in exchange for 'conviction o' sins' and 'justification by faith,' ye know."

"I'm afraid," said Mr. Brooks, smiling at the thought of displacing the Church's "mysteries" for certain corybantic displays and thaumaturgical exhibitions he had witnessed at the Dissenters' camp meeting, "that I must leave all that to you, and I must caution you to be careful what you do lest you also shake her faith in the alphabet and the multiplication table."

"Mebbee you're right," said Mrs. Hoover, mystified but good-natured; "but thar's one thing more we oughter tell ye. She's—she's a trifle dark complected."

The schoolmaster smiled. "Well?" he said patiently.

"She isn't a nigger nor an Injin, ye know, but she's kinder a half-Spanish, half-Mexican Injin, what they call 'mes—mes'"—

"Mestiza," suggested Mr. Brooks; "a half-breed or mongrel."

"I reckon. Now thar wouldn't be any objection to that, eh?" said Mr. Hoover a little uneasily.

"Not by me," returned the schoolmaster cheerfully. "And although this school is state-aided it's not a 'public school' in the eye of the law, so you have only the foolish prejudices of your neighbors to deal with." He had recognized the reason of their hesitation and knew the strong racial antagonism held towards the negro and Indian by Mr. Hoover's Southwestern compatriots, and he could not refrain from "rubbing it in."

"They kin see," interposed Mrs. Hoover, "that she's not a nigger, for her hair don't 'kink,' and a furrin Injin, of course, is different from one o' our own."

"If they hear her speak Spanish, and you simply say she is a foreigner, as she is, it will be all right," said the schoolmaster smilingly. "Let her come, I'll look after her."

Much relieved, after a few more words the couple took their departure, the schoolmaster promising to call the next afternoon at the Hoovers' ranch and meet his new scholar. "Ye might give us a hint or two how she oughter be fixed up afore she joins the school."

The ranch was about four miles from the schoolhouse, and as Mr. Brooks drew rein before the Hoovers' gate he appreciated the devotion of the couple who were willing to send the child that distance twice a day. The house, with its outbuildings, was on a more liberal scale than its neighbors, and showed few of the makeshifts and half-hearted advances towards permanent occupation common to the Southwestern pioneers, who were more or less nomads in instinct and circumstance. He was ushered into a well-furnished sitting room, whose glaring freshness was subdued and repressed by black-framed engravings of scriptural subjects. As Mr. Brooks glanced at them and recalled the schoolrooms of the old missions, with their monastic shadows which half hid the gaudy, tinseled saints and flaming or ensanguined hearts upon the walls, he feared that the little waif of Mother Church had not gained any cheerfulness in the exchange.

As she entered the room with Mrs. Hoover, her large dark eyes—the most notable feature in her small face—seemed to sustain the schoolmaster's fanciful fear in their half-frightened wonder. She was clinging closely to Mrs. Hoover's side, as if recognizing the good woman's maternal kindness even while doubtful of her purpose; but on the schoolmaster addressing her in Spanish, a singular change took place in their relative positions. A quick look of intelligence came into her melancholy eyes, and with it a slight consciousness of superiority to her protectors that was embarrassing to him. For the rest he observed merely that she was small and slightly built, although her figure was hidden in a long "check apron" or calico pinafore with sleeves—a local garment—which was utterly incongruous with her originality. Her skin was olive, inclining to yellow, or rather to that exquisite shade of buff to be seen in the new bark of the madrono. Her face was oval, and her mouth small and childlike, with little to suggest the aboriginal type in her other features.

The master's questions elicited from the child the fact that she could read and write, that she knew her "Hail Mary" and creed (happily the Protestant Mrs. Hoover was unable to follow this questioning), but he also elicited the more disturbing fact that her replies and confidences suggested a certain familiarity and equality of condition which he could only set down to his own youthfulness of appearance. He was apprehensive that she might even make some remark regarding Mrs. Hoover, and was not sorry that the latter did not understand Spanish. But before he left he managed to speak with Mrs. Hoover alone and suggested a change in the costume of the pupil when she came to school. "The better she is dressed," suggested the wily young diplomat, "the less likely is she to awaken any suspicion of her race."

"Now that's jest what's botherin' me, Mr. Brooks," returned Mrs. Hoover, with a troubled face, "for you see she is a growin' girl," and she concluded, with some embarrassment, "I can't quite make up my mind how to dress her."

"How old is she?" asked the master abruptly.

"Goin' on twelve, but,"—and Mrs. Hoover again hesitated.

"Why, two of my scholars, the Bromly girls, are over fourteen," said the master, "and you know how they are dressed;" but here he hesitated in his turn. It had just occurred to him that the little waif was from the extreme South, and the precocious maturity of the mixed races there was well known. He even remembered, to his alarm, to have seen brides of twelve and mothers of fourteen among the native villagers. This might also account for the suggestion of equality in her manner, and even for a slight coquettishness which he thought he had noticed in her when he had addressed her playfully as a muchacha. "I should dress her in something Spanish," he said hurriedly, "something white, you know, with plenty of flounces and a little black lace, or a black silk skirt and a lace scarf, you know. She'll be all right if you don't make her look like a servant or a dependent," he added, with a show of confidence he was far from feeling. "But you haven't told me her name," he concluded.

"As we're reckonin' to adopt her," said Mrs. Hoover gravely, "you'll give her ours."

"But I can't call her 'Miss Hoover,'" suggested the master; "what's her first name?"

"We was thinkin' o' 'Serafina Ann,'" said Mrs. Hoover with more gravity.

"But what is her name?" persisted the master.

"Well," returned Mrs. Hoover, with a troubled look, "me and Hiram consider it's a heathenish sort of name for a young gal, but you'll find it in my brother's letter." She took a letter from under the lid of a large Bible on the table and pointed to a passage in it.

"The child was christened 'Concepcion,'" read the master. "Why, that's one of the Marys!"

"The which?" asked Mrs. Hoover severely.

"One of the titles of the Virgin Mary; 'Maria de la Concepcion,'" said Mr. Brooks glibly.

"It don't sound much like anythin' so Christian and decent as 'Maria' or 'Mary,'" returned Mrs. Hoover suspiciously.

"But the abbreviation, 'Concha,' is very pretty. In fact it's just the thing, it's so very Spanish," returned the master decisively. "And you know that the squaw who hangs about the mining camp is called 'Reservation Ann,' and old Mrs. Parkins's negro cook is called 'Aunt Serafina,' so 'Serafina Ann' is too suggestive. 'Concha Hoover' 's the name."

"P'r'aps you're right," said Mrs. Hoover meditatively.

"And dress her so she'll look like her name and you'll be all right," said the master gayly as he took his departure.

Nevertheless, it was with some anxiety the next morning he heard the sound of hoofs on the rocky bridle path leading to the schoolhouse. He had already informed his little flock of the probable addition to their numbers and their breathless curiosity now accented the appearance of Mr. Hoover riding past the window, followed by a little figure on horseback, half hidden in the graceful folds of a serape. The next moment they dismounted at the porch, the serape was cast aside, and the new scholar entered.

A little alarmed even in his admiration, the master nevertheless thought he had never seen a more dainty figure. Her heavily flounced white skirt stopped short just above her white-stockinged ankles and little feet, hidden in white satin, low-quartered slippers. Her black silk, shell-like jacket half clasped her stayless bust clad in an under-bodice of soft muslin that faintly outlined a contour which struck him as already womanly. A black lace veil which had protected her head, she had on entering slipped down to her shoulders with a graceful gesture, leaving one end of it pinned to her hair by a rose above her little yellow ear. The whole figure was so inconsistent with its present setting that the master inwardly resolved to suggest a modification of it to

Mrs. Hoover as he, with great gravity, however, led the girl to the seat he had prepared for her. Mr. Hoover, who had been assisting discipline as he conscientiously believed by gazing with hushed, reverent reminiscence on the walls, here whispered behind his large hand that he would call for her at "four o'clock" and tiptoed out of the schoolroom. The master, who felt that everything would depend upon his repressing the children's exuberant curiosity and maintaining the discipline of the school for the next few minutes, with supernatural gravity addressed the young girl in Spanish and placed before her a few slight elementary tasks. Perhaps the strangeness of the language, perhaps the unwonted seriousness of the master, perhaps also the impassibility of the young stranger herself, all contributed to arrest the expanding smiles on little faces, to check their wandering eyes, and hush their eager whispers. By degrees heads were again lowered over their tasks, the scratching of pencils on slates, and the far-off rapping of Woodpeckers again indicated the normal quiet of the schoolroom, and the master knew he had triumphed, and the ordeal was past.

But not as regarded himself, for although the new pupil had accepted his instructions with childlike submissiveness, and even as it seemed to him with childlike comprehension, he could not help noticing that she occasionally glanced at him with a demure suggestion of some understanding between them, or as if they were playing at master and pupil. This naturally annoyed him and perhaps added a severer dignity to his manner, which did not appear to be effective, however, and which he fancied secretly amused her. Was she covertly laughing at him? Yet against this, once or twice, as her big eyes wandered from her task over the room, they encountered the curious gaze of the other children, and he fancied he saw an exchange of that freemasonry of intelligence common to children in the presence of their elders even when strangers to each other. He looked forward to recess to see how she would get on with her companions; he knew that this would settle her status in the school, and perhaps elsewhere. Even her limited English vocabulary would not in any way affect that instinctive, childlike test of superiority, but he was surprised when the hour of recess came and he had explained to her in Spanish and English its purpose, to see her quietly put her arm around the waist of Matilda Bromly, the tallest girl in the school, as the two whisked themselves off to the playground. She was a mere child after all!

Other things seemed to confirm this opinion. Later, when the children returned from recess, the young stranger had instantly become a popular idol, and had evidently dispensed her favors and patronage generously. The elder Bromly girl was wearing her lace veil, another had possession of her handkerchief, and a third displayed the rose which had adorned her left ear, things of which the master was obliged to take note with a view of returning them to the prodigal little barbarian at the close of school. Later he was, however, much perplexed by the mysterious passage under the desks of some unknown object which apparently was making the circuit of the school. With the annoyed consciousness that he was perhaps unwittingly participating in some game, he finally "nailed it" in the possession of Demosthenes Walker, aged six, to the spontaneous outcry of "Cotched!" from the whole school. When produced from Master Walker's desk in company with a horned toad and a piece of gingerbread, it was found to be Concha's white satin slipper, the young girl herself, meanwhile, bending demurely over her task with the bereft foot tucked up like a bird's under her skirt. The master, reserving reproof of this and other enormities until later, contented himself with commanding the slipper to be brought to him, when he took it to her with the satirical remark in Spanish that the schoolroom was not a dressing room—Camara para vestirse. To his surprise, however, she smilingly held out the tiny stockinged foot with a singular combination of the spoiled child and the coquettish senorita, and remained with it extended as if waiting for him to kneel and replace the slipper. But he laid it carefully on her desk.

"Put it on at once," he said in English.

There was no mistaking the tone of his voice, whatever his language. Concha darted a quick look at him like the momentary resentment of an animal, but almost as quickly her eyes became suffused, and with a hurried movement she put on the slipper.

"Please, sir, it dropped off and Jimmy Snyder passed it on," said a small explanatory voice among the benches.

"Silence!" said the master.

Nevertheless, he was glad to see that the school had not noticed the girl's familiarity even though they thought him "hard." He was not sure upon reflection but that he had magnified her offense and had been unnecessarily severe, and this feeling was augmented by his occasionally finding her looking at him with the melancholy, wondering eyes of a chidden animal. Later, as he was moving among the desks' overlooking the tasks of the individual pupils, he observed from a distance that her head was bent over her desk while her lips were moving as if repeating to herself her lesson, and that afterwards, with a swift look around the room to assure herself that she was unobserved, she made a hurried sign of the cross. It occurred to him that this might have followed some penitential prayer of the child, and remembering her tuition by the padres it gave him an idea. He dismissed school a few moments earlier in order that he might speak to her alone before Mr. Hoover arrived.

Referring to the slipper incident and receiving her assurances that "she" (the slipper) was much too large and fell often "so," a fact really established by demonstration, he seized his opportunity. "But tell me, when you were with the padre and your slipper fell off, you did not expect him to put it on for you?"

Concha looked at him coyly and then said triumphantly, "Ah, no! but he was a priest, and you are a young caballero."

Yet even after this audacity Mr. Brooks found he could only recommend to Mr. Hoover a change in the young girl's slippers, the absence of the rose-pinned veil, and the substitution of a sunbonnet. For the rest he must trust to circumstances. As Mr. Hoover—who with large paternal optimism had professed to see already an improvement in her—helped her into the saddle, the schoolmaster could not help noticing that she had evidently expected him to perform that act of courtesy, and that she looked correspondingly reproachful.

"The holy fathers used sometimes to let me ride with them on their mules," said Concha, leaning over her saddle towards the schoolmaster.

"Eh, what, missy?" said the Protestant Mr. Hoover, pricking up his ears. "Now you just listen to Mr. Brooks's doctrines, and never mind them Papists," he added as he rode away, with the firm conviction that the master had already commenced the task of her spiritual conversion.

The next day the master awoke to find his little school famous. Whatever were the exaggerations or whatever the fancies carried home to their parents by the children, the result was an overwhelming interest in the proceedings and personnel of the school by the whole district. People had already called at the Hoover ranch to see Mrs. Hoover's pretty adopted daughter. The master, on his way to the schoolroom that morning, had found a few woodmen and charcoal burners lounging on the bridle path that led from the main road. Two or three parents accompanied their children to school, asserting they had just dropped in to see how "Aramanta" or "Tommy" were "gettin' on." As the school began to assemble several unfamiliar faces passed the windows or were boldly flattened against the glass. The little schoolhouse had not seen such a gathering since it had been borrowed for a political meeting in the previous autumn. And the master noticed with some concern that many of the faces were the same which he had seen uplifted to the glittering periods of Colonel Starbottle, "the war horse of the Democracy."

For he could not shut his eyes to the fact that they came from no mere curiosity to see the novel and bizarre; no appreciation of mere picturesqueness or beauty; and alas! from no enthusiasm for the progression of education. He knew the people among whom he had lived, and he realized the fatal question of "color" had been raised in some mysterious way by those Southwestern emigrants who had carried into this "free state" their inherited prejudices. A few words convinced him that the unhappy children had variously described the complexion of their new fellow pupil, and it was believed that the "No'th'n" schoolmaster, aided and abetted by "capital" in the person of Hiram Hoover, had introduced either a "nigger wench," a "Chinese girl," or an "Injin baby" to the same educational privileges as the "pure whites," and so contaminated the sons of freemen in their very nests. He was able to reassure many that the child was of Spanish origin, but a majority preferred the evidence of their own senses, and lingered for that purpose. As the hour for her appearance drew near and passed, he was seized with a sudden fear that she might not come, that Mr. Hoover had been prevailed upon by his compatriots, in view of the excitement, to withdraw her from the school. But a faint cheer from the bridle path satisfied him, and the next moment a little retinue swept by the window, and he understood. The Hoovers had evidently determined to accent the Spanish character of their little charge. Concha, with a black riding skirt over her flounces, was now mounted on a handsome pinto mustang glittering with silver trappings, accompanied by a vaquero in a velvet jacket, Mr. Hoover bringing up the rear. He, as he informed the master, had merely come to show the way to the vaquero, who hereafter would always accompany the child to and from school. Whether or not he had been induced to this display by the excitement did not transpire. Enough that the effect was a success. The riding skirt and her mustang's fripperies had added to Concha's piquancy, and if her origin was still doubted by some, the child herself was accepted with enthusiasm. The parents who were spectators were proud of this distinguished accession to their children's playmates, and when she dismounted amid the acclaim of her little companions, it was with the aplomb of a queen.

The master alone foresaw trouble in this encouragement of her precocious manner. He received her quietly, and when she had removed her riding skirt, glancing at her feet, said approvingly, "I am glad to see you have changed your slippers; I hope they fit you more firmly than the others."

The child shrugged her shoulders. "Quien sabe. But Pedro (the vaquero) will help me now on my horse when he comes for me."

The master understood the characteristic non sequitur as an allusion to his want of gallantry on the previous day, but took no notice of it. Nevertheless, he was pleased to see during the day that she was paying more attention to her studies, although they were generally rehearsed with the languid indifference to all mental accomplishment which belonged to her race. Once he thought to stimulate her activity through her personal vanity.

"Why can you not learn as quickly as Matilda Bromly? She is only two years older than you," he suggested.

"Ah! Mother of God!—why does she then try to wear roses like me? And with that hair. It becomes her not."

The master became thus aware for the first time that the elder Bromly girl, in "the sincerest form of flattery" to her idol, was wearing a yellow rose in her tawny locks, and, further, that Master Bromly with exquisite humor had burlesqued his sister's imitation with a very small carrot stuck above his left ear. This the master promptly removed, adding an additional sum to the humorist's already overflowing slate by way of penance, and returned to Concha. "But wouldn't you like to be as clever as she?—you can if you will only learn."

"What for should I? Look you; she has a devotion for the tall one—the boy Brown! Ah! I want him not."

Yet, notwithstanding this lack of noble ambition, Concha seemed to have absorbed the "devotion" of the boys, big and little, and as the master presently discovered even that of many of the adult population. There were always loungers on the bridle path at the opening and closing of school, and the vaquero, who now always accompanied her, became an object of envy. Possibly this caused the master to observe him closely. He was tall and thin, with a smooth complexionless face, but to the master's astonishment he had the blue gray eye of the higher or Castilian type of native Californian. Further inquiry proved that he was a son of one of the old impoverished Spanish grant holders whose leagues and cattle had been mortgaged to the Hoovers, who now retained the son to control the live stock "on shares." "It looks kinder ez ef he might hev an eye on that poorty little gal when she's an age to marry," suggested a jealous swain. For several days the girl submitted to her school tasks with her usual languid indifference and did not again transgress the ordinary rules. Nor did Mr. Brooks again refer to their hopeless conversation. But one afternoon he noticed that in the silence and preoccupation of the class she had substituted another volume for her text-book and was perusing it with the articulating lips of the unpracticed reader. He demanded it from her. With blazing eyes and both hands thrust into her desk she refused and defied him. Mr. Brooks slipped his arms around her waist, quietly lifted her from the bench—feeling her little teeth pierce the back of his hand as he did so, but secured the book. Two of the elder boys and girls had risen with excited faces.

"Sit down!" said the master sternly.

They resumed their places with awed looks. The master examined the book. It was a little Spanish prayer book. "You were reading this?" he said in her own tongue.

"Yes. You shall not prevent me!" she burst out. "Mother of God! THEY will not let me read it at the ranch. They would take it from me. And now YOU!"

"You may read it when and where you like, except when you should be studying your lessons," returned the master quietly. "You may keep it here in your desk and peruse it at recess. Come to me for it then. You are not fit to read it now."

The girl looked up with astounded eyes, which in the capriciousness of her passionate nature the next moment filled with tears. Then dropping on her knees she caught the master's bitten hand and covered it with tears and kisses. But he quietly disengaged it and lifted her to her seat. There was a sniffling sound among the benches, which, however, quickly subsided as he glanced around the room, and the incident ended.

Regularly thereafter she took her prayer book back at recess and disappeared with the children, finding, as he afterwards learned, a seat under a secluded buckeye tree, where she was not disturbed by them until her orisons were concluded. The children must have remained loyal to some command of hers, for the incident and this custom were never told out of school, and the master did not consider it his duty to inform Mr. or Mrs. Hoover. If the child could recognize some check—even if it were deemed by some a superstitious one—over her capricious and precocious nature, why should he interfere?

One day at recess he presently became conscious of the ceasing of those small voices in the woods around the schoolhouse, which were always as familiar and pleasant to him in his seclusion as the song of their playfellows— the birds themselves. The continued silence at last awakened his concern and curiosity. He had seldom intruded upon or participated in their games or amusements, remembering when a boy himself the heavy incompatibility of the best intentioned adult intruder to even the most hypocritically polite child at such a moment. A sense of duty, however, impelled him to step beyond the schoolhouse, where to his astonishment he found the adjacent woods empty and soundless. He was relieved, however, after penetrating its recesses, to hear the distant sound of small applause and the unmistakable choking gasps of Johnny Stidger's pocket accordion. Following the sound he came at last upon a little hollow among the sycamores, where the children were disposed in a ring, in the centre of which, with a handkerchief in each hand, Concha the melancholy!—Concha the devout!—was dancing that most extravagant feat of the fandango—the audacious sembicuaca!

Yet, in spite of her rude and uncertain accompaniment, she was dancing it with a grace, precision, and lightness that was wonderful; in spite of its doubtful poses and seductive languors she was dancing it with the artless gayety and innocence—perhaps from the suggestion of her tiny figure—of a mere child among an audience of children. Dancing it alone she assumed the parts of the man and woman; advancing, retreating, coquetting, rejecting, coyly bewitching, and at last yielding as lightly and as immaterially as the flickering shadows that fell upon them from the waving trees overhead. The master was fascinated yet troubled. What if there had been older spectators? Would the parents take the performance as innocently as the performer and her little audience? He thought it necessary later to suggest this delicately to the child. Her temper rose, her eyes flashed.

"Ah, the slipper, she is forbidden. The prayer book—she must not. The dance, it is not good. Truly, there is nothing."

For several days she sulked. One morning she did not come to school, nor the next. At the close of the third day the master called at the Hoovers' ranch.

Mrs. Hoover met him embarrassedly in the hall. "I was sayin' to Hiram he ought to tell ye, but he didn't like to till it was certain. Concha's gone."

"Gone?" echoed the master.

"Yes. Run off with Pedro. Married to him yesterday by the Popish priest at the mission."

"Married! That child?"

"She wasn't no child, Mr. Brooks. We were deceived. My brother was a fool, and men don't understand these things. She was a grown woman—accordin' to these folks' ways and ages—when she kem here. And that's what bothered me."

There was a week's excitement at Chestnut Ridge, but it pleased the master to know that while the children grieved for the loss of Concha they never seemed to understand why she had gone.

# DICK BOYLE'S BUSINESS CARD

The Sage Wood and Dead Flat stage coach was waiting before the station. The Pine Barrens mail wagon that connected with it was long overdue, with its transfer passengers, and the station had relapsed into listless expectation. Even the humors of Dick Boyle, the Chicago "drummer,"—and, so far, the solitary passenger—which had diverted the waiting loungers, began to fail in effect, though the cheerfulness of the humorist was unabated. The ostlers had slunk back into the stables, the station keeper and stage driver had reduced their conversation to impatient monosyllables, as if each thought the other responsible for the delay. A solitary Indian, wrapped in a commissary blanket and covered by a cast-off tall hat, crouched against the wall of the station looking stolidly at nothing. The station itself, a long, rambling building containing its entire accommodation for man and beast under one monotonous, shed-like roof, offered nothing to attract the eye. Still less the prospect, on the one side two miles of arid waste to the stunted, far-spaced pines in the distance, known as the "Barrens;" on the other an apparently limitless level with darker patches of sage brush, like the scars of burnt-out fires.

Dick Boyle approached the motionless Indian as a possible relief. "YOU don't seem to care much if school keeps or not, do you, Lo?"

The Indian, who had been half crouching on his upturned soles, here straightened himself with a lithe, animal-like movement, and stood up. Boyle took hold of a corner of his blanket and examined it critically.

"Gov'ment ain't pampering you with A1 goods, Lo! I reckon the agent charged 'em four dollars for that. Our firm could have delivered them to you for 2 dols. 37 cents, and thrown in a box of beads in the bargain. Suthin like this!" He took from his pocket a small box containing a gaudy bead necklace and held it up before the Indian.

The savage, who had regarded him—or rather looked beyond him—with the tolerating indifference of one interrupted by a frisking inferior animal, here suddenly changed his expression. A look of childish eagerness came into his gloomy face; he reached out his hand for the trinket.

"Hol' on!" said Boyle, hesitating for a moment; then he suddenly ejaculated, "Well! take it, and one o' these," and drew a business card from his pocket, which he stuck in the band of the battered tall hat of the aborigine. "There! show that to your friends, and when you're wantin' anything in our line"—

The interrupting roar of laughter, coming from the box seat of the coach, was probably what Boyle was expecting, for he turned away demurely and walked towards the coach. "All right, boys! I've squared the noble red man, and the star of empire is taking its westward way. And I reckon our firm will do the 'Great Father' business for him at about half the price that it is done in Washington."

But at this point the ostlers came hurrying out of the stables. "She's comin'," said one. "That's her dust just behind the Lone Pine—and by the way she's racin' I reckon she's comin' in mighty light."

"That's so," said the mail agent, standing up on the box seat for a better view, "but darned ef I kin see any outside passengers. I reckon we haven't waited for much."

Indeed, as the galloping horses of the incoming vehicle pulled out of the hanging dust in the distance, the solitary driver could be seen urging on his team. In a few moments more they had halted at the lower end of the station.

"Wonder what's up!" said the mail agent.

"Nothin'! Only a big Injin scare at Pine Barrens," said one of the ostlers. "Injins doin' ghost dancin'—or suthin like that—and the passengers just skunked out and went on by the other line. Thar's only one ez dar come—and she's a lady."

"A lady?" echoed Boyle.

"Yes," answered the driver, taking a deliberate survey of a tall, graceful girl who, waiving the gallant assistance of the station keeper, had leaped unaided from the vehicle. "A lady—and the fort commandant's darter at that! She's clar grit, you bet—a chip o' the old block. And all this means, sonny, that you're to give up that box seat to HER. Miss Julia Cantire don't take anythin' less when I'm around."

The young lady was already walking, directly and composedly, towards the waiting coach—erect, self-contained, well gloved and booted, and clothed, even in her dust cloak and cape of plain ashen merino, with the unmistakable panoply of taste and superiority. A good-sized aquiline nose, which made her handsome mouth look smaller; gray eyes, with an occasional humid yellow sparkle in their depths; brown penciled eyebrows, and brown tendrils of hair, all seemed to Boyle to be charmingly framed in by the silver gray veil twisted around her neck and under her oval chin. In her sober tints she appeared to him to have evoked a harmony even out of the dreadful dust around them. What HE appeared to her was not so plain; she looked him over—he was rather short; through him—he was easily penetrable; and then her eyes rested with a frank recognition on the driver.

"Good-morning, Mr. Foster," she said, with a smile.

"Mornin', miss. I hear they're havin' an Injin scare over at the Barrens. I reckon them men must feel mighty mean at bein' stumped by a lady!"

"I don't think they believed I would go, and some of them had their wives with them," returned the young lady indifferently; "besides, they are Eastern people, who don't know Indians as well as WE do, Mr. Foster."

The driver blushed with pleasure at the association. "Yes, ma'am," he laughed, "I reckon the sight of even old 'Fleas in the Blanket' over there," pointing to the Indian, who was walking stolidly away from the station, "would frighten 'em out o' their boots. And yet he's got inside his hat the business card o' this gentleman—Mr. Dick Boyle, traveling for the big firm o' Fletcher & Co. of Chicago"—he interpolated, rising suddenly to the formal heights of polite introduction; "so it sorter looks ez ef any SKELPIN' was to be done it might be the other way round, ha! ha!"

Miss Cantire accepted the introduction and the joke with polite but cool abstraction, and climbed lightly into the box seat as the mail bags and a quantity of luggage—evidently belonging to the evading passengers—were quickly transferred to the coach. But for his fair companion, the driver would probably have given profane voice to his conviction that his vehicle was used as a "d———d baggage truck," but he only smiled grimly, gathered up his reins, and flicked his whip. The coach plunged forward into the dust, which instantly rose around it, and made it thereafter a mere cloud in the distance. Some of that dust for a moment overtook and hid the Indian, walking stolidly in its track, but he emerged from it at an angle, with a quickened pace and a peculiar halting trot. Yet that trot was so well sustained that in an hour he had reached a fringe of rocks and low bushes hitherto invisible through the irregularities of the apparently level plain, into which he plunged and disappeared. The dust cloud which indicated the coach—probably owing to these same irregularities—had long since been lost on the visible horizon.

The fringe which received him was really the rim of a depression quite concealed from the surface of the plain,—which it followed for some miles through a tangled trough-like bottom of low trees and underbrush,—and was a natural cover for wolves, coyotes, and occasionally bears, whose half-human footprint might have deceived a stranger. This did not, however, divert the Indian, who, trotting still doggedly on, paused only to examine another footprint—much more frequent—the smooth, inward-toed track of moccasins. The thicket grew more dense and difficult as he went on, yet he seemed to glide through its density and darkness—an obscurity that now seemed to be stirred by other moving objects, dimly seen, and as uncertain and intangible as sunlit leaves thrilled by the wind, yet bearing a strange resemblance to human figures! Pressing a few yards further, he himself presently became a part of this shadowy procession, which on closer scrutiny revealed itself as a single file of Indians, following each other in the same tireless trot. The woods and underbrush were full of them; all moving on, as he had moved, in a line parallel with the vanishing coach. Sometimes through the openings a bared painted limb, a crest of feathers, or a strip of gaudy blanket was visible, but nothing more. And yet only a few hundred yards away stretched the dusky, silent plain—vacant of sound or motion!

Meanwhile the Sage Wood and Pine Barren stage coach, profoundly oblivious—after the manner of all human invention—of everything but its regular function, toiled dustily out of the higher plain and began the grateful descent of a wooded canyon, which was, in fact, the culminating point of the depression, just described, along which the shadowy procession was slowly advancing, hardly a mile in the rear and flank of the vehicle. Miss Julia Cantire, who had faced the dust volleys of the plain unflinchingly, as became a soldier's daughter, here stood upright and shook herself—her pretty head and figure emerging like a goddess from the enveloping silver cloud. At least Mr. Boyle, relegated to the back seat, thought so—although her conversation and attentions had been chiefly directed to the driver and mail agent. Once, when he had light-heartedly addressed a remark to her, it had been received with a distinct but unpromising politeness that had made him desist from further attempts, yet without abatement of his cheerfulness, or resentment of the evident amusement his two male companions got out of his "snub." Indeed, it is to be feared that Miss Julia had certain prejudices of position, and may have thought that a "drummer"—or commercial traveler—was no more fitting company for the daughter of a major than an ordinary peddler. But it was more probable that Mr. Boyle's reputation as a humorist—a teller of funny stories and a boon companion of men—was inconsistent with the feminine ideal of high and exalted manhood. The man who "sets the table in a roar" is apt to be secretly detested by the sex, to say nothing of the other obvious reasons why Juliets do not like Mercutios!

For some such cause as this Dick Boyle was obliged to amuse himself silently, alone on the back seat, with those liberal powers of observation which nature had given him. On entering the canyon he had noticed the devious route the coach had taken to reach it, and had already invented an improved route which should enter the depression at the point where the Indians had already (unknown to him) plunged into it, and had conceived a road through the tangled brush that would shorten the distance by some miles. He had figured it out, and believed that it "would pay." But by this time they were beginning the somewhat steep and difficult ascent of the canyon on the other side. The vehicle had not crawled many yards before it stopped. Dick Boyle glanced around. Miss Cantire was getting down. She had expressed a wish to walk the rest of the ascent, and the coach was to wait for her at the top. Foster had effusively begged her to take her own time—"there was no hurry!" Boyle glanced a little longingly after her graceful figure, released from her cramped position on the box, as it flitted youthfully in and out of the wayside trees; he would like to have joined her in the woodland ramble, but even his good nature was not proof against her indifference. At a turn in the road they lost sight of her, and, as the driver and mail agent were deep in a discussion about the indistinct track, Boyle lapsed into his silent study of the country. Suddenly he uttered a slight exclamation, and quietly slipped from the back of the toiling coach to the ground. The action was, however, quickly noted by the driver, who promptly put his foot on the brake and pulled up. "Wot's up now?" he growled.

Boyle did not reply, but ran back a few steps and began searching eagerly on the ground.

"Lost suthin?" asked Foster.

"Found something," said Boyle, picking up a small object. "Look at that! D——d if it isn't the card I gave that Indian four hours ago at the station!" He held up the card.

"Look yer, sonny," retorted Foster gravely, "ef yer wantin' to get out and hang round Miss Cantire, why don't yer say so at oncet? That story won't wash!"

"Fact!" continued Boyle eagerly. "It's the same card I stuck in his hat—there's the greasy mark in the corner. How the devil did it—how did HE get here?"

"Better ax him," said Foster grimly, "ef he's anywhere round."

"But I say, Foster, I don't like the look of this at all! Miss Cantire is alone, and"—

But a burst of laughter from Foster and the mail agent interrupted him. "That's so," said Foster. "That's your best holt! Keep it up! You jest tell her that! Say thar's another Injin skeer on; that that thar bloodthirsty ole 'Fleas in His Blanket' is on the warpath, and you're goin' to shed the last drop o' your blood defendin' her! That'll fetch her, and she ain't bin treatin' you well! G'lang!"

The horses started forward under Foster's whip, leaving Boyle standing there, half inclined to join in the laugh against himself, and yet impelled by some strange instinct to take a more serious view of his discovery. There was no doubt it was the same card he had given to the Indian. True, that Indian might have given it to another—yet by what agency had it been brought there faster than the coach traveled on the same road, and yet invisibly to them? For an instant the humorous idea of literally accepting Foster's challenge, and communicating his discovery to Miss Cantire, occurred to him; he could have made a funny story out of it, and could have amused any other girl with it, but he would not force himself upon her, and again doubted if the discovery were a matter of amusement. If it were really serious, why should he alarm her? He resolved, however, to remain on the road, and within convenient distance of her, until she returned to the coach; she could not be far away. With this purpose he walked slowly on, halting occasionally to look behind.

Meantime the coach continued its difficult ascent, a difficulty made greater by the singular nervousness of the horses, that only with great trouble and some objurgation from the driver could be prevented from shying from the regular track.

"Now, wot's gone o' them critters?" said the irate Foster, straining at the reins until he seemed to lift the leader back into the track again.

"Looks as ef they smelt suthin—b'ar or Injin ponies," suggested the mail agent.

"Injin ponies?" repeated Foster scornfully.

"Fac'! Injin ponies set a hoss crazy—jest as wild hosses would!"

"Whar's yer Injin ponies?" demanded Foster incredulously.

"Dunno," said the mail agent simply.

But here the horses again swerved so madly from some point of the thicket beside them that the coach completely left the track on the right. Luckily it was a disused trail and the ground fairly good, and Foster gave them their heads, satisfied of his ability to regain the regular road when necessary. It took some moments for him to recover complete control of the frightened animals, and then their nervousness having abated with their distance from the thicket, and the trail being less steep though more winding than the regular road, he concluded to keep it until he got to the summit, when he would regain the highway once more and await his passengers. Having done this, the two men stood up on the box, and with an anxiety they tried to conceal from each other looked down the canyon for the lagging pedestrians.

"I hope Miss Cantire hasn't been stampeded from the track by any skeer like that," said the mail agent dubiously.

"Not she! She's got too much grit and sabe for that, unless that drummer hez caught up with her and unloaded his yarn about that kyard."

They were the last words the men spoke. For two rifle shots cracked from the thicket beside the road; two shots aimed with such deliberateness and precision that the two men, mortally stricken, collapsed where they stood, hanging for a brief moment over the dashboard before they rolled over on the horses' backs. Nor did they remain there long, for the next moment they were seized by half a dozen shadowy figures and with the horses and their cut traces dragged into the thicket. A half dozen and then a dozen other shadows flitted and swarmed over, in, and through the coach, reinforced by still more, until the whole vehicle seemed to be possessed, covered, and hidden by them, swaying and moving with their weight, like helpless carrion beneath a pack of ravenous wolves. Yet even while this seething congregation was at its greatest, at some unknown signal it as suddenly dispersed, vanished, and disappeared, leaving the coach empty—vacant and void of all that had given it life, weight, animation, and purpose—a mere skeleton on the roadside. The afternoon wind blew through its open doors and ravaged rack and box as if it had been the wreck of weeks instead of minutes, and the level rays of the setting sun flashed and blazed into its windows as though fire had been added to the ruin. But even this presently faded, leaving the abandoned coach a rigid, lifeless spectre on the twilight plain.

An hour later there was the sound of hurrying hoofs and jingling accoutrements, and out of the plain swept a squad of cavalrymen bearing down upon the deserted vehicle. For a few moments they, too, seemed to surround and possess it, even as the other shadows had done, penetrating the woods and thicket beside it. And then as suddenly at some signal they swept forward furiously in the track of the destroying shadows.

Miss Cantire took full advantage of the suggestion "not to hurry" in her walk, with certain feminine ideas of its latitude. She gathered a few wild flowers and some berries in the underwood, inspected some birds' nests with a healthy youthful curiosity, and even took the opportunity of arranging some moist tendrils of her silky hair with something she took from the small reticule that hung coquettishly from her girdle. It was, indeed, some twenty minutes before she emerged into the road again; the vehicle had evidently disappeared in a turn of the long, winding ascent, but just ahead of her was that dreadful man, the "Chicago drummer." She was not vain, but she made no doubt that he was waiting there for her. There was no avoiding him, but his companionship could be made a brief one. She began to walk with ostentatious swiftness.

Boyle, whose concern for her safety was secretly relieved at this, began to walk forward briskly too without looking around. Miss Cantire was not prepared for this; it looked so ridiculously as if she were chasing him! She hesitated slightly, but now as she was nearly abreast of him she was obliged to keep on.

"I think you do well to hurry, Miss Cantire," he said as she passed. "I've lost sight of the coach for some time, and I dare say they're already waiting for us at the summit."

Miss Cantire did not like this any better. To go on beside this dreadful man, scrambling breathlessly after the stage—for all the world like an absorbed and sentimentally belated pair of picnickers—was really TOO much. "Perhaps if YOU ran on and told them I was coming as fast as I could," she suggested tentatively.

"It would be as much as my life is worth to appear before Foster without you," he said laughingly. "You've only got to hurry on a little faster."

But the young lady resented this being driven by a "drummer." She began to lag, depressing her pretty brows ominously.

"Let me carry your flowers," said Boyle. He had noticed that she was finding some difficulty in holding up her skirt and the nosegay at the same time.

"No! No!" she said in hurried horror at this new suggestion of their companionship. "Thank you very much—but they're really not worth keeping—I am going to throw them away. There!" she added, tossing them impatiently in the dust.

But she had not reckoned on Boyle's perfect good-humor. That gentle idiot stooped down, actually gathered them up again, and was following! She hurried on; if she could only get to the coach first, ignoring him! But a vulgar man like that would be sure to hand them to her with some joke! Then she lagged again—she was getting tired, and she could see no sign of the coach. The drummer, too, was also lagging behind—at a respectful distance, like a groom or one of her father's troopers. Nevertheless this did not put her in a much better humor, and halting until he came abreast of her, she said impatiently: "I don't see why Mr. Foster should think it necessary to send any one to look after me."

"He didn't," returned Boyle simply. "I got down to pick up something."

"To pick up something?" she returned incredulously.

"Yes. THAT." He held out the card. "It's the card of our firm."

Miss Cantire smiled ironically. "You are certainly devoted to your business."

"Well, yes," returned Boyle good-humoredly. "You see I reckon it don't pay to do anything halfway. And whatever I do, I mean to keep my eyes about me." In spite of her prejudice, Miss Cantire could see that these necessary organs, if rather flippant, were honest. "Yes, I suppose there isn't much on that I don't take in. Why now, Miss Cantire, there's that fancy dust cloak you're wearing—it isn't in our line of goods—nor in anybody's line west of Chicago; it came from Boston or New York, and was made for home consumption! But your hat—and mighty pretty it is too, as YOU'VE fixed it up—is only regular Dunstable stock, which we could put down at Pine Barrens for four and a half cents a piece, net. Yet I suppose you paid nearly twenty-five cents for it at the Agency!"

Oddly enough this cool appraisement of her costume did not incense the young lady as it ought to have done. On the contrary, for some occult feminine reason, it amused and interested her. It would be such a good story to tell her friends of a "drummer's" idea of gallantry; and to tease the flirtatious young West Pointer who had just joined. And the appraisement was truthful—Major Cantire had only his pay—and Miss Cantire had been obliged to select that hat from the government stores.

"Are you in the habit of giving this information to ladies you meet in traveling?" she asked.

"Well, no!" answered Boyle—"for that's just where you have to keep your eyes open. Most of 'em wouldn't like it, and it's no use aggravating a possible customer. But you are not that kind."

Miss Cantire was silent. She knew she was not of that kind, but she did not require his vulgar indorsement. She pushed on for some moments alone, when suddenly he hailed her. She turned impatiently. He was carefully examining the road on both sides.

"We have either lost our way," he said, rejoining her, "or the coach has turned off somewhere. These tracks are not fresh, and as they are all going the same way, they were made by the up coach last night. They're not OUR tracks; I thought it strange we hadn't sighted the coach by this time."

"And then"—said Miss Cantire impatiently.

"We must turn back until we find them again."

The young lady frowned. "Why not keep on until we get to the top?" she said pettishly. "I'm sure I shall." She stopped suddenly as she caught sight of his grave face and keen, observant eyes. "Why can't we go on as we are?"

"Because we are expected to come back to the COACH—and not to the summit merely. These are the 'orders,' and you know you are a soldier's daughter!" He laughed as he spoke, but there was a certain quiet deliberation in his manner that impressed her. When he added, after a pause, "We must go back and find where the tracks turned off," she obeyed without a word.

They walked for some time, eagerly searching for signs of the missing vehicle. A curious interest and a new reliance in Boyle's judgment obliterated her previous annoyance, and made her more natural. She ran ahead of him with youthful eagerness, examining the ground, following a false clue with great animation, and confessing her defeat with a charming laugh. And it was she who, after retracing their steps for ten minutes, found the diverging track with a girlish cry of triumph. Boyle, who had followed her movements quite as interestedly as her discovery, looked a little grave as he noticed the deep indentations made by the struggling horses. Miss Cantire detected the change in his face; ten minutes before she would never have observed it. "I suppose we had better follow the new track," she said inquiringly, as he seemed to hesitate.

"Certainly," he said quickly, as if coming to a prompt decision. "That is safest."

"What do you think has happened? The ground looks very much cut up," she said in a confidential tone, as new to her as her previous observation of him.

"A horse has probably stumbled and they've taken the old trail as less difficult," said Boyle promptly. In his heart he did not believe it, yet he knew that if anything serious had threatened them the coach would have waited in the road. "It's an easier trail for us, though I suppose it's a little longer," he added presently.

"You take everything so good-humoredly, Mr. Boyle," she said after a pause.

"It's the way to do business, Miss Cantire," he said. "A man in my line has to cultivate it."

She wished he hadn't said that, but, nevertheless, she returned a little archly: "But you haven't any business with the stage company nor with ME, although I admit I intend to get my Dunstable hereafter from your firm at the wholesale prices."

Before he could reply, the detonation of two gunshots, softened by distance, floated down from the ridge above them. "There!" said Miss Cantire eagerly. "Do you hear that?"

His face was turned towards the distant ridge, but really that she might not question his eyes. She continued with animation: "That's from the coach—to guide us—don't you see?"

"Yes," he returned, with a quick laugh, "and it says hurry up—mighty quick—we're tired waiting—so we'd better push on."

"Why don't you answer back with your revolver?" she asked.

"Haven't got one," he said.

"Haven't got one?" she repeated in genuine surprise. "I thought you gentlemen who are traveling always carried one. Perhaps it's inconsistent with your gospel of good-humor."

"That's just it, Miss Cantire," he said with a laugh. "You've hit it."

"Why," she said hesitatingly, "even I have a derringer—a very little one, you know, which I carry in my reticule. Captain Richards gave it to me." She opened her reticule and showed a pretty ivory-handled pistol. The look of joyful surprise which came into his face changed quickly as she cocked it and lifted it into the air. He seized her arm quickly.

"No, please don't, you might want it—I mean the report won't carry far enough. It's a very useful little thing, for all that, but it's only effective at close quarters." He kept the pistol in his hand as they walked on. But Miss Cantire noticed this, also his evident satisfaction when she had at first produced it, and his concern when she was about to discharge it uselessly. She was a clever girl, and a frank one to those she was inclined to trust. And she began to trust this stranger. A smile stole along her oval cheek.

"I really believe you're afraid of something, Mr. Boyle," she said, without looking up. "What is it? You haven't got that Indian scare too?"

Boyle had no false shame. "I think I have," he returned, with equal frankness. "You see, I don't understand Indians as well as you—and Foster."

"Well, you take my word and Foster's that there is not the least danger from them. About here they are merely grown-up children, cruel and destructive as most children are; but they know their masters by this time, and the old days of promiscuous scalping are over. The only other childish propensity they keep is thieving. Even then they only steal what they actually want,— horses, guns, and powder. A coach can go where an ammunition or an emigrant wagon can't. So your trunk of samples is quite safe with Foster."

Boyle did not think it necessary to protest. Perhaps he was thinking of something else.

"I've a mind," she went on slyly, "to tell you something more. Confidence for confidence: as you've told me YOUR trade secrets, I'll tell you one of OURS. Before we left Pine Barrens, my father ordered a small escort of cavalrymen to be in readiness to join that coach if the scouts, who were watching, thought it necessary. So, you see, I'm something of a fraud as regards my reputation for courage."

"That doesn't follow," said Boyle admiringly, "for your father must have thought there was some danger, or he wouldn't have taken that precaution."

"Oh, it wasn't for me," said the young girl quickly.

"Not for you?" repeated Boyle.

Miss Cantire stopped short, with a pretty flush of color and an adorable laugh. "There! I've done it, so I might as well tell the whole story. But I can trust you, Mr. Boyle." (She faced him with clear, penetrating eyes.) "Well," she laughed again, "you might have noticed that we had a quantity of baggage of passengers who didn't go? Well, those passengers never intended to go, and hadn't any baggage! Do you understand? Those innocent-looking heavy trunks contained carbines and cartridges from our post for Fort Taylor"—she made him a mischievous curtsy—"under MY charge! And," she added, enjoying his astonishment, "as you saw, I brought them through safe to the station, and had them transferred to this coach with less fuss and trouble than a commissary transport and escort would have made."

"And they were in THIS coach?" repeated Boyle abstractedly.

"Were? They ARE!" said Miss Cantire.

"Then the sooner I get you back to your treasure again the better," said Boyle with a laugh. "Does Foster know it?"

"Of course not! Do you suppose I'd tell it to anybody but a stranger to the place? Perhaps, like you, I know when and to whom to impart information," she said mischievously.

Whatever was in Boyle's mind he had space for profound and admiring astonishment of the young lady before him. The girlish simplicity and trustfulness of her revelation seemed as inconsistent with his previous impression of her reserve and independence as her girlish reasoning and manner was now delightfully at variance with her tallness, her aquiline nose, and her erect figure. Mr. Boyle, like most short men, was apt to overestimate the qualities of size.

They walked on for some moments in silence. The ascent was comparatively easy but devious, and Boyle could see that this new detour would take them still some time to reach the summit. Miss Cantire at last voiced the thought in his own mind. "I wonder what induced them to turn off here? and if you hadn't been so clever as to discover their tracks, how could we have found them? But," she added, with feminine logic, "that, of course, is why they fired those shots."

Boyle remembered, however, that the shots came from another direction, but did not correct her conclusion. Nevertheless he said lightly: "Perhaps even Foster might have had an Indian scare."

"He ought to know 'friendlies' or 'government reservation men' better by this time," said Miss Cantire; "however, there is something in that. Do you know," she added with a laugh, "though I haven't your keen eyes I'm gifted with a keen scent, and once or twice I've thought I SMELT Indians—that peculiar odor of their camps, which is unlike anything else, and which one detects even in their ponies. I used to notice it when I rode one; no amount of grooming could take it away."

"I don't suppose that the intensity or degree of this odor would give you any idea of the hostile or friendly feelings of the Indians towards you?" asked Boyle grimly.

Although the remark was consistent with Boyle's objectionable reputation as a humorist, Miss Cantire deigned to receive it with a smile, at which Boyle, who was a little relieved by their security so far, and their nearness to their journey's end, developed further ingenious trifling until, at the end of an hour, they stood upon the plain again.

There was no sign of the coach, but its fresh track was visible leading along the bank of the ravine towards the intersection of the road they should have come by, and to which the coach had indubitably returned. Mr. Boyle drew a long breath. They were comparatively safe from any invisible attack now. At the end of ten minutes Miss Cantire, from her superior height, detected the top of the missing vehicle appearing above the stunted bushes at the junction of the highway.

"Would you mind throwing those old flowers away now?" she said, glancing at the spoils which Boyle still carried.

"Why?" he asked.

"Oh, they're too ridiculous. Please do."

"May I keep one?" he asked, with the first intonation of masculine weakness in his voice.

"If you like," she said, a little coldly.

Boyle selected a small spray of myrtle and cast the other flowers obediently aside.

"Dear me, how ridiculous!" she said.

"What is ridiculous?" he asked, lifting his eyes to hers with a slight color. But he saw that she was straining her eyes in the distance.

"Why, there don't seem to be any horses to the coach!"

He looked. Through a gap in the furze he could see the vehicle now quite distinctly, standing empty, horseless and alone. He glanced hurriedly around them; on the one side a few rocks protected them from the tangled rim of the ridge; on the other stretched the plain. "Sit down, don't move until I return," he said quickly. "Take that." He handed back her pistol, and ran quickly to the coach. It was no illusion; there it stood vacant, abandoned, its dropped pole and cut traces showing too plainly the fearful haste of its desertion! A light step behind him made him turn. It was Miss Cantire, pink and breathless, carrying the cocked derringer in her hand. "How foolish of you—without a weapon," she gasped in explanation.

Then they both stared at the coach, the empty plain, and at each other! After their tedious ascent, their long detour, their protracted expectancy and their eager curiosity, there was such a suggestion of hideous mockery in this vacant, useless vehicle—apparently left to them in what seemed their utter abandonment—that it instinctively affected them alike. And as I am writing of human nature I am compelled to say that they both burst into a fit of laughter that for the moment stopped all other expression!

"It was so kind of them to leave the coach," said Miss Cantire faintly, as she took her handkerchief from her wet and mirthful eyes. "But what made them run away?"

Boyle did not reply; he was eagerly examining the coach. In that brief hour and a half the dust of the plain had blown thick upon it, and covered any foul stain or blot that might have suggested the awful truth. Even the soft imprint of the Indians' moccasined feet had been trampled out by the later horse hoofs of the cavalrymen. It was these that first attracted Boyle's attention, but he thought them the marks made by the plunging of the released coach horses.

Not so his companion! She was examining them more closely, and suddenly lifted her bright, animated face. "Look!" she said; "our men have been here, and have had a hand in this—whatever it is."

"Our men?" repeated Boyle blankly.

"Yes!—troopers from the post—the escort I told you of. These are the prints of the regulation cavalry horseshoe—not of Foster's team, nor of Indian ponies, who never have any! Don't you see?" she went on eagerly; "our men have got wind of something and have galloped down here—along the ridge—see!" she went on, pointing to the hoof prints coming from the plain. "They've anticipated some Indian attack and secured everything."

"But if they were the same escort you spoke of, they must have known you were here, and have"—he was about to say "abandoned you," but checked himself, remembering they were her father's soldiers.

"They knew I could take care of myself, and wouldn't stand in the way of their duty," said the young girl, anticipating him with quick professional pride that seemed to fit her aquiline nose and tall figure. "And if they knew that," she added, softening with a mischievous smile, "they also knew, of course, that I was protected by a gallant stranger vouched for by Mr. Foster! No!" she added, with a certain blind, devoted confidence, which Boyle noticed with a slight wince that she had never shown before, "it's all right! and 'by orders,' Mr. Boyle, and when they've done their work they'll be back."

But Boyle's masculine common sense was, perhaps, safer than Miss Cantire's feminine faith and inherited discipline, for in an instant he suddenly comprehended the actual truth! The Indians had been there FIRST; THEY had despoiled the coach and got off safely with their booty and prisoners on the approach of the escort, who were now naturally pursuing them with a fury aroused by the belief that their commander's daughter was one of their prisoners. This conviction was a dreadful one, yet a relief as far as the young girl was concerned. But should he tell her? No! Better that she should keep her calm faith in the triumphant promptness of the soldiers—and their speedy return.

"I dare say you are right," he said cheerfully, "and let us be thankful that in the empty coach you'll have at least a half-civilized shelter until they return. Meantime I'll go and reconnoitre a little."

"I will go with you," she said.

But Boyle pointed out to her so strongly the necessity of her remaining to wait for the return of the soldiers that, being also fagged out by her long climb, she obediently consented, while he, even with his inspiration of the truth, did not believe in the return of the despoilers, and knew she would be safe.

He made his way to the nearest thicket, where he rightly believed the ambush had been prepared, and to which undoubtedly they first retreated with their booty. He expected to find some signs or traces of their spoil which in their haste they had to abandon. He was more successful than he anticipated. A few steps into the thicket brought him full upon a realization of more than his worst convictions—the dead body of Foster! Near it lay the body of the mail agent. Both had been evidently dragged into the thicket from where they fell, scalped and half stripped. There was no evidence of any later struggle; they must have been dead when they were brought there.

Boyle was neither a hard-hearted nor an unduly sensitive man. His vocation had brought him peril enough by land and water; he had often rendered valuable assistance to others, his sympathy never confusing his directness and common sense. He was sorry for these two men, and would have fought to save them. But he had no imaginative ideas of death. And his keen perception of the truth was consequently sensitively alive only to that grotesqueness of aspect which too often the hapless victims of violence are apt to assume. He saw no agony in the vacant eyes of the two men lying on their backs in apparently the complacent abandonment of drunkenness, which was further simulated by their tumbled and disordered hair matted by coagulated blood, which, however, had lost its sanguine color. He thought only of the unsuspecting girl sitting in the lonely coach, and hurriedly dragged them further into the bushes. In doing this he discovered a loaded revolver and a flask of spirits which had been lying under them, and promptly secured them. A few paces away lay the coveted trunks of arms and ammunition, their lids wrenched off and their contents gone. He noticed with a grim smile that his own trunks of samples had shared a like fate, but was delighted to find that while the brighter trifles had attracted the Indians' childish cupidity they had overlooked a heavy black merino shawl of a cheap but serviceable quality. It would help to protect Miss Cantire from the evening wind, which was already rising over the chill and stark plain. It also occurred to him that she would need water after her parched journey, and he resolved to look for a spring, being rewarded at last by a trickling rill near the ambush camp. But he had no utensil except the spirit flask, which he finally emptied of its contents and replaced with the pure water—a heroic sacrifice to a traveler who knew the comfort of a stimulant. He retraced his steps, and was just emerging from the thicket when his quick eye caught sight of a moving shadow before him close to the ground, which set the hot blood coursing through his veins.

It was the figure of an Indian crawling on his hands and knees towards the coach, scarcely forty yards away. For the first time that afternoon Boyle's calm good-humor was overswept by a blind and furious rage. Yet even then he was sane enough to remember that a pistol shot would alarm the girl, and to keep that weapon as a last resource. For an instant he crept forward as silently and stealthily as the savage, and then, with a sudden bound, leaped upon him, driving his head and shoulders down against the rocks before he could utter a cry, and sending the scalping knife he was carrying between his teeth flying with the shock from his battered jaw. Boyle seized it—his knee still in the man's back—but the prostrate body never moved beyond a slight contraction of the lower limbs. The shock had broken the Indian's neck. He turned the inert man on his back—the head hung loosely on the side. But in that brief instant Boyle had recognized the "friendly" Indian of the station to whom he had given the card.

He rose dizzily to his feet. The whole action had passed in a few seconds of time, and had not even been noticed by the sole occupant of the coach. He mechanically cocked his revolver, but the man beneath him never moved again. Neither was there any sign of flight or reinforcement from the thicket around him. Again the whole truth flashed upon him. This spy and traitor had been left behind by the marauders to return to the station and avert suspicion; he had been lurking around, but being without firearms, had not dared to attack the pair together.

It was a moment or two before Boyle regained his usual elastic good-humor. Then he coolly returned to the spring, "washed himself of the Indian," as he grimly expressed it to himself, brushed his clothes, picked up the shawl and flask, and returned to the coach. It was getting dark now, but the glow of the western sky shone unimpeded through the windows, and the silence gave him a great fear. He was relieved, however, on opening the door, to find Miss Cantire sitting stiffly in a corner. "I am sorry I was so long," he said, apologetically to her attitude, "but"—

"I suppose you took your own time," she interrupted in a voice of injured tolerance. "I don't blame you; anything's better than being cooped up in this tiresome stage for goodness knows how long!"

"I was hunting for water," he said humbly, "and have brought you some." He handed her the flask.

"And I see you have had a wash," she said a little enviously. "How spick and span you look! But what's the matter with your necktie?"

He put his hand to his neck hurriedly. His necktie was loose, and had twisted to one side in the struggle. He colored quite as much from the sensitiveness of a studiously neat man as from the fear of discovery. "And what's that?" she added, pointing to the shawl.

"One of my samples that I suppose was turned out of the coach and forgotten in the transfer," he said glibly. "I thought it might keep you warm."

She looked at it dubiously and laid it gingerly aside. "You don't mean to say you go about with such things OPENLY?" she said querulously.

"Yes; one mustn't lose a chance of trade, you know," he resumed with a smile.

"And you haven't found this journey very profitable," she said dryly. "You certainly are devoted to your business!" After a pause, discontentedly: "It's quite night already—we can't sit here in the dark."

"We can take one of the coach lamps inside; they're still there. I've been thinking the matter over, and I reckon if we leave one lighted outside the coach it may guide your friends back." He HAD considered it, and believed that the audacity of the act, coupled with the knowledge the Indians must have of the presence of the soldiers in the vicinity, would deter rather than invite their approach.

She brightened considerably with the coach lamp which he lit and brought inside. By its light she watched him curiously. His face was slightly flushed and his eyes very bright and keen looking. Man killing, except with old professional hands, has the disadvantage of affecting the circulation.

But Miss Cantire had noticed that the flask smelt of whiskey. The poor man had probably fortified himself from the fatigues of the day.

"I suppose you are getting bored by this delay," she said tentatively.

"Not at all," he replied. "Would you like to play cards? I've got a pack in my pocket. We can use the middle seat as a table, and hang the lantern by the window strap."

She assented languidly from the back seat; he was on the front seat, with the middle seat for a table between them. First Mr. Boyle showed her some tricks with the cards and kindled her momentary and flashing interest in a mysteriously evoked but evanescent knave. Then they played euchre, at which Miss Cantire cheated adorably, and Mr. Boyle lost game after game shamelessly. Then once or twice Miss Cantire was fain to put her cards to her mouth to conceal an apologetic yawn, and her blue-veined eyelids grew heavy. Whereupon Mr. Boyle suggested that she should make herself comfortable in the corner of the coach with as many cushions as she liked and the despised shawl, while he took the night air in a prowl around the coach and a lookout for the returning party. Doing so, he was delighted, after a turn or two, to find her asleep, and so returned contentedly to his sentry round.

He was some distance from the coach when a low moaning sound in the thicket presently increased until it rose and fell in a prolonged howl that was repeated from the darkened plains beyond. He recognized the voice of wolves; he instinctively felt the sickening cause of it. They had scented the dead bodies, and he now regretted that he had left his own victim so near the coach. He was hastening thither when a cry, this time human and more terrifying, came from the coach. He turned towards it as its door flew open and Miss Cantire came rushing toward him. Her face was colorless, her eyes wild with fear, and her tall, slim figure trembled convulsively as she frantically caught at the lapels of his coat, as if to hide herself within its folds, and gasped breathlessly,—

"What is it? Oh! Mr. Boyle, save me!"

"They are wolves," he said hurriedly. "But there is no danger; they would never attack you; you were safe where you were; let me lead you back."

But she remained rooted to the spot, still clinging desperately to his coat. "No, no!" she said, "I dare not! I heard that awful cry in my sleep. I looked out and saw it—a dreadful creature with yellow eyes and tongue, and a sickening breath as it passed between the wheels just below me. Ah! What's that?" and she again lapsed in nervous terror against him.

Boyle passed his arm around her promptly, firmly, masterfully. She seemed to feel the implied protection, and yielded to it gratefully, with the further breakdown of a sob. "There is no danger," he repeated cheerfully. "Wolves are not good to look at, I know, but they wouldn't have attacked you. The beast only scents some carrion on the plain, and you probably frightened him more than he did you. Lean on me," he continued as her step tottered; "you will be better in the coach."

"And you won't leave me alone again?" she said in hesitating terror.

"No!"

He supported her to the coach gravely, gently—her master and still more his own for all that her beautiful loosened hair was against his cheek and shoulder, its perfume in his nostrils, and the contour of her lithe and perfect figure against his own. He helped her back into the coach, with the aid of the cushions and shawl arranged a reclining couch for her on the back seat, and then resumed his old place patiently. By degrees the color came back to her face—as much of it as was not hidden by her handkerchief.

Then a tremulous voice behind it began a half-smothered apology. "I am SO ashamed, Mr. Boyle—I really could not help it! But it was so sudden—and so horrible—I shouldn't have been afraid of it had it been really an Indian with a scalping knife—instead of that beast! I don't know why I did it—but I was alone—and seemed to be dead—and you were dead too and they were coming to eat me! They do, you know—you said so just now! Perhaps I was dreaming. I don't know what you must think of me—I had no idea I was such a coward!"

But Boyle protested indignantly. He was sure if HE had been asleep and had not known what wolves were before, he would have been equally frightened. She must try to go to sleep again—he was sure she could—and he would not stir from the coach until she waked, or her friends came.

She grew quieter presently, and took away the handkerchief from a mouth that smiled though it still quivered; then reaction began, and her tired nerves brought her languor and finally repose. Boyle watched the shadows thicken around her long lashes until they lay softly on the faint flush that sleep was bringing to her cheek; her delicate lips parted, and her quick breath at last came with the regularity of slumber.

So she slept, and he, sitting silently opposite her, dreamed—the old dream that comes to most good men and true once in their lives. He scarcely moved until the dawn lightened with opal the dreary plain, bringing back the horizon and day, when he woke from his dream with a sigh, and then a laugh. Then he listened for the sound of distant hoofs, and hearing them, crept noiselessly from the coach. A compact body of horsemen were bearing down upon it. He rose quickly to meet them, and throwing up his hand, brought them to a halt at some distance from the coach. They spread out, resolving themselves into a dozen troopers and a smart young cadet-like officer.

"If you are seeking Miss Cantire," he said in a quiet, businesslike tone, "she is quite safe in the coach and asleep. She knows nothing yet of what has happened, and believes it is you who have taken everything away for security against an Indian attack. She has had a pretty rough night—what with her fatigue and her alarm at the wolves—and I thought it best to keep the truth from her as long as possible, and I would advise you to break it to her gently." He then briefly told the story of their experiences, omitting only his own personal encounter with the Indian. A new pride, which was perhaps the result of his vigil, prevented him.

The young officer glanced at him with as much courtesy as might be afforded to a civilian intruding upon active military operations. "I am sure Major Cantire will be greatly obliged to you when he knows it," he said politely, "and as we intend to harness up and take the coach back to Sage Wood Station immediately, you will have an opportunity of telling him."

"I am not going back by the coach to Sage Wood," said Boyle quietly. "I have already lost twelve hours of my time—as well as my trunk—on this picnic, and I reckon the least Major Cantire can do is to let me take one of your horses to the next station in time to catch the down coach. I can do it, if I set out at once."

Boyle heard his name, with the familiar prefix of "Dicky," given to the officer by a commissary sergeant, whom he recognized as having met at the Agency, and the words "Chicago drummer" added, while a perceptible smile went throughout the group. "Very well, sir," said the officer, with a familiarity a shade less respectful than his previous formal manner. "You can take the horse, as I believe the Indians have already made free with your samples. Give him a mount, sergeant."

The two men walked towards the coach. Boyle lingered a moment at the window to show him the figure of Miss Cantire still peacefully slumbering among her pile of cushions, and then turned quietly away. A moment later he was galloping on one of the troopers' horses across the empty plain.

Miss Cantire awoke presently to the sound of a familiar voice and the sight of figures that she knew. But the young officer's first words of explanation—a guarded account of the pursuit of the Indians and the recapture of the arms, suppressing the killing of Foster and the mail agent—brought a change to her brightened face and a wrinkle to her pretty brow.

"But Mr. Boyle said nothing of this to me," she said, sitting up. "Where is he?"

"Already on his way to the next station on one of our horses! Wanted to catch the down stage and get a new box of samples, I fancy, as the braves had rigged themselves out with his laces and ribbons. Said he'd lost time enough on this picnic," returned the young officer, with a laugh. "Smart business chap; but I hope he didn't bore you?"

Miss Cantire felt her cheek flush, and bit her lip. "I found him most kind and considerate, Mr. Ashford," she said coldly. "He may have thought the escort could have joined the coach a little earlier, and saved all this; but he was too much of a gentleman to say anything about it to ME," she added dryly, with a slight elevation of her aquiline nose.

Nevertheless Boyle's last words stung her deeply. To hurry off, too, without saying "good-by," or even asking how she slept! No doubt he HAD lost time, and was tired of her company, and thought more of his precious samples than of her! After all, it was like him to rush off for an order!

She was half inclined to call the young officer back and tell him how Boyle had criticised her costume on the road. But Mr. Ashford was at that time entirely preoccupied with his men around a ledge of rock and bushes some yards from the coach, yet not so far away but that she could hear what they said. "I'll swear there was no dead Injin here when we came yesterday! We searched the whole place—by daylight, too—for any sign. The Injin was killed in his tracks by some one last night. It's like Dick Boyle, lieutenant, to have done it, and like him to have said nothin' to frighten the young lady. He knows when to keep his mouth shut—and when to open it."

Miss Cantire sank back in her corner as the officer turned and approached the coach. The incident of the past night flashed back upon her—Mr. Boyle's long absence, his flushed face, twisted necktie, and enforced cheerfulness. She was shocked, amazed, discomfited—and admiring! And this hero had been sitting opposite to her, silent all the rest of the night!

"Did Mr. Boyle say anything of an Indian attack last night?" asked Ashford. "Did you hear anything?"

"Only the wolves howling," said Miss Cantire. "Mr. Boyle was away twice." She was strangely reticent—in complimentary imitation of her missing hero.

"There's a dead Indian here who has been killed," began Ashford.

"Oh, please don't say anything more, Mr. Ashford," interrupted the young lady, "but let us get away from this horrid place at once. Do get the horses in. I can't stand it."

But the horses were already harnessed and mounted, postilion-wise, by the troopers. The vehicle was ready to start when Miss Cantire called "Stop!"

When Ashford presented himself at the door, the young lady was upon her hands and knees, searching the bottom of the coach. "Oh, dear! I've lost something. I must have dropped it on the road," she said breathlessly, with pink cheeks. "You must positively wait and let me go back and find it. I won't be long. You know there's 'no hurry.'"

Mr. Ashford stared as Miss Cantire skipped like a schoolgirl from the coach and ran down the trail by which she and Boyle had approached the coach the night before. She had not gone far before she came upon the withered flowers he had thrown away at her command. "It must be about here," she murmured. Suddenly she uttered a cry of delight, and picked up the business card that Boyle had shown her. Then she looked furtively around her, and, selecting a sprig of myrtle among the cast-off flowers, concealed it in her mantle and ran back, glowing, to the coach. "Thank you! All right, I've found it," she called to Ashford, with a dazzling smile, and leaped inside.

The coach drove on, and Miss Cantire, alone in its recesses, drew the myrtle from her mantle and folding it carefully in her handkerchief, placed it in her reticule. Then she drew out the card, read its dryly practical information over and over again, examined the soiled edges, brushed them daintily, and held it for a moment, with eyes that saw not, motionless in her hand. Then she raised it slowly to her lips, rolled it into a spiral, and, loosening a hook and eye, thrust it gently into her bosom.

And Dick Boyle, galloping away to the distant station, did not know that the first step towards a realization of his foolish dream had been taken!

———————

Original title:
Happy Choices

Copyright © 2024 Creative Arts Management OÜ
All rights reserved.

Author: Tim Wood
ISBN HARDBACK: 978-9916-88-162-0
ISBN PAPERBACK: 978-9916-88-163-7

## Fulfilling the Heart

In quiet moments, whispers speak,
A gentle touch, a bond unique.
With every laugh, our spirits sway,
A dance of love in bright array.

Through storms and sun, we find our way,
Together strong, come what may.
In shared glances, worlds collide,
With open hearts, we will abide.